Cowbells Down the Zambezi

David Lemon

Grosvenor House
Publishing Limited

The right of David Lemon to be identified as the author of this
work has been asserted by him in accordance with Section 78
of the Copyright, Designs and Patents Act 1988

The book cover picture is copyright to David Lemon

This book is published by
Grosvenor House Publishing Ltd
28-30 High Street, Guildford, Surrey, GU1 3EL.
www.grosvenorhousepublishing.co.uk

A CIP record for this book
is available from the British Library

ISBN 978-1-78148-640-5

Dedication

This one is for **Zara Taylor** – a much loved
young lady.
I am proud of you Little Babe.

Other Books by David Lemon

Ivory Madness	:	The College Press 1983.
Africa's Inland Sea	:	Modus Press 1987.
Kariba Adventure	:	The College Press 1988.
Rhino	:	Puffin Books 1989.
Man Eater	:	Viking Books 1990.
Hobo Rows Kariba	:	African Publishing Group 1997.
Killer Cat	:	The College Press 1998
Never Quite a Soldier	:	Albida Books 2000.
Never Quite a Soldier (South African Edition)	:	Galago Books 2006.
Blood Sweat and Lions	:	Grosvenor House Publishing 2008.
Two Wheels and a Tokoloshe	:	Grosvenor House Publishing 2008.
Hobo	:	Grosvenor House Publishing 2009.
Soldier No More	:	Grosvenor House Publishing 2011.

Cover design by Gillian Lemon.

Acknowledgements

No journey such as the one described in these pages can ever be a totally solo affair. I took the knocks perhaps, but I also had the fun and was privileged to meet some incredible people. Almost without exception, the people of Zambia took me to their hearts and although I have mentioned a few of them in this book, there were so many folk who helped my little adventure along.

In Zambia there were of course my Cowbell team. I have mentioned them from time to time in the text, but let me introduce you to them properly. Under the captaincy of Andy Taylor, they were – in no particular order - David Shula, Tara Allin, Victor Mwansa, Martin Mwale, Albert Kapatwa and Estime Tshovu. Without them, I probably would not have survived.

Also in Zambia were Talitha Ullrich, Sean and Ronnie Whittome, Graham, Terri and Lesley Gwilliam, Monica Mwenda, Alpha Ngoma, Priscilla Rainey, Shelagh and Katrina (Kaz) Brown, Sam Craven, Sport Beattie, Rachel Murton and a host of others who jumped in to assist when assistance was needed. There were many others who helped in one way or another and whether mentioned or not, please be assured that you are remembered and I am truly grateful.

In Britain, many folk looked at me with vague sympathy when I mentioned that I was going to walk the Zambezi, but my family as always were supportive (they are accustomed to my occasional eccentricities) and my wife, Lace greeted news of my latest escapade with the wry patience, she has developed over the years.

Paul Henshaw of the Together Agency deserves special mention and his sister Sarah sent me a reading that I carried with me and referred to on occasion throughout the days of my walk. Gillian Lemon designed the cover of this book and sorted out the photographs for me, while my son Brian and Andy Reynolds struggled in vain to teach me something about the GPS. Of special assistance with the typescript were Audrey McGeorge, Ruth Pulis and the team at Grosvenor House. Once again, if I have not mentioned someone who assisted in whatever way, please be assured that I am very grateful.

In South Africa, assistance came from many quarters. Tom Naude and his happy band at Fluxcon were generous with their time and equipment, Jean Gaiser and I had long discussions on what to take, while Nicola Featonby-Smith took time out from her hectic schedule to help and advise whenever she could.

Susan and John Hammill in Johannesburg and Sue and Marque Dalais in Durban put up with my untidiness in their homes and kept me sane when my mind ached with worry. Peter Cawood, Heather Badenhorst and Paul Matulavitch assisted where they could and my two lovely nieces Monique and Tanya cheered me up by giving birth while I was walking through the bush. Barry and Marina Woan – and Granny bless her – entertained me right royally in Margate and Gale Rice with John Sharp also deserve special mention.

And of course there were the Promasidor Team in Johannesburg. They are too numerous to mention, but they made me feel at home and nobody made any comments about my age or my then portly build, which gave me huge encouragement.

Last but not least is Short Joan Edridge, who thanks to the miracles of email, ploughed doggedly through my manuscript in search of errors and mistakes – of which she found a number.

All I can say to you all is 'thank you from the bottom of my heart.'

Sponsor's Foreword

Driving away from the source of the mighty Zambezi River, I felt a sense of awe at what we had just put into motion. Behind us, we had left David Lemon to start his epic adventure and I wasn't sure that he would survive the months ahead.

Hours earlier we had bounced our way through North Western Zambia with a Land Cruiser full of Cowbell staff, an avid photographer and a few well-wishers. Now we quietly pondered the enormity of the task our intrepid adventurer had set himself. I couldn't help wondering how an elderly man could possibly walk alone through three thousand kilometres of very wild Africa and survive.

But survive he has and so far, his Zambezi Cowbell Trek has taken David through some of the most remotely beautiful parts of the continent. Although a major aim of the walk is to publicise the plight of elephants, David's efforts will also be a big boost for Zambian tourism. The wonders of the Victoria Falls are known around the world, but there remain many hidden gems such as the Mongu River Market and the Sioma Ngonye Falls that are featured in this book.

Probably the best part of the adventure for Cowbell as sponsors, has been our re-supply efforts. This has taken the team to many wonderful parts of Zambia that we probably would not have seen any other way. We have watched our adventurer lose a great deal of weight, while seemingly growing stronger by the day. His spirits have flagged on occasion, but his indomitable will to succeed has kept him going.

Now that David is over halfway to the ocean and journey's end, the first part of his story needs to be told. As sponsors of the walk, we sincerely hope that **Cowbells Down the Zambezi** will become part of the curriculum in Zambian and other African schools. My generation and generations before have had their chance to enjoy and develop our environment, but none of us have done a very good job. Perhaps our children can do better and reading this book will give them an idea as to exactly what needs sorting out in our beautiful country.

David Lemon is very much an 'Elephant Man' and it is with pride and excitement that Cowbell is giving support to his attempts to show the world what is happening to Africa's elephants. Regrettably, they are in serious trouble and only a few folk seem to care. Governments give us platitudes that are accepted worldwide, but it needs people on the ground to tell us exactly what is happening. This is a major aim of the Zambezi Cowbell Trek.

Promasidor is the parent company of Cowbell and we believe that the finest milk powder in the world has kept David going on his walk. He complains in the book about the banner that we used, but I am sure he secretly enjoyed parading in front of it.

Cowbells Down the Zambezi is a book about people and places, so we at Cowbell hope you enjoy walking through the wild Zambezi valley with David and spending time with the River People of Zambia.

Andy Taylor
Managing Director
Cowbell,
Zambia.

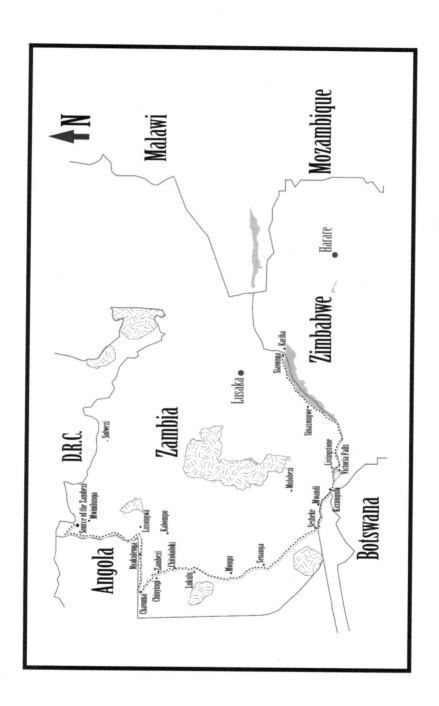

"We go into the wilderness with our whole selves. It asks no less of us. It asks the utmost of our bodies. It asks that we perceive it with accuracy. The price can be high if we do not."
Margaret P. Stark.

Prologue

(The Unanswerable Question)

The glow from dancing flames flickered across his face and I could feel his eyes upon me as we ate. With over a thousand kilometres behind me, I was not in good shape and my host was concerned.

"Why are you doing this?" Simeon asked quietly, reaching for another handful of *nshima*. "You are very old to be walking in the bush."

He was right of course and as I rolled a small amount of the stodgy porridge in my palm, I pondered the answer.

Why was I doing it? What would motivate an elderly man to walk three thousand kilometres along an African river? Would it mean anything to anyone other than myself? Probably not, but I felt it was something I needed to do – if only to prove to myself that I was not yet in my dotage.

One young man who had asked the question had been closer to the mark than anyone else.

"Is it like climbing a mountain?"

That seemed to sum it up. The Zambezi had become my personal mountain and while nobody ever 'conquers' mountain or river, there is always the prospect of reaching the top or the end to keep one going and add fuel to dreams.

But Simeon knew nothing about mountains and waited intently for my answer. Behind him, I could see his womenfolk sitting in the shadows and they too seemed to be listening for some satisfactory explanation for what they obviously regarded as madness.

Thinking on it, I dipped my rolled handful of *nshima* into the smaller pot, soaked it in fish gravy and using one finger, attached a tiny piece of fish to the parcel. Transferring it to my mouth, I chewed slowly and the world seemed to be waiting on my reply. Simeon's dark eyes glowed in the firelight and the night was silent apart from the occasional muffled squawk from insomniac chickens and the grunt of a dreaming goat. In the middle distance, a cowbell pealed softly and I wondered what I could say.

"I am certainly old," I told Simeon as falling logs hissed into the fire. "But this is something I want to do, so I must do it while I still can."

His expression told me that he might understand the words, but not the motivation behind them. I didn't myself and wondered somewhat bleakly just what I was trying to prove and to whom. I was desperately thin, permanently hungry and in bad shape. My heels were split and bleeding, my arms and legs were a mass of cuts and bruises while my shoulders had a permanent ache from the weight of my pack. My teeth rattled like rabid castanets, my mouth was full of ulcers and my progress had slowed from a brisk walk when I started out, to what was little more than a hobbling shuffle. Nevertheless, I was still making progress and even my assorted aches and pains did nothing to spoil the feeling of freedom that bubbled in my chest.

I could do what I want and when I wanted it. Few modern folk have that opportunity and if I took another few months over my walk, it didn't matter in the slightest. It is often said that there is no hurry in Africa and that had to be worth a little hardship.

Lying beneath my blanket later that evening, I looked up at the vast array of African stars and they added to my enjoyment. The stars of Africa are the same stars one sees everywhere else, but when one is in the bush, they seem so much brighter and more numerous. I felt privileged to be able to watch them night after night and knew that with the dawn, I would be walking through a wild world, cleansed by morning dew and looking as freshly welcome to the wanderer as anywhere on earth.

I would meet more folk like Simeon and sample friendship and hospitality that was purely African.

This was surely what my walk was all about.

A fiery-necked nightjar delivered his descending, six-note call to the darkness, fragrant mopani smoke from the fire drifted across my face and a skops owl chirruped sweetly from a nearby tree. A lone hippopotamus gurgled upstream and I felt supremely content with my lot. Despite my physical problems, the sounds of Africa soothed my soul and were an obvious answer to the doubters. If only I could find the words to convey this to people.

In my day to day conversation I struggled to do this, but I hope that in the following pages, you will gain some understanding of what motivates a sixty-seven year old man to walk three thousand kilometres down the Mighty Zambezi.

Chapter One

(Gentle Beginnings)

In the north western corner of Zambia where three countries meet, a tree stands on the edge of a swamp. It is an ordinary msasa tree and looking at it, I wasn't sure whether to be overawed or disappointed. Straight-trunked and middle aged the only aspect of the tree that seemed different was that the root system was above ground and looked vaguely like an upturned candelabra. It was difficult to see the tree as one of the most iconic spots in Africa.

Among those tangled roots, water bubbled from the ground to form a small brown pool, from which it overflowed to trickle through black, swampy ground where it became a tiny stream. A thick covering of leaves had collected on the surface but the stream was too small to be impressive. It was a drab beginning to the fourth longest and most romantic of Africa's rivers – the Mighty Zambezi.

The swamp was covered in miombo woodland and my senses quailed as I looked around me. This was not the open countryside I had been expecting. This was more like rain forest and walking through it would be difficult. The canopy towered above my head, the silence was oppressive and I wondered what I was letting myself in for.

In my *naiveté*, I had envisaged a gentle stroll along open banks with water always to hand. This was altogether more daunting.

"There was a larger tree here," Mr Chiwaya who ran the Heritage Site understood my bewilderment. "When it grew old and died, this one took its place."

We had left Mwinilunga two hours previously and I was impatient to be on my way, but felt suddenly scared about the days ahead. They looked like being considerably more difficult than I had anticipated. My companions obviously shared my misgivings, as everyone had been subdued on the drive to the source. Andy Taylor was struggling to be his usual cheerful self while Talitha was busy with her camera. A small entourage of interested newspaper reporters and local officials had accompanied us to the start, keen to find out what it was all about. I was the centre of attraction, but at that moment, I wanted only to be away from all the fuss.

"How far does this woodland stretch?" I asked Mr Chiwaya. He shrugged burly shoulders and looked worried.

"You will not be able to start from here," He said. "It is too thick to walk through. Other expeditions have always begun at Kaleni Hill."

Kaleni Hill was forty kilometres north of us. I wanted to walk and even though the forest was thick, I felt that with my experience I could surely force my way through it.

"No I will start from here," I told the curator. "I must walk from the source to the sea."

Official photographs were taken and I posed beside the spring, taking the obligatory sip of water, before donning my boots and hefting my pack. The pack contained everything I would need for ten months 'on the road,' as well as sufficient food to keep me going for eight to ten weeks. As I strapped it across my chest, my knees creaked beneath the weight. Fully laden, it weighed thirty kilograms, which was too much for my ancient muscles. I would have to lighten it somehow, but brushing burgeoning doubts aside I said farewell to Andy and Talitha, as well as the assembled media men and spectators.

Taking a deep breath to combat fluttering nerves, I walked down the trickling stream. With one final wave for the cameras, I was on my way.

Three thousand kilometres to go and I had already made my first major mistake.

*　　　*　　　*

Of course, it started a long time before that afternoon at the source. As my sixty-seventh birthday approached, I was becoming ever more restless. It was two years since I had done anything out of the ordinary and that had been a nine week kayaking trip around Lake Kariba. It had been fun, but did little to suppress my adventurous urges.

With the dreaded three score years and ten around the corner, I needed another adventure and when Ed Stafford walked the length of the Amazon, I wondered how he would have coped with the Zambezi. Stafford was a former soldier and half my age, but I felt I could emulate his feat on a river I knew well. I had read Mike Boon's account of kayaking the Zambezi and wondered if anyone had walked it. I wrote to the Royal Geographic Society and according to their records, such a walk had never been done.

Could I do it? At my advanced age, it would be a major undertaking, but the more I thought about it, the more I felt it was possible. According to which accounts I read, the river was between two thousand, seven hundred and three thousand six hundred kilometres in length. It rose in Zambia, ran for two hundred and forty kays through Angola, meandered south and then east before heading into Mozambique and the sea. On the way, it bordered Zambia, Namibia, Zimbabwe and Botswana, so I could face the inevitable hassles of crossing borders in Africa.

That was a daunting prospect, but if I stuck to the northern bank, I would only need visas for Zambia, Angola and Mozambique. Zambia was easy. I had visited the country many times and never experienced problems getting in and out. Angola and Mozambique were another matter and visits to their Embassies in London did nothing to ease my worries.

The Angolans told me that there would be no problem with permits, provided I could supply two references from Angolan residents. When I explained that I knew nobody in their country, the man dealing with my query smiled and told me that I would be able to get the necessary permits at the Embassy in Lusaka or at the border itself.

"We Angolans are friendly people," He assured me. "You will be made welcome in my country."

They were fatefully wrong words, but I didn't know it then.

The Mozambique officials were more dogmatic. They wanted exact dates of my entry to their country and that was something I had no way of knowing. Would I be able to get myself a visa at the border? The answer was unequivocal. I would not. The border post at Zumbo on the Zambezi was not equipped to issue entry permits, so I would need to apply either in London, Lusaka or Tete. It was a problem, but there had to be a way around it.

Another major problem was how to carry the food necessary to keep me alive. I would find food and be fed along the way, but I might spend weeks away from humanity, so would need to have enough for at least two months. Everything would have to be carried, so the logistical problems were depressing. What I needed was someone to resupply me along the way, but I didn't know who I could ask.

Then there was the problem of sponsorship. Ed Stafford had been heavily sponsored on his Amazon walk and without that, could not have succeeded. According to his book, a major sponsor had been Sir Rannulf Fiennes' Trans Global Expedition Trust and their web site told me they sponsored anything that seemed 'mad but marvellous.' That seemed to describe what I was attempting, so I sent a long letter to the Trans Global people, outlining my aims and asking to be considered for one of their thousand pound sponsorships.

They probably thought I was a crank when they read my age, because I never even received an acknowledgement. Dismissing thoughts of sponsorship from my mind, I concentrated on the other problems involved in a Zambezi Walk.

It was Christmas 2011 when Andy Taylor approached me in England. Based in Zambia, he was on holiday and his expression was quizzical as he asked about my proposed venture.

"I suppose, you are going to do the usual David Lemon thing and disappear for months on end so that nobody knows where you are or how you are doing?"

I acknowledged that indeed I was and told him about my abortive search for sponsorship and support.

"Cowbell could sponsor you," He offered. Cowbell were producers of powdered milk in Zambia and Andy was their Managing Director, but I laughed the offer off. I didn't need sponsorship. I had never had it before in my little adventures and always muddled through, so I would survive without it.

"We will give you any help you require in Zambia, provide you with Zambian kwacha and resupply you from time to time. We will even give you a thousand pounds to prepare for the trip." Andy expanded his offer and my ears perked up. I think it was the offer of resupplies that convinced me.

"You're on," I told him and so I became a sponsored adventurer. There were drawbacks to that though. On my arrival at Ndola, I was greeted by cheering schoolchildren, a media circus and a huge blue and white banner that was to dog my footsteps for months to come.

I would not have survived without Cowbell's sponsorship however and they were always there for me when problems cropped up. To Andy and his little team, I will be forever grateful.

In Johannesburg, I spoke with nutritionists about the problems I was going to face and was given samples of supplements that were too heavy to carry in bulk. Jeannine Stokes-Waller, a lovely Afrikaans lady warned me about the dangers I was submitting my body to, but I was forced to ignore her advice, well-meaning though it was. Eventually, I flew to Zambia with a number of packets of vitamin supplement and some small cartons of Cellfood to boost my health.

I also gave a number of interviews and endured a photo shoot, organised by my publicity-orientated friend, Nicola Featonby-Smith. With everything done, I flew to Ndola.

There I spent five enjoyable days meeting people, talking to journalists and stocking up on the lightest food I could find. That was a Southern African breakfast cereal, known as Pro Nutro that I had used before, sweetening tablets for my tea and of course a few sticks of *biltong* – the dried meat of Africa.

I gave talks to local groups and was flown to Lusaka for a press conference with Given Lubinda, Zambia's Tourism Minister and Minister for Foreign Affairs. A burly man who exuded a formidable air of power, he was extremely supportive and gave me a letter, entreating all Zambians to assist me in my efforts. That letter was to rescue me from trouble on more than one occasion.

The press conference itself was also useful and over subsequent months, I was often stopped by Zambians who told me they had seen me on television and were anxious to help and have their photographs taken with me.

But I was becoming ever more fretful and anxious to start walking, so it was with a sense of relief that I set off for Mwinilunga with Andy, Talitha and two pretty young ladies, Lesley and Terri Gwilliam who had come along to see me off. I gave another talk at Solwezi Mine and on the 26th April 2012, Andy drove us to the source of the Mighty Zambezi.

*   *   *

Walking through tangled trees and undergrowth I was immediately in trouble. My boots sank deep into soft mulch underfoot while foliage ripped at my face and body. Trees of varying size formed a solid, unyielding curtain. Time and again, I was beaten back when I didn't have the strength to force my bulky pack between apparently slender trunks. A branch ripped a deep gash in my arm and another snapped the collapsible fishing rod, strapped to my backpack. In the first long hour, I made about sixty metres of forward progress.

Eventually acknowledging to myself that I had been pig-headed, I turned sorrowfully round and went back, forcing myself through that clinging barrier of whip-like trees and easing my feet from the soggy mulch. My shirt was sodden with blood, sweat and water from the trees and my heart pounded with the effort of moving forward. As I approached the source again, I prayed that everyone had gone home, as the thought of explanations and admissions that I was a stubborn old fool were not appealing.

The ramshackle building that was the visitor centre had been left unlocked, so my first camp on the Zambezi Cowbell Trek of 2012 was on the floor of a large building. I went to sleep that night feeling extremely sorry for myself.

It had hardly been an auspicious start.

*   *   *

After a restless night, I was guided down a rough road by a friendly night watchman, called Aaron. He assured me that it would take me around the worst of the thickets and I could rejoin the river some kilometres further on. It was not difficult walking, but my pack was far too heavy. My legs were buckling as I walked and the ache in my back was crippling. At one point, Aaron told me that the right hand verge of the road was in the DRC (Democratic Republic of Congo) so of course I had to walk on that side for a while, so I could say that my walk had taken in another country. It was a pity I couldn't get the requisite stamp in my passport.

After a couple of hours, we came back to the Zambezi - not quite the river of my dreams, but a pathetic little stream trickling unhappily between wooded banks. It was two foot wide at its widest and I wondered at the kayaking tales, wherein boatmen claimed to have started at the source - surely a physical impossibility.

Aaron went home and to show my appreciation - and lighten my load - I gave him some packets of food to take home. His eyebrows rose at the vitamin supplement, but I lied and told him that when mixed with water, the stuff made a delicious porridge. I often wonder whether he tried it.

The road deteriorated into a path that went in the same direction as the stream (it could hardly be called a river) but climbed into a range of shallow hills. It wasn't hard going, but my shoulders ached and the pressure of the pack straps cut off circulation to my fingers. Gritting my teeth, I plodded on. I would have to get used to the discomfort as it was unlikely to lessen.

I passed through a number of villages, where children flocked at my heels, women peeped shyly at me from their cooking fires and men greeted me with jovial concern. My explanations that I was walking to the sea were brushed aside as the ravings of a demented soul and concerned citizens pressed sweet potatoes on me to make me feel better.

They didn't. I enjoy most African bush foods, but have never liked sweet potatoes. However, the offers were genuine and I have always made a point of accepting whatever hospitality is given, so sweet potatoes I ate in abundance. I slept my second night on the front step of a bush school and was given a tour of the area by the acting headmaster. For me, it was a depressing exercise. The Zambezi seemed determined not to grow into a proper river and it meandered around hills and fields without ever getting wider. In most places, I was able to step across and my host assured me that it went on like this for a long way.

"It gets bigger after iKelengi town," He assured me and out came my map. iKelengi was twenty kilometres from the school.

"Can I go straight to iKelengi?" I asked and was told that it was not only possible, but a guide could be arranged to take me there.

So it was that the following morning, I was up with the lark and following a narrow path through delightfully forested countryside with my teacher friend and a couple of strapping youngsters. They set a brisk pace - so brisk that eventually I had to tell them to slow down or carry my pack for me. Much to my delight, they chose the latter course, although they took it in turns to carry the damned thing. For me, the relief of walking without that weight on my back was enormous and I strode out, enjoying the fresh morning air and the countryside around me.

I caught occasional glimpses of the Zambezi, but in the main we stuck to forests and fields, skirting the Fisher farm at Kaleni Hill, a beautifully laid out property that had been the first mission station in Zambia well over a century previously. It all looked very civilised and I even saw the occasional motor vehicle, reminding me that it is never easy to leave the real world for any length of time.

We had done exactly sixteen kilometres by the pedometer on my belt when we reached the outskirts of iKelengi - a typically African town with buildings, ranging from mud huts to modern houses with big gardens. Plots of maize grew on both sides of the road and I wondered how the locals differentiated one from another.

Having bought cokes for my guides at a roadside store, we parted after they had pointed out a path that would take me back to the river. Deciding that there was no hurry in Africa, I wandered into town to enjoy the noisy, dusty ambience. Shopkeepers called greetings and offered chairs for me to sit on, but I eventually found a comfortable roadside wall, where I held court for an hour or so. Mine was the only white face on view and I soon had a crowd of locals around me, all 'oohing' and 'ahing' when I told them my plans. From snotty-nosed urchins to dignified elders, everyone seemed impressed and I preened inwardly at the attention. The winter sun was pleasantly warm and I was thinking about making a move when two men pushed their way through the throng.

"The chief wants to see you," I was told and I wondered what he wanted. Was this going to be one of Africa's bureaucratic tussles or was the chief merely interested in a passing wanderer?

Whatever the case, tribal chieftains would be part of my life over the next few months so I followed the men to the Royal

Palace. Despite the fact that my morning had gone well, I had a fluttering of nervousness in my stomach. Chiefs in rural Africa are powerful people and although I had my letter from Minister Lubinda, I hoped this fellow would appreciate what I was doing.

The Royal Palace was a large house, probably built for some government official in the colonial era. It was surrounded by a six-foot fence made from thatching grass and as we slipped through a gap, my companions warned me to do exactly as they did when in the presence of the chief. I knew from experience that tribal etiquette is extremely important in rural Africa, so promised to do as I was told.

We waited for the chief on a wide, gauzed-in veranda, where I was allowed to sit on a wooden chair, while my companions squatted on the floor. Facing us and about three metres away were two armchairs. Ten minutes later, these were occupied by a thin man, wearing a threadbare suit and a motherly-looking woman who appeared from inside the house. My companions prostrated themselves on the floor, but I stood up and gave a little bow toward the couple.

Somewhat to my surprise, it was the woman who turned out to be Chief Kaleni and the man - who said not a word throughout - was her consort. I studied her with interest. Dressed in a colourful *chitenge* - a wrap around garment worn by most rural women (and a few men) in Zambia - she had a sweet face and looked like everyone's favourite aunt. For all that, there was an indefinable air of command about her and her voice when she spoke was quietly authoritative. She knew all about my Zambezi Walk and questioned me in excellent English as to my plans, my motives and what I hoped to get out of it.

Her questioning was gentle though and throughout it, she gazed at me from a pair of truly lovely brown eyes. She might have been fairly plain in looks, but the authority of her chieftainship was evident in her gaze and I felt that this was a lady worthy of respect. That was certainly shown by my companions who greeted her every utterance with soft claps and bobbed up and down in poses of humble prostration that might have been embarrassing in other circumstances, but seemed natural in the presence of Chief Kaleni.

The questioning seemed to take an age, but it was probably only ten minutes before the chief rose to her feet and with a small smile on her face wished me good luck and asked me to come back and tell her about it when my walk was over. There was more clapping and putting faces to the floor while I thanked her and gave her another small bow.

About to leave the veranda, the chief turned back to me and indicated my hat. **Zambezi Cowbell Trek 2012** was emblazoned on the front of it and I explained that Cowbell were my official sponsors.

"The milk people?" She queried softly and I was surprised that she knew of them in this isolated spot, but I suppose chiefs need to have their fingers on all sorts of pulses. I told her how Cowbell were an offshoot of Promasidor in Johannesburg and how good they were being to me.

With another smile and a little wave over her shoulder, she disappeared into the house itself, her silent consort still dutifully in tow.

I was to meet other chiefs over succeeding months, but Chief Kaleni was my first experience of Zambian royalty and to say that I was impressed with her charm and natural authority would be an understatement. The lady was a star and I went on my way feeling good about myself and my Zambezi Cowbell Trek.

Back in town, it was hot and dusty, but I had a river to catch up with, so hefting my pack on to my shoulders and waving to the throng of locals who had gathered to see me go, I set off along a narrow path through fields of straggly cassava plants.

The Zambezi was beginning to look more like a river and after an hour, I reached a spot where it thundered through five great pipes beneath a road. There was a wide pool below the bridge, sandy beaches on either bank and it seemed the ideal spot to camp for the night.

A minor drawback was the crowd of curious children who appeared from nowhere to follow me with wide-eyed curiosity and whispered comments to each other. They offered no threat and in time, I would take village children for granted, but at that early stage, they were an embarrassing nuisance. At one stage, I chased them away by running a few steps toward them waving my arms. They ran off squealing with what sounded like terror but were soon back, circumspectly at first but as their curiosity got the better of them, standing around me, just out of reach and staring intently.

Eventually I ignored them and got on with setting up camp on the sand. It was a comfortable camp in delightful surroundings and I slept well, lulled by the thunder of falling water, but I learned one lesson that night. The air was filled with invisible spray that slowly soaked through my bedding, my clothes and even my hat. When I got out of bed in the morning, everything was saturated and took an hour or two to dry out, making an uncomfortable start to the day.

Nevertheless, I left my sandy beach shortly after first light and headed north, feeling comfortable with my progress. I was eighty kilometres from the source and averaging twenty odd kays a day, which wasn't bad for an old fellow. I knew that would drop off in time, but felt confident that I could manage the three thousand or so kilometres that lay ahead of me.

Perhaps I should not have been so complacent because it was to be a bad day. Three kilometres downstream, I came to a foaming little tributary that tumbled into the Zambezi. It looked rocky and fairly shallow, so wouldn't provide much of an obstacle, but before tackling it, I needed a drink. Shrugging off my pack, I loosened my belt before sitting down on a rock. On the belt was a first aid kit, my leatherman and a pouch containing my camera. As I took it from my waist, I inadvertently let go of one end, the Nikon pouch slipped off and I watched helplessly as the camera bounced off a rock and plopped into the stream.

With a yell of frustration I jumped in after it, my boots slipping and sliding on wet rocks and icy water battering at my clothing. Scrabbling frantically under the torrent, I could only feel rocks and these were moving with the force of the water. Despairingly I put my head right under, but the water was too muddy and fast-flowing for me to see anything. With a groan, I came up again to find myself surrounded by curious locals.

I had thought myself alone in the world when I stopped beside that stream, but in Zambia one is rarely without company. This lot looked vaguely apprehensive and doubtless wondered at this weird *mzungu*, taking a bath in such inauspicious circumstances. Haltingly I explained what had happened and a number of youngsters jumped into the water to assist. It was another aspect of this fascinating country that I was to grow accustomed to over the months ahead. No effort was too much for Zambian folk when they thought I needed help. These young men were enduring extreme cold and discomfort, merely because I had been a fool and they wanted to assist. Would that happen in the West I wonder? Probably not for a camera.

But it was a hopeless task, even though my assistants widened the search area and were going deep into the Zambezi itself. I asked whether there were crocs in the area and one of them waved his hand dismissively, but I was worried and called them out. The camera was gone and although I had another one, it was a major disaster so early in the trek. Thanking my very wet helpers, I resumed my walk, feeling cold, disgruntled and angry with myself.

Drawing closer to the border post with Angola, worries started to flutter in my stomach. I have travelled through Africa in various forms of transport, but almost all my problems have occurred when crossing from one country into another. I have been held up for hours, been arrested, knocked about and asked for many a bribe - none of which I have paid. I don't suppose it is peculiar to Africa, but border officials seem to have a universally inflated idea of their own importance and love to make life difficult for the solitary traveller. I didn't suppose the formalities at iZhimbe would be any different.

Suddenly there it was. A battered wooden sign pointed north and informed me that the border post was two kilometres away. It seemed too good to be true and I wondered whether to keep going along the river and bypass officialdom altogether. It was a tough decision, but Angola had only just emerged from a bitter civil war and I didn't want to spend the next few weeks hiding from the authorities. That was not the point of my trip.

Tempting though it was to stick with the river, I walked in the direction indicated by the ramshackle sign. I would be honest. I would go through the formalities. I would pay for the necessary permit and add a few American dollars from my bribe fund if necessary. I needed to keep going forward, so would do whatever was necessary to maintain my progress.

I should have followed my instincts and kept to the river.

CHAPTER TWO

(Shorts and a Ministerial Convoy)

The path emerged on what purported to be a main road, although potholes and puddles made it look more like a minefield. Nevertheless, there were signs of heavy traffic on its rutted surface and turning my face resolutely to the left I plodded toward the border.

I hadn't gone more than a hundred metres when a minibus taxi roared up behind me, the passengers staring at this bedraggled *mzungu* plodding through the dust with his house on his back. The driver shouted that he would take me to the border post for 'five pin.' With the Zambian kwacha used in units of a thousand, each such unit was known as a 'pin,' so this fellow was asking five thousand kwacha to carry me little more than a kilometre. That was less than one pound sterling, but it doesn't take long to begin assessing value in the local currency.

I smilingly waved the offer aside and in no way abashed, he crashed the minibus into gear and roared away, covering me in thick yellow dust. His passengers waved pityingly.

iZhimbe was a typical bush hamlet with a few brick buildings and bedraggled trees offering shade at the side of the road. Women sold fruit and vegetables, ragged urchins ran around and chickens squawked indignantly at any interruption to their foraging. The first major building in town was a police station, so in keeping with my guise as an honest traveller, I called in to announce my presence. The officer in charge examined my letter of authority from Minister Lubinda, then invited me into his office for a chat. It was very pleasant and when he saw me out later, he shook me by the hand and wished me luck and 'all God's blessings.'

Greatly encouraged, I walked across the road to the Zambian border post. The official on the desk obviously didn't like the look of me and even the magic letter did nothing to sway his opinion, but eventually I managed to see the man in charge - a thin fellow who introduced himself as Aaron.

"I am David," I told him and went through my story again.

Unlike his minion, Aaron was understanding and told me that although he was pleased with what I was doing for Zambia (it was being done for me, but I didn't shatter his illusions) he was not sure the Angolans would let me in.

"Sometimes they are friendly and helpful those people, but on other occasions they even give me problems. However, I will take you across and see what we can do to help."

This was generous indeed and not what I expected from officialdom in Africa, so I jumped at his offer. While Aaron stopped to speak with his surly subordinate, I moved across to my pack, but he waved me on.

"Leave that here and we will come back to it," I felt suddenly doubtful. "While I am happy to stamp your passport, we had better see how the Angolians react before I do."

I found the Zambian habit of inserting an 'i' into the word quite comical, but suppressed my mirth and followed Aaron across the iZhimbe River and into Angola.

If life moved slowly on the Zambian side of the border, it was almost at a standstill in Angola. There were the same ramshackle buildings, the same raggedly dressed children and even the same chickens, but there was no sense of urgency about the place. People sat under trees and talked, music blared from a store and two smartly dressed young women greeted Aaron with enthusiasm.

"They are Zambians, here to see what Angola is like," He explained as we went into the immigration post. "I think they will come back with us."

I felt that the girls were probably 'ladies of the night' looking for Angolan – or even Angolian - custom. They examined me with unfeigned curiosity and I resolved to keep my hand on my wallet and my virtue intact.

The Chief of Immigration greeted us with a beer bottle in his hand and a beam on his face. He was overweight and sweating badly in the stifling heat of the border post. The windows were shut and an overhead fan made desultory efforts to keep the place cool, but it moved so slowly that a small army of flies rested on the blades, enjoying a free ride to nowhere.

Aaron explained the problem. My passport and ministerial letter were handed over and read with great solemnity by the fat man. I waited anxiously for his verdict which wasn't long in coming.

"I don't mind you coming through," He told me through Aaron. "I will have to clear it with my headquarters though, as the army are working along the river and you might need a special permit."

After a long discussion in the local language, Aaron told me that we should wait in the shade till decisions were made. Out we went and made our way to the noisy store. It wasn't well stocked, but there were a few chairs and tables, while a sign told me that smoking was prohibited but cold beer was on sale. The Zambian women smiled at me as we walked in. I tried to ignore them.

Sitting me down at another table, Aaron told me to wait while he tried to sweeten up the Angolan officials, so I ordered a beer each for us and a couple for the said officials as a boost to the sweetening process. The ladies looked soulfully at our beers, so I ordered a coke each for them as well. It looked like being an expensive day.

Time seemed to creak by in the heat and I made desultory conversation with the ladies, who came from Choma and worked as hairdressers. Quite what they were doing in isolated iZhimbe they didn't say and I was so hot, sweaty and nervous that I wasn't interested.

At last Aaron returned and motioned to me to accompany him. To my dismay, he headed back toward the bridge, with me struggling to keep up.

"They are checking with Head Office," he said as we walked, "and it could take time, so we will go back and our friend will come across when he has news."

There was little for me to do in iZhimbe so I wandered among the trees, answering questions from friendly locals and looking at the wares on sale. They were the normal array of tomatoes, cabbage, dried fish and a few packets of square biscuits, known as chico biscuits. I bought one of these from the crone who was selling it and put it in my pocket for future eating. It was the start of a strange love affair - and I don't mean with the crone. Hard and tasteless though they were, those biscuits kept me going through some very bad times.

For a while, I sat with the Choma ladies who as forecast, had come back into Zambia. We chatted amicably, although the afternoon heat began to press down on me as the day wore on. There was nothing I could do but wait.

I didn't see the Angolan official come across the bridge, but the surly immigration chappie suddenly materialised with the news that Aaron wanted to see me. Bidding farewell and good luck to the ladies, I hurried to the office where I found the fat man cuddling another beer and Aaron looking forlorn.

"You will need a special permit to continue," He told me. "Everyone is frightened that you will be shot by soldiers or step on a landmine, so you will need special authorisation from Luanda."

"How will I get that?" I asked plaintively. "And what will it cost?"

Aaron shrugged.

"I don't know what it will cost, but the only place you can obtain such a permit is in Solwezi."

I was aghast. Solwezi was two hundred kilometres behind me. Here I was, stranded in one of the most isolated corners of

Zambia and I had to get back to a town that was even further away than the Zambezi source.

"How can I get to Solwezi from here?" I protested and Aaron shrugged. The Angolan swigged from his bottle.

"You can take the minibus out there." (it was the one, I had seen that morning) "They will take you to iKelengi and from there you can find buses to Solwezi."

There was no point in arguing. Officialdom had struck again and it was hardly Aaron's fault. Thanking him and promising to see him in a few days time, I hurried out to the minibus, which almost as though I was expected, stood with its engine running in the shade of a tree. Explaining my needs to the driver, I asked his advice and he seemed unfazed.

"I will take you to iKelengi and from there, my brother can carry you to Mwinilunga." I shuddered in mounting despair. Mwinilunga was the closest town to the Zambezi source, so the end result would be that at the end of four hard days, I would be back where I started.

Resigning myself to the inevitable, I put my pack in the minibus and wedged myself into a seat beside an elderly lady with a basket of dried fish on her lap. Fortunately I was beside a window and to the consternation of other passengers, I kept this open so that a modicum of hot air could flow over my face.

The journey was a nightmare. In places, the potholes were like craters and the vehicle had to be inched around them, tilting and swaying so that the elderly lady and I were soon firm friends. The bus was filled with the smell of sweaty bodies - mine included - fish, chickens and dust. We reached iKelengi around five in the evening and I was beginning to worry about money. Andy had given me a handful of kwacha, but I would need somewhere to spend the night and there wouldn't be enough for that after I had paid the minibus driver and his brother.

There was worse to come. My transport to Mwinilunga, forty-five kilometres away was a Chinese-made motor cycle and I gazed at it in horrified trepidation.

"But how will that take me and my pack?" I cried plaintively. "We will crash and be killed."

"I am a good driver and it will be easy," My new chauffeur's name was Gideon. "Besides, The Lord will look after us, so we will be alright."

The early Christian missionaries did a good job in Zambia. Almost without exception, those folk I met in the course of my walk were devoutly religious and there were occasions when I prayed too, in the hope that their faith in God's divine assistance wasn't misplaced.

This was one such occasion and as we chugged into the evening, I clung grimly to the frame beneath my bottom and shut my eyes. Although the road was better than it had been further north, there were potholes to avoid and I wondered what would happen if we met oncoming traffic and a pothole at the same time. Fortunately, it didn't happen and whether that was due to God's guidance or plain old Lemon's Luck, I wasn't sure.

We arrived at Mwinilunga in darkness and Gideon pointed out a ramshackle lodge in the town centre where I could sleep. I still had the problem of cash, but with some reluctance, the owner of the lodge changed fifty American dollars for me - at an extortionately bad rate - and that was sorted out. I was sure Andy and Cowbell would rescue me when I told them where I was.

I was given a comfortable room in an annexe and went to bed feeling tired and frustrated, but knowing that things could have been worse. Africa has a habit of throwing up unexpected problems to the unwary traveller and sometimes, they provide far more of a challenge than the adventure itself.

In one day, I had walked in two different countries, met a huge assortment of people, endured a rib-shattering ride in a minibus, a terrifying journey on a motorcycle and ended up in a Mwinilinga flea pit - out of pocket, out of patience and with all sorts of problems ahead of me. Surely things couldn't get worse?

Little did I know it, but they could and would - considerably worse!

*   *   *

Victor Kayekezi was the District Commissioner of Mwinilunga and he rose from his desk to greet me. A short, well-built man in his thirties, he had heard about my troubles at the border and subsequent arrival in town the previous evening. Obviously worried about the geriatric *mzungu* in his domain, he had sent his driver Augustus and personal assistant, Kenneth Katawa around to the Muzina Lodge to collect me.

Both men were charming and suggested that the DC would love to meet me, but I had no doubt that it was a summons rather than a request. Having nothing better to do with my Saturday morning but make enquiries about buses to Solwezi, I climbed into the government Land Rover and here I was, meeting the Great Man himself.

Victor read my ministerial letter and listened to my tale of woe in attentive silence. When I finished, he propped his chin on manicured fingers and studied me across the desk.

"I will take you to Solwezi myself," That solved one problem, "There, we will see the Portuguese Consul and sort this matter out within the hour. We will leave tomorrow and in the meantime, my men can show you the town."

There wasn't much to see in Mwinilunga, but I wandered around for a while, had broken eggs and soggy chips in Kenneth Katawa's eating house and with my visa problems apparently solved, generally enjoyed my day. The sun was pleasantly warm and like the DC, most Mwinilunga citizens seemed to know about my border hassles, so I was a minor celebrity wherever I went. Many people approached for a chat and to express their sympathy at my treatment from the 'Angolians.'

It was all very pleasant and I even stood myself to a couple of cold beers that evening. I wasn't going to risk Kenneth's cafe again, so bought paw paw from a street vendor and enjoyed that in my room. The following day we drove to Solwezi.

We arrived well after dark and as I had arranged with Andy to be met by the local Cowbell representative, the first stop was outside a local supermarket. There was Albert huddling in the shadows and he had a wad of cash for me, which he handed over after glancing over his shoulder to ensure we were not being watched. With a couple of million kwacha (the exchange rate was eight thousand to the pound) in my pocket, I felt better and confident that my problems would be sorted out on the morrow.

I was being naive. This was Africa and despite Victor Kayekezi's authority, the matter was not to be resolved that easily.

We were driven into the government offices on Monday morning. There I was introduced to Permanent Secretary, Douglas Ngimbe as well as most of the staff. The building also housed the office of the Minister for the North West, but she was not available. I enjoyed tea from a china cup in Douglas' office and then I waited for something to happen - and waited - and waited. I know there is no hurry in Africa, but there are times when the lack of it tries my patience.

While I waited around the government building, I couldn't help wondering to myself why it was that despite having one of the nicest climates in the world, Zambians rarely opened their windows to allow the light in. Curtains were kept shut and lights were needed in even the most palatial of rooms. Victor's office in Mwinilunga was a prime example, as was Douglas Ngimbe's. It seemed strange, particularly as I live in a foul climate, yet open my windows and curtains at every opportunity.

But there were more important things to worry about than the Zambian predilection for dark conditions and I was relieved when Victor reappeared from an inner sanctum and announced that we were going to see the Portuguese Consul. Jumping back in the Land Rover, we travelled four hundred metres before pulling up at a ramshackle cottage, set back from the road. A grubby flag hung limply from a pole outside and a security guard bit his nails behind a boom.

Striding forward, Victor nodded to the guard and was allowed to walk past him, but I was stopped by a hand held out in my path. Turning to see what was wrong, Victor snapped at the guard, to be answered with a torrent of Lunda.

"What is the matter?" I asked plaintively. "Why won't he let me through?"

The DC smiled grimly and the guard picked up a telephone receiver in his guardhouse.

"You are wearing shorts," Victor told me, "and everyone is required to wear trousers when entering the consulate."

I looked at the shabby little building in amazement. Paint peeled from the walls, the garden was overgrown and the corrugated-iron roof had huge areas of rust where the coating had come off. The place was a mess and even though I had washed and ironed my clothing in Muzinga Lodge, I was not to be allowed entry because I wasn't wearing trousers. It did not make sense.

With Victor's influence, we were eventually allowed through and met the Consul in a back office. My bare legs provoked a barely-concealed sneer from the man, but I was not impressed by him either. Another small man, he did not have the presence of Victor Kayekezi and I decided that he was merely a bully, taking advantage of his probably undeserved status. I was being unfair and smiled to myself at the thought, but His Excellency - or whatever one calls Consuls - caught my smile and snapped angrily at Victor.

"He says that the dress rule is there for a purpose," I was told. "It keeps the riff raff out who merely want to waste time."

As ninety-nine percent of Zambians wore long trousers, I couldn't follow that, but bit back the retort that sprang to my lips. I had to stay calm and not let officialdom rattle me if I wanted to resume my walk. I listened humbly as Victor explained my problem to the Consul. Eventually I was called in on the discussion, but the Consul himself wouldn't talk to me, directing his comments through my companion. An official was summoned to deal with me and I made the acquaintance of Madeleina Kamalonga. It was not to be a happy relationship.

Ms Kamalonga - a not unattractive lady - plonked a pile of forms down on the counter and stood over me while I completed them. When I asked a question, she sneered visibly and explained slowly as though speaking to some senile old goat. Her command of English was excellent, but - perhaps it was the shorts - she obviously felt that dealing with my problem was beneath her dignity. I could feel my temper rising and glanced across to see whether Victor would spring to my rescue again, but he was engaged in deep conversation with the Angolan Consul. They were probably talking football - the one subject on which everyone in Zambia was totally agreed.

At last the forms were completed to Madeleina's satisfaction and she asked for two hundred US dollars. I was struck dumb for a moment. I was travelling on a shoestring and losing that amount of money would leave me dangerously short. When I queried the amount, the lady's sneer reappeared.

"It is one hundred dollars for the special permit and another hundred for express delivery," She told me witheringly. "If you don't want express delivery, it could take up to six months to come through. With the payment, we should receive it tomorrow."

I paid up, but not without a huge sense of despondency enveloping my shoulders. I would be left without financial reserves for emergencies and when travelling alone in rural Africa, those reserves are very necessary. I didn't seem to have a choice though and the cash having been squirreled away in a desk, Victor and I returned to the government offices, where he handed me over to Douglas Ngimbe.

"I must get back to Mwinilunga," He explained. "The Minister is visiting tomorrow, but Ngimbe will assist you with the Angolans and arrange for you to be brought back once the permit has been issued."

In the meantime, I had to find somewhere to stay within walking distance of both the government offices and the Portuguese Consulate, so with the assistance of Eugene Sibote - Police Commissioner for the North Western District - I landed up at Ngongo Lodge. Inside it was comfortable and the staff were friendly. There was even a beer garden which gladdened my heart, but the lodge was set right in the middle of downtown Solwezi and my spirits plummeted again. I had no choice however and could only make the best of the situation. As he drove away, Eugene promised to exert whatever influence he had on my behalf, so I had plenty of big guns on my side.

For twelve long days, I hung around Solwezi and the Ngongo Lodge. Every morning, I walked to the government offices, had a chat with Douglas or whoever happened to be around and then walked to the Portuguese Consulate, there to be stopped and told that I could not enter while wearing shorts. Every morning, I protested that I had no long trousers, had already spoken to the Consul and been allowed to enter the hallowed building. Every morning, the security man telephoned someone inside the building before I was reluctantly allowed through and every morning, Madeleina Kamalonga gave a wordless shrug as soon as she saw me and my heart dropped a little further into my boots.

"The papers are still with the people in Luanda," Was all she would say and there was nothing I could do about it.

The same series of events happened every afternoon and eventually, I would wander back to Ngongo Lodge, picking my way through raucous side streets where the noise was deafening, the crowds terrifying in their volume and piles of smelly rubbish had to be carefully circumvented. I spoke daily on the phone to Douglas, imploring him to make something happen and he kept promising that things would be resolved the following day. They never were and one morning, I phoned Minister Lubinda in Lusaka and asked him to do something with the Angolan authorities. He promised to do what he could and Douglas later told me that the Angolan Ambassador had rung the Consul and asked him to let me through, but apparently the holdup was in Luanda, not Solwezi.

It was hugely frustrating, made infinitely more so by the twice daily confrontations over my shorts. When I queried the constant harassing with the Kamalonga woman, she smirked and told me that I could always buy a pair of trousers. Once again, I had to bite my tongue before I dropped myself in further trouble.

The days came and the days went, each one the same as the one before and each one adding to my frustration. People in Lusaka were apparently working hard on my behalf and I knew Douglas (he always called me 'My Dear') was doing his best, but I seemed to be getting nowhere. For all that extra hundred dollars, this was hardly 'express delivery.'

One morning, I was approached by a shaven-headed man in camouflage uniform with an AK47 slung across his shoulder. He made directly for me and I wondered what sort of trouble I was in this time.

"You are Mr Lemon," He announced and I agreed that I was. As mine was the only white face in town, it was hardly a clever deduction on his part.

"'I am George."

"Hello George," I muttered. "Nice to meet you."

"Those Angolians are stupid people Mr Lemon," I immediately warmed to George. "We Zambians were taught by the British, so we know how to do things properly, but the Angolians were taught by the Portuguese, so they remain stupid."

If ever there was an oblique compliment to Cecil Rhodes and the minions of Britain's one-time Empire, this was it and I smiled at the thought of George addressing some of the liberal apologists for Empire that abound in Britain. I shook him warmly by the hand.

"Thank you George. You have made my day for me." And we went our separate ways, but I felt much better for meeting George of Solwezi.

Another interlude was provided by a bus driver called Bob and his friend, Chinga. They hailed me in the market and invited me to share their pork chops and *nshima*. Chinga told me that he owned a camp in South Luangwa and was in Solwezi to investigate the possibility of opening a back packers' lodge in the town. I hadn't seen a single back packer during my stay and told him so. He agreed rather sadly.

"'It would be a good place to work though."

With that, I couldn't agree. I was fed up with the town, its people and its amenities, but we enjoyed a nice lunch and they wished me luck when we parted.

After ten days of frustration, I had had enough. I told Douglas I would give it another two days, but that would be that. I would take the Kabompo Road from Mwinilunga, which led down the Angolan border, then head East to Chavuma where I would rejoin the Zambezi. It was a longer walk than the two hundred and forty kilometres of river that went through Angola and would mean my dream of becoming the first person to walk the length of the Zambezi would come to nothing.

"I cannot go on like this, Douglas," I told my important friend. "Not only am I going mad, but I am costing my sponsors a fortune."

It didn't seem right to keep using Cowbell cash on what might yet turn out to be a fruitless quest. Douglas promised to have one more attempt to exert whatever influence he could muster.

It didn't work and on 7th May, I marched into the consulate after the usual row about shorts and demanded to see Madeleina Kamolonga. When she made her customary sneering entrance, I demanded my two hundred dollars and told her that she could keep her ruddy country and her consulate with its silly delusions of grandeur. She raised supercilious eyebrows, produced my money and waved me away.

As I wandered out for the last time, the gate guard beamed at me - he had given me the usual hard time ten minutes previously - and I spared him a sarcastic scowl. I couldn't help wondering whether trouble might have been avoided, had I followed Ms Kamalonga's advice and bought a pair of trousers.

Rules in Africa can rarely be circumvented.

*   *   *

At last I was on my way. I left Solwezi in high dudgeon and endured a five hour ride to Mwinilunga in a seriously overcrowded and overloaded - and late - Kiliki bus. For the second time, I arrived in town after dark, but I knew where the Muzina Lodge was this time, so booked myself in. Unfortunately, the only room available was beside the bar, so sleep was a long time coming that night.

Victor Kayekezi greeted my return with effusive apologies for the inefficiency of the 'Angolian' civil servants and his own government's inability to help. I waved it off with the assurance that I wasn't too worried as it took the pressure off my walk.

I was lying. I felt sick inside. My preparations, the worries and pain I had been through in the lead up to this adventure had all been in vain. I would not be the first person to walk the length of the Zambezi River. The dream was over.

But I still had a long walk ahead of me and explained to Victor how I would make my way to Chavuma. He summoned his Heads of Department to a meeting in which my route and possible pitfalls were discussed at length. Maps were drawn up, alternatives were discussed and I was told that the shortest route meant travelling South toward Kabompo until I reached the Courthouse at Lusongwa. There I should take a new road that went straight to Chavuma, but if I missed this, I would have to make for Kabompo itself and then up through Zambezi toward my destination.

To be honest, I didn't care. After hanging around for nearly two weeks, I wanted to be on my way and making progress. Still, it was kind of them to concern themselves and I appreciated the handshakes and expressions of encouragement I received.

The Immigration Officer, Mr Zulu even stamped my passport for a full ninety days, thereby saving me looking for an immigration centre when my thirty day permit expired.

"After that, you will need a special permit," He told me solemnly but I didn't care. Given Lubinda had assured me that there would be no problems with immigration, so that was not a worry. I asked Victor the best way of getting out of town, but he wasn't having that.

"I shall take you in my Land Rover," he told me, "and drop you off where the Kabompo road begins. We will give you a proper send off, My Friend."

He was a nice young man, Victor Kayekezi. District Commissioners in Zambia are political appointments and with his driving personality, capacity for hard work, charm and helpfulness, I felt he would go far. When I told him that he would one day be president of Zambia, he took my hand and looked into my eyes.

"David, that is a true compliment for my future," He told me. "I thank you from my heart for saying that."

Victor dropped me off on the road to Kabompo early one morning and I felt suddenly daunted by the task I had set myself. The sun shone, the dusty road stretched into infinity and I had a long walk ahead of me. Augustus took numerous photographs of Victor and I, then with a final wave they drove back to Mwinilunga, I took a deep breath, shrugged my pack into position on my back and started walking.

For the second time in less than three weeks, I only had three thousand kilometres to go.

*　　　*　　　*

With my muscles relatively fresh, I made good progress on that first day. I spent an hour at an army checkpoint, chatting with the soldiers about my walk and their duties in this remote spot. There were few villages near the road and dark forests seemed to stretch for a long way in every direction. Nice looking spots to camp were everywhere, but there was always one major problem. I have a deeply ingrained fear of running out of water. It is heavy stuff to carry and I had filled up with two litres at the check point, which was more than enough to see me through a night, but I was scared to stray too far from the precious substance. As I walked, I scanned the bush for any signs of moisture, but the ground looked parched and there was little undergrowth between the trees. I would have to rely on villages.

I covered well over twenty kilometres that first day and eventually made camp in deep forest. I used a little precious water in my vitamin supplement - I thought of it as gruel - but didn't dare make tea in case I couldn't find water the following day. I had bought more chico biscuits before leaving Mwinilunga, so they - there were two in a packet - were my breakfast, my mouth washed out with a sip or two of water.

Chicos are hard square biscuits that come in a variety of flavours that all taste very similar. They remind me of the hardtack biscuits, contained in military ration packs, but over the months of my walk, I developed a taste for them and bought them whenever I could. At one pin a packet, they were a bargain, though I sometimes smiled at the thought that in normal life, I would not have touched the ruddy things. They were dry, tasteless and not a lot of fun, although at the time, they were a marvellous supplement to my gruel.

With over twelve kays under my belt on the second day, I was sitting on my pack under a tree, when I heard the sound of engines. The only vehicle I had seen was an army truck at the check point, but suddenly a cloud of thick dust was approaching and I watched with interest, without stirring from my perch.

A land cruiser thundered past, enveloping me in dust. It was followed by another and then another. This was obviously an official party on their way to something important, but I was not too interested, apart from having to keep my mouth firmly closed against the dust. Seven vehicles sped past then slid to a stop a hundred metres up the road. I wondered if this meant trouble.

Figures loomed through the dust, but I wasn't going to move from my seat. Suddenly I was surrounded by people, including Mrs Limate, the government minister for the North West province. I had met her in Solwezi and wondered whether I should stand out of respect for her office. She didn't seem to mind me seated though, so I stayed where I was.

"How are you doing Mr Lemon?" She asked and I explained that apart from worries about water, life was good and I was making excellent progress. She snapped something in Lunda to her entourage, most of whom were staring at me as though I was some exotic species of man eater. One man stepped out from the throng and it was Victor, my friendly DC.

"The Minister says you are obviously a very strong man," He grinned at me and I solemnly agreed that I was.

"But she says that strong as you are, we are going to give you a lift to the crossroads ahead. We are going to visit a new border post with Angola and it will save you twenty kilometres."

In normal circumstances, this would have been cheating, but Angolan officialdom had prevented me from walking the entire Zambezi and the river was many kilometres away in any case. In some ways, the Angolans had taken the pressure off me, so I accepted the ride and for the first time in my life, was part of an African ministerial cavalcade.

We were the last vehicle in line, so took the brunt of the dust, but I couldn't help wondering what would happen if one of the vehicles had a problem. Visibility was but a few metres and we were travelling at well over eighty kays an hour, so the carnage could have been horrendous. I might have been better off walking.

Victor laughed at my discomfiture and assured me that all the drivers were trained and experienced in bush conditions. "We have to travel fast," he commented, "because the Minister is such a busy lady that she is always in a hurry."

I reflected that the sense of power such cavalcades must engender probably had a lot to do with the speed, but they were being kind to me so I kept my thoughts to myself. Besides, it was nice to sit in comfort and not have the weight of that pack tugging at my shoulders.

All too soon, we arrived at a crossroads, where whitewashed shops stood back from the road. Augustus fought the Land Rover to a halt and Victor and I piled out. I could understand his need for haste as the rest of the convoy didn't even slow down.

"We will leave you here," He gripped my hand again. "These people will look after you."

Some locals were wandering across the road to see what was going on and he directed a stream of Lunda at them. Then with a final shake of my hand, Victor pushed me toward a thin young man and climbed back into the vehicle. He waved and then this hopefully future president of Zambia was gone and this time, the parting was final.

Dumping my pack under a tree, I wandered across the road with my new companion.

*   *   *

Most roadside settlements in rural Zambia look much the same - a collection of small, ramshackle buildings a little way off the thoroughfare, one or two of which might show signs of recent painting or development and a tree or other landmark, around which the settlement has sprung up.

This one was no different and crossing the road, I made my way to the smartest looking of the shops. My companion looked pleased.

"This is my place," he told me, "and it is not ready yet, but if you need anything, my cousin has a shop over here."

I didn't and Joe Kapinga showed me on to his veranda where a number of older men were taking advantage of sparse shade. My approach was regarded with evident curiosity, but

Joe announced that I was very tired and needed quiet. Quite how he knew that, I wasn't sure but he was right.

A chair was produced and Joe proceeded to regale me with stories about himself, his family - he seemed to be distantly related to Chief Chibwiko - and his hopes and plans for the future.

"I have a mine as well as this shop," He passed that news from the side of his mouth and I grinned at the subterfuge. The men around us were hanging on every word, although their eyes were on me and I didn't think Joe's mine could remain a secret much longer. "When I have enough money to develop it, I will build more stores right around this area.

'I am looking for a partner at the moment too."

I had to give him credit for not asking for money, but I have spent most of my life in Africa and am too old to fall for stories of instant wealth waiting to be found.

"Don't look at me Joe," I laughed. "I haven't got any money and I don't know anything about mining or the retail business."

He showed no disappointment at my rebuff. Food was called for and his wife, Goodness appeared from inside the store. She was a large lady with a baby hanging from one breast and smiled at me before wandering off to make a fire for *nshima*.

Despite his importuning, Joe Kapinga was a nice young man and insisted that I spent the night on his veranda. Goodness apologised because the only relish she could produce with the *nshima* was made from boiled rape, but despite a lifelong antipathy toward vegetables, I managed to get my share down.

As evening drew in, the talk became more general and one elderly fellow, who had directed a stream of Lunda at me initially, suddenly switched to French and I had to dig into my memory for long forgotten remnants of that language. He had learned his French while working in the Congo and eventually, we had quite an enjoyable conversation. A radio was produced and hitched to a car battery, so the evening peace was shattered by the strident sounds of an African disco. A couple of old men danced on the dusty ground and my French-speaking friend displayed a talent for old fashioned jiving that I would never have suspected.

Just before the sun went down, I saw the ministerial convoy hurtling back toward Mwinilunga and moments later, a pall of dust drifted up from the road and coated us all with its rough embrace. Chief Chibikwo's son arrived in a smart 4 x 4 and when I was introduced, he took it as the cue for another photo shoot. The evening light was still good and we posed beside the store, on the road, leaning against his vehicle and beside the road sign directing traffic to the border post.

"I will put these on your web site," He promised, writing my details in a note book before roaring away into the gathering gloom. As far as I know, he never did.

I have to admit that I did enjoy the evening. It was redolent of old time Africa and everyone was friendly and helpful. The only problem was that I was dying for a hot drink but felt it would be rude to make one for myself alone and I didn't have enough tea or coffee to satisfy everyone. I went to bed with a glass of tepid water to allay my thirst.

I was away before Joe and Goodness woke up and I made good time along that dusty road. The morning was fresh, birds sang in the trees and there were few signs of life in the villages I passed.

I felt good and after my lift in the ministerial cavalcade, my attitude to this part of the walk had changed. I was a long way from the Zambezi and decided that while I was walking along the road, I would accept any lift that was offered. Once I reached the river, it would be different, but that was many days away and for the moment, I wanted to start the proper walk as soon as I could. If that meant accepting lifts, then so be it.

The only problem was that there was nobody to offer me a lift. Although the road to Kabompo was nominally a highway, I could see from the dusty surface and deep corrugations that it was rarely used and I walked through that day without seeing anything more than a few roadside goats. Villages became fewer and further between, but when I did pass one, I made sure to fill my water bottles, even though the extra weight on my shoulders made life difficult.

I spent another night in the forest, enjoying the peace, the dazzling array of stars overhead and the various sounds of the night. I even risked a water shortage by making myself a cup of tea, so my sleep was good and I looked forward to the morrow.

It didn't take long for my days to fall into a pattern. I would rise at five, build a fire, more to protect myself against the morning cold than for culinary purposes and be on the road as daylight arrived. In the first two hours, I reckoned to complete at least six kilometres and then as the sun grew warmer, my pace slackened and I would stroll through the day, my eyes on the lookout for water sources and my soul singing with the joys of walking in Africa. The only thing missing from this idyllic lifestyle was the presence of elephants and the countryside I was passing through seemed ideal for the great grey giants.

When I stopped at a rural school, I quizzed the head teacher about the absence of wild life and he told me that when his father had been a boy, the area had been full of elephants and buffalo.

"It was dangerous for people to move far from their villages," He said slowly.

"So what happened to them all?"

He shrugged.

"Hunters, poachers, people needing meat or frightened for their own safety - everyone had a hand in killing off the wild life. Guns coming into the country made it easier and even now..."

His voice tailed off, but I knew what he meant. Even now, anything that moved in the bush and wasn't human would be killed on sight and if it wasn't eaten, the carcass would be given to dogs. It was very sad but part of the tragedy that is modern Africa. For millennia, African tribesmen lived with wild life in peaceful cohabitation. They killed what they needed to eat and the herds survived and multiplied. Occasionally the tables were turned and people died, but that was regarded as part and parcel of living in the bush.

Then the white man arrived with his spurious civilisation and problems began. With the best will in the world, the colonialists tried to preserve wild life by evicting locals from their homes and designating specific areas as game reserves or parks. People were forbidden to feed off the animals, forbidden to use wood for their fires and forbidden to enter areas that had always been theirs by right. It was a recipe for disaster and modern Zambia is proof of this. Apart from a few small pockets in remote areas, wild life in the country has all but disappeared and although there are plans afoot to create new parks, a major re-education of the populace will be needed if wild animals are to have any chance of surviving.

But during those initial days of walking, the absence of wild life was just a tiny blot on my enjoyment of life. I could feel my muscles strengthening and I was enjoying the ambience and rugged nature of the country I was passing through. The people were friendly and when I was overtaken by a scotch cart, pulled by four oxen, I asked the men walking beside it whether I could put my pack on the cart and accompany them. They were only too pleased to oblige and for five kilometres, I was able to walk without that dreadful weight tugging on my shoulders. It was a magical interlude and although I was to take advantage of many more scotch carts over succeeding months that first ride lives on in my memory.

I still had water worries, but villages always seemed to appear when I was beginning to get desperate. I enjoyed some marvellous camping spots and one Sunday, I spent the day at Kansinsi School, chatting with teachers and admiring the way the place was run. Many of these fellows were city types, but had been transferred to remote Kansinsi, where there was no electricity and water had to be drawn from a nearby river. They were sanguine about this and merely looked forward to future transfers back to more civilised spots.

The day after Kansinsi, I was toiling up a hill, when my right leg slipped in sand and a muscle in my calf made an audible twanging sound. I had already walked a good eight kilometres and the road stretched straight and empty ahead of me, so I had no alternative but to keep going. The leg hurt and I hobbled along, using my walking pole as a makeshift crutch, but eventually everything seemed to go dead on me. Although it was still painful, I was able to make progress. It was worrying, as I could not afford a major injury so early in my walk.

It took me nine days to reach the outskirts of Lusongwa, the place where Victor had told me to branch off on a new road.

"Just find the Courthouse," he told me blithely, "and ask one of the messengers to show you the short cut. They will know the way."

I was full of confidence as I entered the scruffy little settlement. There were few people around, but I did see a hospital. Eventually, I asked a man where I could find the Courthouse and without saying a word, he pointed to a building, set back from the road.

I was horrified. The place had not been used in years. The windows were broken and the outer walls showed signs of damage and decay. I was not going to find any court messengers here.

Turning back to the man, I asked about the short cut to Chavuma and still without saying a word, he pointed back the way I had come.

"How far back?" I asked and he thought for a moment.

"Maybe ten kilometres."

I didn't know what to do. Evening was drawing in and I was a long way from anywhere. Lusongwa was hardly the place to spend a night and I wondered whether they would put me up in the hospital. It was probably worth a try, but I didn't want to bother the nursing staff unnecessarily.

Somewhat sadly, I looked around for somewhere to make a camp. The entire village was stark, with little or no vegetation and it all looked horribly uncomfortable. I was tired and didn't know what to do with myself.

It looked like being a sad end to what had been a reasonably successful day.

CHAPTER THREE

(Back on the River)

They had offered me a lift - for payment - earlier in the day and I had turned them down as I was only a kilometre or two from my goal - the Courthouse at Lusongwa. Now, they chugged out of the evening and slowed when they spotted my forlorn figure beside the road in that God-forsaken centre.

'They' were a gentleman named Cassius and his mate who were operating a mobile store from the rear of a minivan. The van itself was dirty and dented, incapable of making fast progress, but definitely transport. At that stage, I would have ridden with the devil to get out of Lusongwa, as it was a depressing place. Apart from the hospital, every building in view was either derelict or falling down, the road was a mass of potholes and people gazed at me with lack-lustre eyes.

"Now do you want a lift?" Cassius greeted me and I allowed that I did. They were heading for Mwiningu, a place I had never heard of, but I was happy to get out of Lusongwa. As my pack went into the van, I sighed with relief and sank back among cartons of cigarettes and cool drink, listening with half an ear to the drunken chatter of a man seated next to me. I was on my way to somewhere and didn't really care where.

It was dark when we pulled into Mwiningu, a raucously noisy centre with a main road running through it. Wondering whether I had jumped from fat into frying pan, I asked Cassius for somewhere to spend the night. He told me of a comfortable hotel that wouldn't cost me much and twenty minutes later, I was ensconced in the Riverside Lodge, which even had electricity and running water.

I was able to charge up various items of equipment - phone, camera and solar-powered charger - and even managed to borrow a kettle for shaving water and tea.

For me, this was luxury indeed and I enjoyed an excellent night, to be walking with hot tea inside me at first light. The main road was crowded with pedestrians and I returned the smiling greetings of workers coming into town with smiles of my own. A youth called Hardy fell into step beside me and told me he was going to Kabompo, where there was a bank and buses going on to Zambezi Town. He offered to carry my pack and I let him do so for a few kilometres, but the weight was obviously a strain on his narrow shoulders and I soon took it back.

We arrived in Kabompo shortly after noon. I found the bank, but the cashier refused to change my US dollars and the manager was called for. He explained that as Kabompo was in the middle of nowhere, there was little demand for foreign currency and if he changed my money, the notes could lie unused in his vaults for years. I showed him my letter from Given Lubinda and his manner softened.

"You have friends in high places," He murmured. "I will see what I can do."

Half an hour later, I left the bank with half a million kwacha in my pocket and a good feeling in my soul for that helpful bank manager. When we parted, I wished him luck and a speedy transfer, but he shook his head. "I shall probably be here for a few years yet." He gave me a warm shake of the hand to speed me on my way.

There was only one road out of town and that was a tarmac highway to Zambezi. Traffic was heavy and having no desire to walk along that busy thoroughfare, I paid for a lift in a battered pickup, loaded to the gunwales with people. Fortunately, I was in the cab where a pouty young woman sat squeezed between the driver and myself. It was a long, uncomfortable journey, enlivened when we stopped at a wayside store and two chickens escaped from the crush of folk - there were sixteen of them - in the back. I laughed as women rushed after the squawking birds, which were only recaptured when an old lady crawled under the vehicle to grab them both by scrawny necks. Chickens in Africa do not have a comfortable life.

Zambezi was another busy little place, but I didn't linger as I would pass through it again once I reached the river. I was sixty kilometres from Chavuma and wasted no time in heading out of town. Having camped in trees, from which I could see the distant Zambezi winding through a plain below me, I started early the next morning and walked as though my life depended on it. A number of drivers offered me lifts, but I turned them all down until late in the afternoon, another minibus pulled up beside me.

"Where are you going Sir?" The driver asked the question while his passengers gaped at me. When I told him, he shook his head.

"'That is thirty kilometres away and it will soon be dark. Jump in and I will only charge you ten pin to take you there."

My legs were rubbery and I was at the limit of my strength so I gladly took up the offer. That thirty kays took another three hours however, as we had to stop repeatedly to let passengers off and take on new ones. Nobody spoke to me and I sat huddled in one corner, my pack an uncomfortable lump on my knees. Drivers coming the other way often stopped for a chat with our driver and I tried to switch my mind off and enjoy the ride, but it wasn't easy.

Daylight had gone when we arrived in Chavuma. I have a horror of arriving in strange places after dark, but the driver gave me directions to 'a very comfortable lodge.'

"It is only three kilometres down the road," He assured me and the prospect of another long walk did not appeal, but I didn't have a choice. Hefting the pack on to my back, I set off for the 'very comfortable lodge,' but when I arrived, the place was full. It was hardly the best time of night to be homeless in Chavuma.

The landlord was a decent chap though and when I asked whether he had a storeroom I could sleep in, he laughed and told me he could do better than that. Off we went again and ten minutes later, climbed a small hill to yet another lodge, which he assured me would have vacancies because it was 'very expensive.'

It did and at a hundred and fifty pin per night it was, but Veronica Chitambo gave me a room with hot water - almost unheard of in Zambia's rural hostelries - and a double bed that was extremely comfortable. There was even a kettle installed and banishing the cost as of no account, I settled in to sleep off the effects of a very long couple of days.

Mind you, I had covered close to a hundred and fifty kilometres over those two days and if the roar of water outside was any indication, I was back beside the Zambezi. With that thought to keep me going, I slept well.

Tomorrow would look after itself and I would have a day off to gaze at the river I had left behind near iZhimbe all those weeks previously.

*   *   *

Standing on the veranda of Veronica's lodge with my morning tea, I looked down on the Zambezi with joy in my heart. I had left the river as a typical African watercourse with no pretensions to grandeur, but it had blossomed and showed signs of becoming a massively magnificent river.

Directly in front of the lodge, it rumbled and roared its way over massive rocks, hurtling through narrow channels and tossing spray contemptuously into the air. Below the rocks, it flattened out, but the surface still boiled and grumbled as the river braced itself for the long journey ahead. Immediately below the rapids, it was four hundred metres wide and downstream, I could see a pontoon, moored to the bank. Workers in yellow overalls wandered below me and a teenager lolled on the edge of a rocky outcrop, a fishing rod dangling negligently while he relaxed in early sunshine. It was all rather idyllic and I decided that another day in these surroundings would not only rest tired muscles, but would soothe my soul with the sights and sounds of rural Africa.

I was on my way early the following morning, pack pressing hard on my shoulders, but a spring in my step that came with the knowledge that at last, the roads were behind me and I was doing what I had travelled many thousands of kilometres to do.

I followed a path that ran parallel to the river and walked hard, fairly eating up the kilometres. On the roads, I had averaged over twenty kilometres a day, but I knew that as the countryside became rougher, that would drop away. It meant I had to take advantage of any easy going that was offered, so I pushed myself whenever I was on a path.

My only worry came when the path meandered away from the river and the spectre of thirst and non availability of water began niggling at my mind. It was ridiculous and I knew it, but it is a phobia that I can never escape. Twenty-first century Man often claims to be thirsty, but few folk in this modern day and age know the meaning of the word. Real thirst makes your tongue swell in your mouth, your vision swim and your nerves shriek for relief. It takes the strength out of muscles and induces a craving for liquid that is almost unbearable. I had been there more than once and had no intention of going there again.

So I worried, but there was water everywhere. The rains had not long ended and there were hundreds of small streams rushing down to take advantage of the Zambezi's patronage and hitch a ride to the sea. I had to wade across many of these and always made sure I had a long drink before continuing on my way. I have never enjoyed the tastelessness of water, but I had to have it, so drank it undiluted. Later on, I would ensure that at least one of my containers was filled with a Cowbell Drink o' Pop sachet (they come in a variety of fruity flavours) and that was more enjoyable than plain water, but during those early days, I drank my water neat.

One tributary was wider than its fellows and I was wondering whether I could get across without making a detour, when a fisherman came down the opposite bank. He shouted at me to stay where I was and shortly afterward, appeared beside me in a dugout canoe.

"I will take you across, Sir," He offered and I looked doubtfully at his boat. It was less than three metres long and very narrow, so I was not at all sure that it would take me and my cumbersome pack. Deciding that it would only be a short ride and was preferable to a long detour, I suggested that my new friend take the pack first, before coming back for me. As he paddled away, I noticed that with the extra weight, the canoe had mere centimetres of freeboard and inwardly marvelled at how trusting I had become. The pack contained everything I owned - including most of my money - yet I had handed it over to the care of a complete stranger without worrying for a moment.

That was one aspect of life that would remain the same throughout my walk. I didn't worry about leaving belongings unattended and had complete trust in the people I walked among. During my journey I would be regaled with tales about the kleptocratic leanings of local people, but at no stage did anyone steal anything of mine, even though some of my kit must have posed great temptations to people with nothing of their own. On one occasion, I left my camp with kit lying around while I went off for a meal with the local headman, but on my return everything was being guarded by a posse of serious-looking six year olds. I thanked them and told them what clever fellows they were and off they went, giggling happily and pleased to be of assistance to the wandering *mzungu*.

But that was in the future and when the fisherman returned to fetch me, I gingerly levered my own bulk into the canoe. The vessel was too narrow for my backside and I was forced to move into the centre of the boat where the gunwales were slightly further apart. This affected the balance and I wondered if we would make it to the opposite bank, fifteen metres away.

We didn't. We were in mid stream when the canoe began to shake. I clung on for dear life, the fisherman stood perfectly still in the stern and over we went. Cold, muddy water closed over my head and despite not having the pack on my back, the weight of the bits and pieces I was carrying dragged me down to the muddy bottom of the stream. I kicked my way back up and emerged, spluttering and snorting to find my Good Samaritan standing in shallows, trying to find his boat.

It was the first time I realised that dugouts don't float when they take in water. They sink like stones and that would cause me many anxious moments over the months ahead. On this occasion, the stream was shallow and unlikely to contain crocodiles, but later on, I would take many a canoe ride over wider and wilder tributaries and the fact that most of the craft I travelled in leaked like the proverbial sieve, was not good for the nerves.

Robert finally located his canoe with one foot and we managed to haul it up from the bottom. Once upturned and empty, it floated again and he suggested that I should get back in and he would try again to get me across the stream.

I laughingly waved him away. I was already so wet that I could walk across without doing further damage, so I ploughed through the mud and pulled myself up the bank to rejoin my pack. I was sure that the damned thing had watched the shenanigans going on in the water with malevolent satisfaction. I was beginning to form an intense dislike for that pack of mine.

Fortunately the sun was up, so I stripped off and hung my clothing from branches around me. Robert sheepishly bade me farewell and went off to check his fishing nets, so I was left alone to sunbathe and hope that nobody came along to see the naked *mzungu* on the edge of the forest. Fortunately, the African sun is good for drying clothing and twenty minutes after the accident, I was dressed and ready to go. A check of my equipment revealed that my pedometer had gone. It had been fixed to my belt and probably been dislodged when I tried to fit my hips between the gunwales of Robert's boat. It was not a serious loss because I still had the track manager on my GPS to tell me how far I travelled, but it was annoying. For a moment,

I debated going back for another look, but I wasn't going to get my feet - or anything else - wet again, so the idea was quickly discarded.

On I walked, vowing that I would only accept lifts in large canoes in future.

On another occasion, I had to cross a stream on a bridge made from tree trunks with their ends propped against the banks. The approaches were muddy and the trunks were wet. I gazed at the makeshift contraption with trepidation, but again the alternative was a long detour, so I moved gingerly on to the 'bridge,' my walking pole outstretched to aid my balance.

I took one step, committing my entire weight to the tree trunks, then another and then another. I was half way across when the inevitable happened. One boot slipped, one tree trunk wobbled and my feet shot out from under me.

I landed with a splash on my back in two feet of muddy water. My pack was under me and I was in much the same position as a dung beetle when it is flipped on to its back. I lay there with my arms and legs waving while my brain struggled to find a solution.

Fortunately nobody came along to witness my humiliation and with a huge heave of my muscles, I managed to get on to my side, from where it was comparatively easy to regain my feet, but once I had done so, I gazed at the water around my shins with considerable disgust. I could have easily waded across that stream. Stripping off and hanging my clothing out to dry again, I pondered the lesson learned. From then on, I always tested the depth of any watercourses I needed to cross before trusting to bridges, boats or any other means of crossing rivers.

But I was making progress and the kilometres were falling away behind me. Local villagers were curious as to my motives for walking through their land, but once they heard my intentions, they gave whatever assistance they could with great enthusiasm. I spent many a happy afternoon, relaxing in the shade and listening to desultory chatter from village elders while children gathered in respectful lines, just to gaze at my face and listen to my voice.

"They have never seen a white person before," John Chipoya told me. "They think you must have come from another world."

I suppose I had, but it was sobering to think that I was the first white person these kids had seen. This was the multi-cultural computer age, yet here in rural Zambia, people still inhabited the world they had lived in for centuries. The children knew nothing about motor vehicles, televisions, computers, power tools or electric lighting. They didn't have books to read and made their own entertainment without electronic toys or video games. None of them had tasted tea or coffee, while chocolate or ice cream were unheard of.

Yet they seemed sublimely happy and wherever I went, I saw radiant smiles and heard the sounds of whistling or singing. Women waved shyly at my passing, while men went out of their way to find out who I was and what I was doing. The children followed me for as long as they could with their eyes wide while they exchanged whispering comments on this strange new creature in their midst.

It all seemed so very innocent and heart warming. I often feel that the sheer inanity of modern life in the West has a lot to answer for.

I arrived back in Zambezi Town (it used to be called Balovale, which sounds much more romantic) on a Sunday morning. I was dirty and unshaven, but my muscles had hardened, the fat around my waist was disappearing and I felt very fit. On the way into town, I was stopped by some men making bricks. They hit me with the usual barrage of questions and as I was walking away, one of them called me back. He put his hands on my shoulders and gazed into my eyes.

"I know who you are," He told me. "You are Jesus Christ and you have come back to walk through the wilderness again."

Dropping to his knees in front of me, he bowed his head while his companions looked vaguely doubtful. Somewhat embarrassed, I pulled him back to his feet.

"I am not Jesus," I told him firmly. "I am David Lemon and I am walking to Mozambique."

Suiting action to the words, I walked away from the bricklayers and headed toward town, marvelling at the encounter, but wishing that I had a few of Jesus' party tricks at my disposal.

If only I could have changed water into wine for instance.

CHAPTER FOUR

(A Strong Man and a Political Princess)

Either side of Zambezi Town, I called in at two widely differing missions. The first was Chinyinge Catholic Mission, which I came upon by chance. Fascinated by a modern-looking suspension bridge across the river, I asked locals about it. With tall towers and hefty cables anchoring the structure, it seemed out of place in such wild surroundings.

Learning that the bridge led to a mission, I walked across, holding tightly to a cable railing as we swayed in the wind. Other people were not nearly so hesitant and children on their way to school ran past me, wrestling, jumping about and doing all the things that children do. They weren't worried about the safety of the bridge and I went on with more confidence. Only a little mind you, as it still felt very precarious.

Father Paul was very welcoming and gave me the use of a small room and a bathroom in which to wash my clothes as well as myself. Tea was brought in a large pot and once I had everything sorted out to my satisfaction, I went on an exploratory tour.

The mission was a sprawling accumulation of houses, a clinic, a school and a church. These were perched on the edge of a traditional village with mud huts and the inevitable store, where I bought chico biscuits to keep me going.

Lunch was taken at a long table and consisted of *nshima* and tiny barbel – a species of catfish, found in most African rivers. I didn't enjoy the fish as they were eaten heads and all. I have a strong stomach, but struggled to get through a plateful of these little monsters. The cook, Benedict noticed my discomfort and gave me a wink as he took my plate away. I wondered whether that indicated sympathy or mischief, but after lunch I sat on the veranda, reading and enjoying the peaceful ambience of the mission.

"Will you be attending Mass this evening?" The question came from Father Paul and I hesitated. Brought up a Catholic, my faith had taken a battering over the years and I had not been to Mass in decades. Nevertheless, I have a strong belief in 'Somebody up There' and needed all the help I could get. A little doubtfully, I agreed that I would indeed be attending Mass.

The service was simple and uplifting. Father Paul conducted the proceedings in Lunda, but for my benefit gave his sermon in English. In it, he spoke about this 'very brave man' who was attempting to do what nobody had done before and asked the congregation to pray for my safety and success. Brown eyes swivelled toward me from all quarters and I felt overwhelmed by all the attention. There was a great deal of singing during the service and not for the first time, I marvelled at the natural harmony, so many Africans possess. Like the Welsh, they are born to sing and looking around me at radiant faces, I wondered whether I had made a mistake by abandoning my religion.

It was a question that I would have time to ponder over succeeding weeks.

After Mass, I sat down with the priests and listened while conversation – most of it in English – flowed around me. Benedict smiled as he placed food in front of me and when I saw what it was, I could have hugged him. Obviously for my benefit, he had prepared a stew of goat and potatoes which was delicious. Oh the joy of tasting my first spuds in weeks. It was heavenly – definitely the correct adjective in those circumstances – and I had two sizeable portions before retiring to bed.

It had been a good day. When I asked about the suspension bridge, I was told it had been built thirty years previously by Brother Vincent, who copied the design from a photograph in National Geographic magazine.

I would have liked to have met Brother Vincent, if only to congratulate him on the sturdy design of his bridge. I would have liked to see Benedict again too, to thank him for my excellent meal, but when I left the following morning, he was nowhere to be found – probably still tucked up in a nice warm bed.

With Zambezi Town behind me, I was well and truly into the plains and pleased to see that the flood waters had receded. Yellow grasslands spread into vast horizons and my only problems came in the mornings when the grasses – some of them chest high – were soaked with dew. My clothing would be saturated within minutes of starting out. I dried off with the sun however and once again, days began to work themselves into a routine.

I would leave my camp as soon as it was light enough to see I had left nothing behind, walk for two hours, then stop for breakfast (if I had it) and a pipe, before setting off at a more leisurely pace. By midday, I would be looking for a place to camp and would spend the afternoon reading my Kindle in the shade, while the wild world of Africa went on around me. Around five in the evening, I would prepare a fire for tea or coffee and make my evening meal of gruel by mixing a sachet of powdered vitamin supplement with water. It was tasteless, but I presumed it was doing me good, although weight was dropping off me with alarming speed. I felt fine however, so didn't let it worry me.

Before leaving Ndola, Andy Taylor had told me about a missionary called Gordon Hanna at a place called Chitokoloki and pointed it out on the map.

"He is an American who does business with Cowbell," He said enthusiastically. "I told him about your walk and he is looking forward to meeting you, so please call in."

Chitokoloki was downstream from Chinyingi and I was camped by the river when I heard the sound of song drifting through evening air. It sounded like a church choir, so I presumed I was close to the mission. I wasn't and it took me another three days to reach the place, but that singing was a nice accompaniment to my dreams as I drifted off to sleep.

To reach Chitokoloki, I had to climb a steep path from the river and after enjoying flat terrain over preceding weeks, that entailed huge effort. I made it though and found a wide road at the top. People were walking in both directions and I enjoyed the customary questions, smiles and expressions of astonishment at what I was trying to do. Nobody offered to carry my pack and sand underfoot made for slow going.

I reached the mission around midday and was warmly greeted by Gordon Hanna. He turned out to be Canadian and had been at Chitokoloki for thirty years. Gordon took me home, where his wife, Ruth clucked over my dirty clothing and I was soon showered, shaved, changed and refreshed, while my offending attire was whisked away to be washed and ironed. Lunch was delicious and a great deal more appetising than my gruel.

An American nurse from the mission hospital was called when I told Gordon that my shoulders still ached from the weight of my pack, even after being on the road for weeks. She gave me some gel to apply, plus a packet of pain killers that came in handy when villagers came to me with their ailments. Another course of antibiotics and yet another malaria 'cure' were also provided and I added them to my already extensive first aid kit.

Chitokoloki means 'silver water' in the Lozi language and when I sat on Gordon's veranda that evening, I could see how the name came about. The Zambezi flowed across my line of vision and it looked like a vast band of burnished metal across the Zambian plains. It was breathtakingly beautiful and I couldn't help feeling that it was no wonder everyone I met in this enchanted spot wore a smile as big as Africa itself.

Showing me around the mission, Gordon talked at length about his life, his plans and his dreams for the future of Chitokoloki.

"We have the best equipped hospital outside Lusaka," He told me proudly. "Patients come from all corners of the country and we deal with everyone who needs treatment. Our medical staff are volunteers and come to us from around the world. Most of them stay six months before going back to their homelands, but while they are here, they do marvellous work. Over the years, we have set up five mission hospitals around the country, but this is the headquarters of our operations."

We both smiled at the unintended pun and I asked Gordon what denomination of Christianity the mission espoused. He shook his head firmly.

"We are just Christians," He said simply. "We have no particular religious bent and no hierarchy such as bishops and priests to use up our money."

"Sort of freelance missionaries then?" I offered and he smiled at the imagery. "But where do you get your funds from?"

"We have benefactors all over the world. When we need something, we pray for it and it usually turns up. For years, we prayed for an aeroplane, not only to transfer patients, but also for us to get around when visiting the hospitals under our care. A couple of years ago, two Americans offered us a plane, I chose what we needed and it was duly delivered. Soon afterwards, I received a letter from a young man in Lusaka, telling me he was an experienced pilot and would love to come and drive our aeroplane for us. We built the airstrip ourselves and were even given a heavy roller to flatten the runway down."

Other much needed items such as vehicles, boats and a five-ton lorry had also been donated and Gordon was obviously proud of the little empire he ran with the power of prayer.

That night, I told him of the problems I was having in understanding my GPS and he produced a modern 'smart phone' on which we studied the route I needed to take when I left Chitokoloki.

"You will be better off crossing the river at Senanga," He pointed it out on the tiny map he had brought up on the screen. "Then you take this road, running parallel to the river."

He paused and squinted at the screen.

"No, look, there is a path that runs even closer to the Zambezi and seems to go all the way to Sesheke."

I peered down in bemusement. He was right. I could see the road he mentioned and between that and the river was a tiny line indicating a footpath. A few weeks later, I was to follow his directions and the path was right where it ought to be. It petered out in places and was often difficult to follow, but it was there and I wondered why I had bought a GPS and not merely a 'smart phone' that could seemingly do everything.

I left early the following morning after an excellent breakfast and a hug from Ruth. It had been a marvellous interlude in my journey and I walked on feeling fresh, well fed and hugely impressed with the quiet conviction of the missionaries at Chitokoloki. There was only one thing that puzzled me. When I asked Gordon what services he held in his church, he told me it was occasionally used by visiting priests, but in general, people used it to offer up personal prayers.

"Do you have a choir?" I queried and he shook his head.

"No, as we don't hold regular services, there is no call for one."

Walking on, I wondered about the singing I had heard before reaching the mission. It had sounded like a religious gathering of some sort, but perhaps it had merely been villagers making their own obeisance to a Deity. I didn't think I had missed any villages between that point and Chitokoloki, but decided that I must have done.

Unless.....?

Shaking my head in wry amusement at the direction of my thoughts, I plodded on.

Two days after I left Chitokoloki, tragedy struck. On a flight from Chavuma, the volunteer pilot, Jay Erickson and his wife Katrina were killed when the aircraft hit power lines and plunged into the river. He was twenty-seven, she a couple of years younger and they left two small children behind. I heard about the accident weeks later and sent a message to Gordon and Ruth, offering my condolences and telling them that I would be praying for them.

In spite of my ready cynicism in matters ecclesiastical, I did pray for those lovely people who had made me so welcome and done their best to help toward the ultimate success of my venture.

Folk like Gordon and Ruth, Father Paul and a few others I was yet to meet, impressed me with their simple piety and the way they spent their lives helping the people around them. This modern world needs more people like them.

*   *   *

It was only a little stream, but the muddy water was rushing along, it looked deep and I was cold. The sensible thing to do would have been to take my boots off and wade across, but the thought of icy water up to my thighs was not appealing. Besides, there was only a metre or so between the banks, so after inspecting the landing area carefully for pitfalls, I gathered myself, took a deep breath and jumped.

What I hadn't allowed for was the weight on my shoulders. Jumping over a metre of water is simple when unencumbered, but with twenty-five kilograms or so weighing me down, I only just made the far bank. My boots thudded into the mud and for a moment or two I teetered, the pack pulling me backwards. Waving my arms frantically, I struggled for balance, but that horrible pack was too heavy and my thigh muscles weren't strong enough to steady me. One boot slipped in the mud and I was lost.

With a huge splash, I landed on my back in the water and once again was forced to do my stranded tortoise act, wriggling myself on to one side and laboriously levering my body upright. It didn't work this time and with freezing fingers, I managed to undo the straps and allowed the pack to fall into the stream. Hauling myself out, I retrieved the ruddy thing and once again was forced to strip off and hang my clothing out to dry. On this occasion the sun was barely up and I spent an uncomfortable half hour walking briskly around in my birthday suit and hoping nobody would come along.

It was not a good start to my day.

Heading south from Chitokoloki, I stuck to footpaths for a while, but these tended to take me away from the Zambezi, although for once it didn't lead to water worries. The plains were filled with pools that had to be skirted and the countryside presented a drab picture of vast grassland with only these ponds and small patches of forest to alleviate the monotony.

They made for excellent camping sites, those inland pools. Night after night, I camped beside them, occasionally wondering where the river was and the only drawback was that the inland water was home to hordes of mosquitoes. I took to using my net at night, but as I was usually up before dawn, that half an hour or so of blundering around in the darkness made me a target for many a million marauding mossies. I would slap ineffectually at them as I waited for water to boil and wasted no time in getting on the road as quickly as I could.

There were no villages to be seen along this stretch and I assumed that I was now well into Lozi country – the area formerly known as Barotseland and home to a proud and independently-minded people. The few people I encountered no longer spoke to me in Luwale, so I had to learn the Lozi words for 'hello,' 'thank you' and 'good bye.'

'Muswili' seemed to cover most greetings and my 'muswilis' were soon ringing out over the plains.

On several occasions, I lost the path I was following and this invariably led me into trouble. One morning, I branched off from a footpath that seemed to be heading directly inland and walked in what I felt was the direction of the Zambezi. It was a mistake. I was soon pushing my way through grass, reaching high above my head in places and seeming to have been tied into ankle-high knots in others. I fell repeatedly, inflicting numerous cuts and grazes to my limbs. For long periods, I had no idea where I was or even what direction I was moving in and when at last I came out on the riverbank, I was met with an impenetrable barrier of thorny vegetation that sent me inland again.

In well over three hours, I covered less than a kilometre and I was feeling ever more desperate. Stopping under a tree, I tried to gather my scattered senses and tensed as a shrill cry rang through the late morning air. Pushing through vegetation to investigate, I startled two young women who were yelling across the river, obviously trying to call up a boat. They reacted to my presence like startled bushbuck, but I spoke soothingly and calmed them down. Neither spoke English and giving up their attempts to attract transport, they moved hurriedly away from me.

They were my only hope of salvation so I followed in their footsteps, often having to crawl on hands and knees through tiny gaps in the foliage which they had slipped through without any problem. How I cursed that pack on my back.

I had no choice however but to go where they went and after wading through streams, slipping and sliding along the muddy banks of ponds among the trees, I was wet through, battered, scratched and decidedly out of sorts.

The girls had been shouting and hallooing at intervals and suddenly, to the delight of us all, their calls were answered from up ahead. I walked with lighter steps and at last we came upon a rude camp beside another muddy stream. Here, two unkempt-looking men and a woman were sorting out a fish catch and I gazed at it in wonderment. There wasn't a decent sized specimen among the fish and most of them were bream fingerlings, a centimetre long and surely not worth eating. The fishermen themselves were skeletally thin, so if indeed these fish provided their daily sustenance, it didn't seem as though they were of great nutritional value.

But one of the men had a smattering of English and when I told him I was heading for Lukulu (it didn't seem worth a deeper explanation) he shrugged and pointed out a well worn path heading south. It was probably the same 'road' I had been following that morning, so I had wasted four or five hours in a pointless and painful detour.

There was nothing for it but to follow the path however and when I camped in a grove of big trees an hour or so later, I discovered that I had lost my plastic mug. It had obviously come adrift during one of my crawls through the undergrowth and although it wasn't serious – I could drink out of a saucepan – it put the seal on what had been an awful day.

According to my map, I was approaching the confluence of the Kabompo River and the Zambezi, which was my first major river obstacle. I would have to find someone to take me across and when I was hailed by a young man with his girlfriend, I asked him where I could find someone with a canoe.

"I have one of my own," His name was Tom and he was cheerfully helpful. "Let me take this lady across the river, then I will come back for you and we will get around the mouth of the Kabompo."

It seemed too good to be true, so with a sigh of relief, I sat down on the bank, took off my boots and watched him paddle his *inamorata* across the Mighty Zambezi. He was soon back and as his was a much larger dug out than the last one I had been in, I settled myself comfortably in the bow with my pack and quite enjoyed the ride across the river.

But Tom had only told me half the story and when we landed, he pointed out a path leading up a steep hill.

"If you take that for only a short distance," He told me, "You will come to a school and then a clinic. At the clinic they will provide you with a boat and take you across the river."

I could feel myself wilting. It was early afternoon and I had learned through experience what 'only a short distance' could mean in rural Zambia. The people tended to be too nice to tell me the truth when it came to how far I had to walk and this could turn out to be a major hike.

It was and the sun burnt my remaining energy away. The path was sandy and I could feel a deep ache in my thighs as my steps grew shorter and my forward momentum ever slower. I passed several villages and people gazed at me with evident curiosity, but I was in no mood for chatter and ignored them all. Eventually I met a well-dressed man, coming the other way and asked him how far I was from the school and the clinic. He frowned.

"You still have about four kilometres to go," my heart sank into my boots, "but you can come back to my village if you like."

It was a nice offer, but the thought of retracing my footsteps did not appeal, so I asked him to show me a way to the Zambezi, which I could see some way below the track I was following.

"I will camp there for the night," I told him. He looked doubtful, but escorted me down a narrow trail that came out beside the river. Thanking him, I looked around for somewhere to camp, but there was thick vegetation along the edge of the river and wherever I spotted a gap in this, I found fishing nets, canoes or people already there. Not wanting company, I walked another five hundred metres and eventually managed to wedge myself into an uninhabited gap in the foliage. It made for an uncomfortable night and for the rest of the day, I was pestered by curious locals, coming to see who I was and what I was doing.

Scratchy-eyed and unrefreshed, I was on my way early the following morning and kept to the bank rather than the path I had been following. It took me nearly an hour to reach the school, but a friendly teacher ordered a pupil called Bosco to escort me to a place where I could cross the river. No mention was made of the clinic or its boats.

As we walked, Bosco told me that he wanted to be either a journalist or a pilot, but couldn't make up his mind. We chatted amiably for a while and he carried my pack, although he was smaller than I was, so I felt guilty about that. Arriving at a riverside store, he explained my problem to the extremely large lady behind the counter. Examining me with evident curiosity, she quickly made up her mind and moving outside, bellowed a summons into the morning air.

Fifteen minutes later, I was ensconced in an almost new canoe and on my way back across the Zambezi. The mouth of the Kabompo drifted past and although I had taken a very round-about way to cross that river, I was pleased to have it behind me. Having been dropped at a point where a path led into trees, it was indicated as the road to Lukulu and I was on my way again, wondering – not for the first time – what I had let myself in for.

Walking along a river is an easy matter in theory, but with the flood plains of the Zambezi in the way, it was proving considerably more difficult that I had anticipated.

*   *   *

The Zambezi seemed at its most violent as I cut away inland. A glance over my shoulder showed the river hurling itself over rocks, cliffs and steep drops as it rushed through the Nyamboma Rapids, but a number of local people advised me to take a path that cut off a wide bend in the river before it reached Lukulu.

The going was easy, but the path twisted and turned to such a degree that I was forced to ask for guidance at a village. An elder called Bernard detailed his teenage son to show me the way and for two hours, the lad walked with me, setting a pace that had me gritting my teeth in my determination to keep up. Fortunately, he didn't seem keen to talk and I had the impression that he was escorting me under sufferance, having far better things to do.

Eventually, he left me on the edge of a plain, pointing out where the path snaked ahead through short yellow grass. I thanked him and with the first genuine smile I had seen from him, he wished me luck on my journey.

"May God guide your footsteps and keep you safe Sir," He said and I wandered on, berating myself for making snap judgements.

The grass might have been short, but it was heavily tangled and I stuck grimly to the path. Another stream barred my passage and as I walked gingerly to the edge of it, I tripped and landed belly down in murky water, that damned pack pushing my face ever further into the ooze. It was cold and I eventually managed to haul myself upright for another drying session. Throwing the pack on to the ground, I wondered whether it possessed a malevolently human streak. Somehow it seemed determined to drag me down – quite literally.

While my clothes were drying, I took out my satellite telephone. It had been loaned to me by some lovely people at Fluxcon in Pretoria, but my previous attempts at getting through to the outside world had failed and I determined that this would be my last try. As it was Sunday morning, I rang Lace, back home in France Lynch and to my joy, I got through. She told me all the news – dogs were well, we had new ducks and the chickens were laying. It all seemed unreal in my wild world, but it was nice to get a brief feeling of home. I sent a few text messages and my daughter Deborah came back to me, but the phone was an expensive toy so I quickly signed off and dressed again.

With their offer to sponsor me with the phone, Fluxcon had included a free hundred minutes of 'air time' and I had naively taken that to mean, speaking time during phone calls. It wasn't though. Air time began when the phone connected to a satellite, so was being used even as I dialled or prepared text messages. This meant that everything had to be rushed, but the phone would be my lifeline if anything went seriously wrong and for that I was grateful to Tom Naude and his colleagues at Fluxcon.

Moving on, somewhat smelly from my immersion in the stream – I didn't dare to think where it came from – I walked hard and an hour later, came out on a wide, dusty road where I sat down to rest weary muscles. I hadn't been there long when a strapping youth who introduced himself as Kenny sat down beside me. At his question, I told him I was heading for Lukulu and he grinned broadly.

"That is also where I am going," He told me. "Would you like me to carry your luggage for you?"

I was tired and had been debating finding somewhere to camp, but this was too good an offer to turn down. Moments later, we strode off toward Lukulu, Kenny stooped beneath the pack while I enjoyed walking without its weight on my shoulders.

There was a steady stream of pedestrians going in both directions and shouted greetings were exchanged as we went along. A number of them laughed at Kenny and his pack, particularly when I referred to him as a 'Number One Explorer.' It was all very jovial, the sun was pleasantly warm on my back and in spite of my weariness, I enjoyed the walk.

As we came into the outskirts of the town, Kenny announced that he was going to church and would have to leave me. Inevitably, we had discussed religion – a favourite subject in Zambia – as we walked and my companion had been overjoyed to discover that we shared the Roman Catholic faith. His was stronger than mine and he told me he went to church three times a week and sang in the choir. I declined his offer to introduce me to the local priest and we parted with wishes from both of us toward the success of the other.

It had been a pleasant interlude, but I had to get through town and find my way back to the river. A phone mast loomed and I took the opportunity to arrange a meeting with the Cowbell team in Mongu the following weekend. It gave me eleven days to cover roughly one hundred kilometres, so I felt I could take things easy for a while. In the meantime, I was hungry and had enough kwacha in my pocket for a reasonable meal, so kept my eyes open for a restaurant.

I had learned through experience that restaurants in Zambian towns were not what the word implied in more advanced countries. All too often, they were one-room establishments with a couple of tables and served nothing but *nshima* with relishes, comprised of fish or vegetables. Anything had to be more filling than my gruel though, so my pace quickened as my taste buds salivated at the prospect of real food.

My culinary reverie was interrupted when a cyclist pulled up beside me and asked where I was going. When I told him what I was looking for, he introduced himself as Brian Matondo and suggested that I climbed on to his luggage rack and he would take me to a 'really nice place.'

That sounded good, but getting on his bike did not. I pointed out that with me and my pack aboard, it would be difficult for him to balance, but he insisted that we try. Moments later, we were sprawling in the road and the bike pinned my legs to the dust, a pedal digging painfully into my calf. Brian was apologetic and we walked on for a while, me limping at the new pain in my already battered body.

The 'really nice place' was yet another poky little room, smoke blackened and claustrophobic. I ordered *nshima* and fish and two portions were brought out from the horrendous kitchen. As always, the fish was a whole bream, served with everything but the entrails and I wolfed it down. I didn't have the heart to ask Brian to pay for his own, so my kwacha stocks took another knock. I wasn't too worried though as I didn't think I would need to buy much – apart from the odd biscuit – before reaching Mongu.

Having enquired as to where I would spend the night, Brian suggested that I stayed with him. He lived on a pig farm and anticipating roast pork for dinner – silly me – I agreed, even though it meant back-tracking along the way I had come into town.

Backtrack we did and for four long kilometres. I had propped my pack on to Brian's bike, so was able to walk unencumbered, but my legs were tired and it seemed a long way. Eventually, we left the road and Brian pointed out an enclosure away to our left.

'My pigs,' he said and shortly afterwards, we came to his house. My heart fell into my boots once again.

During my wanderings in Africa, I have slept in a variety of houses, but with the exception of a Masai *manyatta* in Kenya, this had to be the most basic building I had ever tried to use as a bedroom.

Built entirely of clay, it comprised four windowless walls and a tin roof. Inside, it was surprisingly well furnished, with a battered lounge suite huddled in one half of the building and a curtain cutting off a bedroom in the other. It was hot and stuffy, but I was committed to staying and had to make the best of it.

That afternoon, Brian took me on a tour of the town and showed me the harbour, where dugouts clustered against the bank and traders hawked their wares, consisting mainly of fish – fresh, dried or smoked. We were offered three large bream on a stick, but they cost fifteen pin and a little regretfully, because they did look delicious, I decided that we could go without.

As for the pigs, they didn't belong to my friendly host at all. He merely kept them fed and watered for a local farmer, for which he was paid fifty thousand kwacha a month. He seemed content with that and was proud to be a 'farm worker,' but it sounded like slave wages to me. Still, it was not my business so I refrained from comment.

Brian's young wife was called Pauline and they had a toddler called Emma which made me smile. Such typically English names in this isolated dwelling in rural Africa seemed somewhat incongruous. Still they were lovely people and while we waited for Pauline to prepare the evening meal, I wondered whether I would indeed be treated to pork.

When the meal was brought in, Brian glanced anxiously at me.

"I hope you eat rat," He said hesitantly and with my fingers firmly crossed, I assured him that I did. When I took the lid off my plate, a fairly large rat was exposed, well roasted but still recognisable for what it was. I have eaten field mice, but this was different. I had no choice though, particularly as Brian was tucking into his roasted rodent with gusto, so I broke a piece off my chappie, put it in my mouth and chewed somewhat hesitantly.

It was delicious and I soon finished off my meal, rolling the *nshima* into small balls with one hand and eating each mouthful with a portion of rat attached. I couldn't help wondering what my mother would have thought, seeing her 'Darling Boy' eating rat with what she would have termed 'an uncultured peasant.' It didn't bear thinking about, but I enjoyed my meal.

Having laid my bedroll between chairs, I managed a fitful sleep, but was on the road early in the morning, a firm handshake from Brian and a shy curtsy from Pauline sending me on my way. They were nice people and my night in their house will provide me with lovely memories right into my dotage.

Yet as I walked down that long road, I found it hard to get over the anomaly that was a little family in Darkest Africa whose names were Brian, Pauline and Emma.

*   *   *

As the year rolled into June, the Zambian winter began to take its toll of my strength. Daytime temperatures were in the twenties and I enjoyed the warmth, but with the advent of darkness, the world became achingly cold. My bedroll consisted of a sheet, sewn up one side and a thin Masai blanket. This was not enough and the chill ate into my bones. It meant that nights were spent muffled in whatever clothing I could find - even to the extent of wearing gloves to bed. Lace had given me a silk balaclava to wear at night and with this, the gloves and my thick socks - plus shorts and a shirt - I must have looked pretty weird, but I didn't care.

With the dawn, I would be up early because lying abed was coldly uncomfortable and while I have always tried to make small fires in the bush, most mornings saw me huddling close to as large a blaze as I could find fuel for. Basic though it had been, the comfortable warmth of Brian and Pauline's shack became a pleasant memory.

Back on the river, I asked a man in his garden which path I should take for Mongu and with one look at my pack, he abandoned what he was doing and walked with me.

"I will show you the short cut," Joseph told me happily and walked with me for over an hour. During that time we discussed Zambian politics, the state of Zimbabwe, the legacy of the old explorers and the joys - or otherwise - of walking through Africa. Time passed quickly and when he left me on a path that seemed to be heading firmly inland, he quelled my fears with a smile.

"The river sweeps around a bend here," he told me. "This path will save you time."

Reasoning that with over a week to do eighty-eight kilometres to Mongu, I didn't want to save too much time, I set out at a considerably slower speed. I was being naive again I'm afraid. When wandering in Africa, it is best to make as good a pace as one can, in case pitfalls lie ahead.

In this case, they certainly did. Two days later, I found myself trapped between streams and pools in one section of the plain. Whichever way I turned, I was confronted by water and I couldn't find my way back to where I had started. Twice I fell into shallows and whenever I tried barging through reeds or grass, harsh blades cut painfully at my skin. I was beginning to panic when I spotted a small village.

Wet, bloodied and close to exhaustion, I met with a party of men and women, talking under a tree and asked for directions - if not to Mongu, at least out of this maze of water.

None of them knew what I was talking about, but someone hailed a herdsman, guiding his cows through the grasslands.

Stephens did speak English and promised to get me out of the predicament in which I found myself. First he needed to eat, so *nshima* was prepared and we ate it with a handful each of the bream fingerlings. Despite their lack of bulk, they were surprisingly tasty.

Stephens was a Lozi and told me that when the river flooded, the area in which we sat would be well underwater. Every year, he was forced to abandon his village and take his family and cattle inland, but it was not a problem.

"When the waters recede and we return," he mused, "we plant our maize and millet in ground that has been fertilized by the Zambezi and cattle grow fat on rich grass."

I had had more than enough of rich grass at that point, but was interested when Stephens showed me his village. Instead of the usual mud and pole huts, every dwelling was made entirely of grass. He told me that constructing them that way made it easy to rebuild when they returned in the dry season. It made sense and despite their flimsy construction, the huts looked as comfortable as their more solid counterparts.

In company with two boys, armed with catapults, we walked a long way that afternoon. On two occasions, our path was blocked by water, but Stephens knew where canoes were kept and the boys paddled us across. I was no longer tense when travelling in dug outs and had discovered that provided one relaxed, they are remarkably stable craft.

For the next two days, I made excellent progress along a succession of paths through the grass. The people I met all confirmed that I was on 'the short cut to Mongu' and I felt pleased with myself, even though it seemed as though I would be there a day or two early.

Silly me!

It was late morning when I stopped in a village to chat with locals, who crowded around me. They were interested in my plans and one youth asked whether I would consider running for President of Zambia. It wasn't the first time I had been asked the question, nor would it be the last, but I smilingly pointed out that I was not a Zambian.

"But you know how we live Sir," He went on. "The politicians have no idea what goes on in the villages or how we struggle to keep ourselves alive."

I tried to explain that politicians are the same everywhere, but he was not convinced. Nevertheless, he walked with me and regaled me with tales as to the difficulties of life in the Lozi lowlands.

It was in the next village that my confidence took a knock. A well dressed matron frowned as my self-appointed guide told the inhabitants what 'My Friend David' had in mind. Turning to me, she asked how I intended to cross the Luena plain.

I shrugged and explained that I had managed so far and didn't see that the Luena should be any more difficult than the rest. Her frown deepened and she explained that the following day, I would be wading through water that reached my neck in places.

Accustomed to African hyperbole, I smiled but her words dampened my mood and that evening, I repacked my kit, placing everything that might be damaged by getting wet into 'dry bags,' the closable containers that are guaranteed to keep their contents dry in the worst of circumstances. If necessary, I would wade across the Luena Plain, even if the water did reach my neck.

I hadn't been walking long the following morning when the path became a stream. The water wasn't deep, but it was annoying and because it was dirty, I could not see what I was walking over. Twice, I tripped over tangled grass and fell full length in that horrid water. There seemed little point in drying off, but I did exchange my boots for 'rafters,' the tough, wrapover bush sandals. With my boots in one hand and my walking pole in the other, I must have made a strange sight as I prodded my way along the stream. There was no escape from the water, as tall grass grew on either side of me and I didn't dare leave what must once have been the path.

It was horribly uncomfortable and having continuously cold legs soon made the rest of me feel cold too. My teeth began to chatter, but I had to wade on. Occasionally, the path would rise and I would be on dry ground for a while, but this never lasted and I was soon up to my knees in water again. Hour followed hour and I cursed myself, the world and the Zambezi with equal fervour.

In mid afternoon, I came across a village on a rise. The inhabitants looked at me with considerable surprise and when I told them what I was doing, one elder shook his head.

"You will not get through," He said, waving one hand at the grassy plain spreading away from the village. "That is the flood plain from the Luena River and even though there are paths, you will need to swim in places."

I was committed though and moved on after a brief rest. The previous day, I had expected to be confronted by a vast sheet of water, but the plain looked exactly like any other African plain. There was grass, grass and more grass, with nary a tree or bush to break the monotony. Surely I could walk across that?

But beneath the grass was water - lots and lots of it. I followed another path that had become a stream and suddenly I was waist deep and soaked to the skin. There was no break in the monotony and I wondered where I would sleep that night.

In the event, I found a spot where a small rise offered an almost dry spot, barely large enough to roll out my blanket. There was no firewood and the evening chill on my saturated body warned of rheumatism and worse to come. Mosquitoes tormented me throughout the night and with no chance of putting my net up, I covered myself with repellent and flapped uselessly as they whined around my head. Like most African mossies, they seemed to regard insect repellent as some exotic cocktail and it did little to keep them at bay. I shook and shivered my way through the night before hitting the 'road' - it could hardly be called that any more - well before first light.

I had tied my boots together by the laces and slung them around my neck, but until the sun was up, that water was cold and the first few hours of wading sapped my spirit as well as my energy. My steps grew slower and a number of falls made me feel ever worse about myself. Why did I put myself through such torment when I could have been safely warm at home with my family? It didn't make sense - even to me.

Wrapped in my own misery, I didn't hear it at first, then a call cut into my reverie. Leaning on my walking pole with water lapping at the legs of my shorts, I looked around me and two hundred metres to my left, saw a man in a canoe. He shouted something, before poling toward me along what must once have been another path. When he arrived, he shook his head at my bedraggled state and asked if I was alright. I assured him that I was, but that I was lost.

"No matter, Sir," His name was Ngenda. "My uncle has a village here so I will take you to him and you can get dry."

His boat was not a large one, but with some difficulty I managed to get my pack and my weary body aboard. Ngenda used his long paddle as a punting pole and we sped through a narrow channel in the grass that brought back awful memories of the morning and the day before.

It must have been around noon that we pulled up beside a collection of canoes and I climbed wearily on to dry land. The village was on a hill, completely surrounded by water and I was introduced to Gilbert Kavitondo. He showed no surprise at my saturated state, but offered me a piece of sugarcane to keep me warm. I sat on a chair, brought by one of the women, while the sun dried me out and brought a spark of life to tired muscles.

"You must stay here tonight," Gilbert told me firmly. "Tomorrow, I will take you in my boat to where there is less water for you to walk through."

It was a wonderful offer and early the following morning, we boarded a larger dugout and Gilbert took me across a chunk of plain that would undoubtedly have broken my heart had I attempted to walk it. He knew the channels and pointed out various villages as we went along. They all seemed to be occupied by his relatives and Gilbert proudly announced that as he was the headman, they were all his.

Although we went on for over an hour, the ride was over all too soon and Gilbert finally pulled in beside another canoe which had a baby donkey shivering in the stern. The poor little mite looked awfully sorry for itself and my heart went out to it.

"On its way to market," Gilbert told me laconically and I marvelled on the difference in outlook between Westerners and the people of Africa. We tend to feel sorry for animals and lavish love and attention on those in our care, but the rural African looks upon them purely as utilities. The donkey was uncomfortable and obviously frightened, but it would raise a few kwacha when it was sold and that was more important to the owner than the animal's well-being. It was a sensibly pragmatic view of what is important in life, but it was difficult for me to get my head around.

"This is as far as I can take you," Gilbert was apologetic. "You can walk on the land for a few kilometres, but then you will be back in the water." My face must have fallen, as he quickly added that I would 'probably get over that water in one day.'

It took me three and they were horrible days indeed. Wet, uncomfortable, hungry and sorry for myself, I ploughed through that awful flood. There was no sign of life on this part of the plain and I used my compass repeatedly, to ensure I was going in the right direction. Grassland - with plentiful water beneath it - stretched into distant horizons and there were no landmarks to show me where I was. I camped on other uncomfortable little rises and spent two nights fighting the cold and mosquitoes.

The sun was well up on the third morning when a spike appeared on the horizon and I veered towards it. The telephone masts of Zambia saved my bacon on a number of occasions, but this one was surely the nicest sight I had seen in days. Gradually, it grew larger and suddenly I felt dry ground underfoot again. With a sense of relief, I pushed myself forward. I still had a great deal of water to cross, but it was in the form of streams and fast-flowing gullies rather than solid sheets of the stuff.

Twice more I fell into muddy water and on the second occasion, my walking pole was ripped from my hand and disappeared. For ten minutes I searched, kneeling in the water and running my fingers through thick, glutinous mud. I was rescued by three young fishermen, one of whom jumped in beside me and quickly found the pole. Why he could do it and I could not, I didn't know but it was annoying.

Thanking him, I climbed from the water and one of the others pointed to my legs with an exclamation that could have been one of disgust. Looking down, I saw five or six black leeches feeding off my body and while I know that one is supposed to burn the things off, I ripped them away, leaving patches of blood on my skin. It was the first time I had encountered the loathsome creatures in my African wanderings, but that was not a 'first' I relished.

The fishermen had built a wind shelter out of dry grass and for an hour, I let my clothes dry out and my muscles regain a little of the life that had been leeched - quite literally - out of them. My companions chatted quietly and the eldest of them gravely informed me that nobody crossed the Luena plain on foot before September at the earliest.

"Yet you have done it Sir and you are very old," Nothing like being direct I suppose. "Truly, you are a great man."

Flattering, but I hardly felt great. I did feel old however and it was on tottery legs that I moved away from that hateful plain. I had no idea how far I was from Mongu, but it no longer seemed to matter. I had survived what must surely have been one of the most difficult and uncomfortable journeys of my life and as I gradually warmed up and felt strength returning to my body, I began to feel pleased with myself.

The Luena Plain was summed up for me by a teacher I met a couple of days later. When I told him about my wet and uncomfortable crossing, he shook his head in wonderment.

"You must have suffered, Sir," was his comment and he was right - I did.

*   *   *

He was a powerfully built young man, but when he first approached, he merely made me laugh.

It was three days since I had left the Luena plain and since then, I had stuck to a road. It was leading me well inland, but locals assured me that it would get me to Mongu and I wasn't going to risk the water again. The problem with the road was that the surface was covered in thick sand that tore at leg muscles and slowed me down. Nevertheless, I was well on course to arrive in Mongu on the Friday, scheduled for my meeting with the Cowbell team. Andy would not be with them, but would meet me in Senanga two weeks later.

Savouring a breakfast of dried fruit chips, I watched the young man approach, pushing a vastly overloaded bicycle. It had fifty kilogram sacks strapped fore and aft and he was struggling to manoeuvre it through the sand. Stopping beside me, he smiled widely. I made some comment about his load and he smiled again.

"I am taking bags of rice to the market at Limilunga," He told me. "I have to do this twice a week and it is hard work."

Allowing that it probably was, I asked him his name and he told me, "Kaluka."

"'And your family name?"

"That is Kaluka."

He had obviously misunderstood me, so I persisted.

"'No, no - what do people call you?"

"Kaluka," His face split into a huge grin. "I am Kaluka Kaluka - Kaluka squared if you like. Would you like me to add your bag to my load and you can walk to Limilunga with me?"

It was tempting, but I looked doubtfully at his overloaded bicycle He brushed my misgivings aside.

"It won't be as heavy as the rice and I am a strong man. I can do it easily."

Stifling my doubts, I helped him strap the pack on to the cross bar, tying it in place with the strips of rubber inner tube that are used for cord throughout Africa. I was left with my bedroll to carry and we were on our way to Limilunga.

After ten weeks on the road, I regarded myself as pretty fit, but Kaluka Squared set a brutal pace and I struggled to keep up. We left the road in places and took narrow paths through forested areas, but he obviously knew where he was going. After walking for an hour, I swallowed my pride and called for a halt to ease burning lungs. Kaluka waited for me to get my breath back, then off we went again. He even managed to talk about his family, his life and his girlfriend while he pushed that enormous load, but my answers were monosyllabic. I did not want to waste my breath on anything other than forcing my body along.

At a T junction, Kaluka indicated a clinic, set back from the road. Spotting a tap outside the building, I walked across for a drink and as I did so, the calf muscle that had given me trouble weeks before suddenly twanged its disapproval of my exertions and I was hobbling again. Kaluka looked concerned, but I fear it was more the prospect of being late for market than worry about my condition.

"I am holding you back," I muttered through my pain. "You go on ahead and I will move slowly from here."

He probably took my comments as a slur on his strength. Watching quietly while I applied soothing gel to the afflicted leg, he waited till I was mobile again and off we went, me hobbling in his wake with my walking pole as a makeshift crutch. Other young men greeted my companion and one of them told me that Kaluka was 'a very strong man.'

That I could agree with.

By the time we arrived on the outskirts of Limilunga, my legs were rubbery and my eyes were blurred with sweat. I was not in a good state, but Kaluka looked as fresh as a daisy - at least to my jaundiced gaze.

"Not far now," He cajoled. "In another ten minutes, we will reach the main road and then we are very close to the market."

Ten minutes grew to thirty minutes, then to three quarters of an hour. I was beginning to stagger when at last, my companion laughed and I saw a row of shops.

"We are here," He crowed happily. "Now you can rest."

While he untied my pack from the bicycle, I looked around me with weary eyes. This was the place where the Lozi Litunga (King) had his rainy season palace, but it was the usual rude main street with dilapidated buildings on either side. There was an excited buzz of conversation as people bartered for produce from the market - an open square on one side of the road. Sacks of fish were on sale and I was surprised to see that many of them contained bream fingerlings. I couldn't help wondering how many of the little fish went to make up one fifty-kilogram bag and what it was doing to future fish stocks in the country.

But that was all too serious for me to worry about and I dumped my pack on the veranda of Musa's Family Shop before slumping in a convenient chair and allowing my legs time to recover. In three hours, we had walked twenty kilometres and that was too much for an old toppie like me. Kaluka Kaluka might take such hikes as a matter of course, but my body felt as though I had been hit by a truck. When I stood up to wish my new friend farewell, my legs buckled and I clung to the back of my chair to stop myself from falling. Kaluka looked concerned, but brightened when I gave him a pen, plus a maglite torch for himself and a packet of needles for his girlfriend.

"That is for bringing me here," I told him but didn't add that it was also for showing me how a truly strong man tackles the long road. Kaluka Kaluka was undoubtedly one of the strongest and fittest men I had ever met.

It was Thursday afternoon and I had to be in Mongu the following morning. My phone battery was flat, but I managed to get through to Andy on the satellite phone and he promised to get his man Victor to liaise with me as to where we could meet. In the meantime, a charming young lady in Musa's emporium allowed me to put my phone on charge and I sat and watched the citizens of Limilunga go about their business. A man who called himself Arnold - I had a feeling that it was not his real name - told me that he was part of the Lozi Freedom movement, who were intent on breaking away from the rest of Zambia.

"We were betrayed by Kaunda's Zambians," He told me hotly. "Now we want a free Loziland with our own leaders and the Litunga as our president."

I had heard murmurings about a Lozi breakaway before leaving Ndola, but it hadn't seemed likely. The fervour of this young man made me think however and I determined to find out more about the issue. Zambia is currently one of the most successful of African countries and has the highest economic growth rate in the continent, but if the Lozi did break away, the country would be halved in size and I wondered how that would affect everyone.

But my more pressing problem was to get out of Limilunga. Mongu was only a few kilometres away. I could walk it in a couple of hours, so would have no problem with getting there - provided I was fit enough to move on.

At that stage, I was not. The walk with Kaluka had taken enormous toll of my strength. My calf muscle niggled and my body ached. When I tried to walk, my head spun and my vision blurred. I didn't have enough cash for an overnight stay in Limilunga, but I wasn't sure that I could walk on. I could feel myself becoming ever more fretful and ill at ease.

A loud hoot from a car drew my attention and a young man stuck his head out of the driver's window.

"Are you Mr David?" He shouted and as mine was the only white face in view, it was not an inspired guess. When I allowed that I was, he introduced himself as Joseph and told me that 'Victor from Cowbell' had sent him to take me into Mongu. It was cheating I suppose as I could have walked the last few kays, but I didn't have a choice. Joseph had another young man with him and I relaxed in the rear, comfortable at last. Wherever we were going, it had to be preferable to spending the night, camped beside the main road.

In Mongu, I was driven into an establishment called The Majesty Lodge, where I was given a room with hot water and *en suite* bathroom. The joy of sinking down on a double bed was an experience that will live long in my memory. In our comfortable modern lives, we forget how wonderful, basic comfort can be to those who are not accustomed to it.

Joseph left me with the news that he would collect me the following morning and I made myself tea - the room had a kettle - and a bowl of health gruel before retiring early and sleeping like the dead. During the night, I got up for a wee, but while on my way to the bathroom, my legs gave way and I crashed to the floor. My head banged against a wall and blood flowed from a gash over my eye. Slowly - ever so slowly - I regained my feet and after doing what I had to, walked carefully back to my bed, where once again I slept like a log.

I didn't bother with breakfast the following morning and when Joseph came to fetch me, I was surprised to see that he was on a bicycle, rather than the car, he had driven the previous day. I didn't ask, but wandered beside him to his house on the other side of town.

After meeting Joseph's family and sitting in his front room - the walls covered with banners and photographs relating to Manchester United - for much of the morning, I met Victor and Martin in downtown Mongu. After another photo call, I was whisked away to a lodge with an impressive view over the plains. My companions took me for a steak supper that evening and a good time was had by all. I spent Saturday resting and sorting out my new supplies and on Sunday morning, we went to the market.

Mongu Market ought to be a 'must' for visitors to Zambia and I am surprised the Tourist Board does nothing to publicise it. Traders come from miles around in their boats and canoes, while stalls are spread out in colourful disorder beside the water. The main channel of the Zambezi is ten kilometres to the East, but that sort of distance is nothing to these hardy boatmen and I found myself entranced by the 'taxis' coming into port, roughly carved gunwales overloaded with supplies and the baggage of passengers. The Lozi paddle their canoes from a standing position and this added to the majesty of the picture. Victor and Martin haggled cheerfully with storekeepers and came away with packets of dried fish, while I sampled fritters that were delicious when fresh, but difficult to chew once that freshness wore off.

While in the market, we spoke to a number of boatmen and my questions as to the feasibility of getting a lift back to the river and walking on from there were laughed off.

"The entire plain is under water," One fellow told me. "Unless you want to swim to Senanga, you will have to take the road."

After three days on the dirt road from Luena, I had had more than enough of highways, but other boatmen said the same thing and reluctantly, I eventually accepted that taking the road to Senanga was the only way I would be able to move on.

It was a depressing decision to make, but there wasn't an alternative.

So it was that on Monday morning, my Cowbell reprobates - Martin was on friendly terms with every woman in Mongu and Victor knew all the dives in town - dropped me on the road to Senanga. New tarmac stretched in front of me and I had one hundred and fifteen kilometres to cover in ten days. My heart was heavy, because this was not what I regarded as walking the Zambezi.

The stretch between Mongu and Senanga was perhaps the most boring part of my entire trip. The road was straight, rarely deviating and with only the occasional gentle gradient.

It was newly laid so there weren't even any potholes to break the monotony. I passed villages from time to time and the residents were polite but wary. I was careful to fill my water containers at every opportunity, trying to ensure that I always had at least two litres on hand. It wasn't much, but enough to keep me going.

There was never enough for washing however and as my beard grew spikier, I decided to endure a dry shave with a new blade. Even as the prospect tumbled around in my mind, I passed a village with a borehole pump right beside the road. Morning traffic was brisk, but this was too good an opportunity to miss, so off came my pack and out came the shaving kit - a disposable razor and my bar of soap. Villagers watched my preparations with evident amazement and I soon had an audience of curious children sitting on the ground around me, big eyes focussed on the skinny old *mukuwa* with his shirt off.

Tiring of feeling like a laboratory specimen, I asked one of the village elders if he could chase the children away and he did so with a torrent of Lozi. Moments later, their places had been taken by adults, who also seemed fascinated by my ministrations. One delightful lady brought a fluffy towel for me to use and handed it to me with a little curtsey that made the gesture all the more agreeable. Despite what seems to be happening in the allegedly civilised world, manners in rural Africa are still held in high regard.

That shave did me the world of good too. I took to the road again feeling considerably better about life. It was probably the only bright spot on this leg of the journey and as I wandered on, I wondered how many other people could boast of having shaved beside a busy main road with two separate audiences to the action.

I was averaging twelve kilometres a day, which was worrying. I didn't want to arrive in Senanga too early, but on the other hand, had learned from my Luena experience so pushed on regardless. On three occasions, I was offered lifts and the occupants of one vehicle had seen me on television, so we spent a cheerful half-hour chatting beside the road. They loaded me up with bananas and went on their way, arms waving from car windows until they were out of sight.

It was on the Wednesday that I was offered yet another lift, this time from a taxi driver buying fish by the side of the road. I told him that I was not in any hurry, so would walk on and he laughingly assured me that I would arrive in Senanga that day. I didn't believe him, but forty minutes later saw a large roundabout ahead and a police road block. Away to my right, I could see the Zambezi and although I had nothing to hide from the cops, I was feeling decidedly anti social, so took a narrow path toward the river.

Close to the water I rested beneath a tree, only to be disturbed by a group of schoolchildren, whispering '*mukuwa*' to each other in tones of wonder. I tried to chase them away, but they were soon back. They were doing me no harm and I ought to have been accustomed to the scrutiny by then, but I was irritable and worried that morning. I had two and a half days before I could realistically hope to meet Andy and apart from making a camp beside the river and indulging in a little fishing, I didn't know how I would occupy myself.

Moving down a path, I wondered what to do. Another tree offered shade and the day was hot, so I moved toward that, but the grass had recently been burned, so it would not make a comfortable camp. Then I spotted an old house sitting on top of a hill. It didn't look occupied, but there were trees around it, so I decided I could probably lie up in whatever garden there was and at least see out the day.

The place seemed deserted when I arrived, but edging my way around what once must have been a very comfortable abode, I saw a group of people chatting around a fire. There was only one man among them and as Zambia is a country where misogyny is the order of the day, I approached him first.

"Would you mind if I rested beneath these trees?" I asked after exhausting my Lozi vocabulary with '*Muswili.*' "I am tired and the day is very hot."

"Why don't you rest in my house?" The invitation came from a small woman in her mid fifties and dressed in tribal attire of a Tee shirt and *chitenge,* wrapped around her body. "It is cool in there and you will be far more comfortable."

Which was how I came to meet Judith Monde Mututwa, a political princess in her own right and a woman who proved to be one of the most interesting characters I have met in a lifetime of African wandering.

Ready to go with nerves aflutter. Photograph
by Talitha Ullrich

Loading up. Photograph by Talitha Ullrich

A village matron prepares nshima.

Learning young - grinding maize will be a life time task

Difficult terrain along the river bank.

'Path' across the Luena flood plain

Before we sank

A typical 'bridge.'

Drying out after another soaking

John Chipoya with his family

Restful afternoon with my Kindle

Interviewing Simamba with Monde as interpreter

CHAPTER FIVE

(Another Wonder of the World)

The house was cool inside and comfortably furnished. Putting my pack down, I studied my surroundings with interest. Everything looked a little run down and when Monde (that was how she liked to be addressed) Mututwa followed me inside, she apologised for the lack of electricity.

"There has been a mix up with payments," She smiled. "They cut us off last Friday, but I wasn't here and will have to wait until they come again. In the meantime, I have gone back to my roots and cook on a fire outside."

A framed photograph in the lounge depicted an elderly gentleman in morning dress being invested with a medal by an equally elderly gentleman and I was studying it when my hostess came in.

"That is my Father, receiving a medal from the late President Mwanawasa," She told me with obvious pride. "You might have heard of Maxwell Mututwa?"

I hadn't, but I was curious. What had he done to deserve the investiture?

Maxwell Mututwa played a major role in Zambian and Barotseland politics for much of his life. He was a former *Ngambela* (Prime Minister) of the Barotse Royal Establishment and held Cabinet roles in successive Zambian parliaments. A fiery orator, he had been arrested for treason at the age of ninety-two and imprisoned for a month, released only because of a public outcry at such an elderly servant of Zambia being thrown into jail.

"That experience killed him," Monde said sadly. "A few weeks later, he was watching television when he died. It was a terrible loss, not only to my family but also to the nation, because my father was a great Zambian."

He sounded an interesting man and I was to learn that he and his brother, Godfrey had virtually built the town of Senanga between them. Later, when Monde and I went for a walk, she pointed out buildings that either belonged to her or Godfrey's half of the Mututwa family.

Monde had been married to Gilbert Nkausu, a man who held two ministerial posts in the Chiluba government a few years previously. She was very much a political animal and regaled me with tales about the great names of Zambia's modern history.

The house too, could have told a lot of stories.

"Most of the liberation leaders have stayed here and where you are sitting, people like Sam Nujoma, Oliver Tambo and both Mugabe and Nkomo from your country have sat. So many great people wanted to speak with my Father and share his views and his wisdom."

Maxwell Mututwa had been buried in the front garden and his grave was covered with a tarpaulin and surrounded by a fence of thatching grass. This was in accordance with tribal custom and when the time was right, the grave would be uncovered so that everyone could see it. I felt the Old Boy would have preferred to be in the sunshine and when I said so, Monde smiled.

"You are right," She murmured. "He loved to sit in the sun with his grandchildren and great grandchildren."

On the way up to the house that morning, I had passed a very old woman struggling up the path with a hoe on her shoulder and carrying a bucket of water. I hadn't dared to offer help for fear of causing offence, but when I asked Monde about her, she laughed.

"That must have been Simamba. She is over a hundred, but still works her fields and carries her own water and firewood. I will take you to meet her this evening."

She did and I came away from my meeting with Simamba Mambo, feeling privileged to have spent time with a special person. It was a typically African interview, with me sitting on a chair, Monde, who was acting as interpreter on a wooden stool and the interviewee herself on the floor. Wrinkled and bowed, she might have been, but Simamba had a simple dignity and her mind was perfectly clear. She told me that she was 'about a hundred and five,' although that could be a couple of years one way or the other. She talked of the past and the Zambezi River which had been a major part of her life. She had been born in Sileli and would die there, but she had spent time in Zimbabwe where her late husband had been working in Bulawayo and Hwange. When I asked what she remembered of my country, she told me that all she could remember was 'nice people and lovely beer.'

With the African custom of caring for the elderly in mind, I asked whether people looked after her and she cackled again.

"I don't need looking after and when they offer, I turn them down. People leave firewood or vegetables in my house" (her home consisted of a sleeping hut and a kitchen, surrounded by the usual grass fence) "and for that I am grateful, but while I can do things myself, I will continue to do so."

And her children - did they ever assist?

"I had six, but only three are still alive and they are very old. I feel younger than them so I don't ask and they don't offer."

Monde told me that someone had tried to burgle the Old Girl's hut and from the glint of amusement in her eye, it was a good story.

"I heard him trying to break through the roof," Simamba was also smiling, "so I picked up the axe I use for cutting firewood and waited for him. I think he must have seen me though, because he slid down and ran away."

The mental picture of this diminutive geriatric confronting an intruder with an axe made me chuckle and the three of us were soon giggling. When I left, I held Simamba's hand for a moment, told her she was a shining example to the rest of us and wished her many more years of happy life. I also told her how I had hesitated to offer help that morning and she hooted with laughter.

"Look at you," She said. "A skinny old man with a big luggage. I can carry more than you anyway."

It summed her up really - an indomitable spirit inside a tiny body. She would probably live forever and she was right - she could carry more than me.

There were other folk in Sileli village and with Monde, I visited them all over the next couple of days. Without exception, they greeted me with a typically Zambian attitude of curiosity, respect without servility and a willingness to assist that was humbling. They lived simple lives in the sunshine and their generosity of spirit was something that people in the western world would do well to emulate.

That night, I slept on the floor, but it was comfortable and I enjoyed an excellent night. With the dawn I wondered whether I ought to move on or spend another day with Monde Mututwa.

She solved the problem for me.

"Where will you go? You are comfortable here, I will feed you and I enjoy your company. It is nice to talk with someone from the outside world."

So it was settled and when I walked into Senanga with my hostess, it felt like a royal procession. She was dressed in a smart beige trouser suit and I felt scruffy beside her in my shorts and wrinkled shirt. It appeared that every woman in Senanga knew Monde and we were forever stopping to talk, often accompanied by giggling. At one stage, I asked why everyone seemed so cheerful and she smiled.

"They are all curious about my new white boyfriend. I think some are looking forward to the wedding."

She seemed amused rather than offended, so we walked on companionably. I wandered around the market, while she collected rent from a couple of small shops. On the way home,

I suggested a cool drink and she took me to the Senanga Safaris Lodge, which belonged to her cousin Charles. He wasn't around, but I presumed Andy would stay there when he arrived.

After an afternoon spent at Maxanaedi School for Orphans, Street Kids and Vulnerable Children, we went down to the river and met Maxwell, a fisherman who told me he had five children and thought Monde Mututwa was a saint.

"If you marry her, I will provide food for the wedding," He grinned and I shifted uneasily. The locals seemed convinced that Monde and I shared more than we did, but when I glanced across, she was smiling, so obviously wasn't offended.

Maxwell showed me some of the fish he caught from his dugout and they were all of good size.

"I catch them with a hand line and sell them here every morning," He said proudly. "I don't need the market and make enough money to keep my family in comfort."

It seemed an excellent arrangement and Maxwell was a happy man, so I wished him luck and we went into the village so that Monde could do her evening rounds. She was greeted everywhere with obvious affection and I decided that fate and the hot sun had led me to meet a remarkable woman.

The house did not have running water, so everything had to be carried up from the river. Nevertheless, water was heated for me to bathe and shave each day and the outside loo was one of the most remarkable I've seen. It was the usual hole in the ground, surrounded by a grass wall, but it had a seat that was the inner wheel of a tractor. It looked strange, but was surprisingly comfortable and when I mentioned it to my hostess, she smiled.

"I might live like a village woman," she said softly, "but I like my comforts."

To me, that summed up Monde Mututwa. A saint to the people around her and a person who worried incessantly about the welfare of her neighbours and the people of Zambia. At the same time, she was a down-to-earth lady who was a pleasure to be with.

We parted on Friday with a hug and I walked toward Senanga, feeling that once again, my steps had been guided toward a meeting that would live on in my memory.

*   *   *

It was around midday when I left Monde and started walking into town. As I went, I pondered on the lass and how much I had enjoyed her company. It sounds snobbish, but after weeks of only the most basic conversations, it had been wonderful to discourse on a variety of subjects with a highly intelligent lady.

But for the moment, there were more pressing problems to cope with. I didn't expect Andy to arrive before late afternoon, so needed a shady spot, where he would be sure to spot me as he drove into town. There were few trees beside the road, but while I was pondering the problem, I became aware of a vehicle slowing behind me.

"Mr Lemon, I presume?"

The unoriginal greeting came from my sponsor who had made better time than I had expected. Talitha was with him and had been photographing my back - and the pack - as they drove behind me.

Beers were opened and both Andy and Talitha commented on the weight I had lost. At that stage, my weight loss wasn't worrying me, but it was to become a problem over succeeding weeks.

When Andy asked whether I knew of a decent hostelry to spend a couple of nights, the obvious answer was the Senanga Safaris Lodge (I have spelt the second word correctly!) where I would have a chance of meeting the other half of the Mututwa family. Twenty minutes later, we were booked into two riverside chalets and I stretched out on a double bed, feeling on top of the world.

Senanga was probably the most picturesque town I passed through in the course of my walk. Smaller than Livingstone or Mongu, the main street was tarred, with jacaranda and flamboyant trees scattered haphazardly around the centre. With the river nearby, the market was full of fish and everyone seemed smilingly content with their lot.

We spent Saturday morning exploring the town, Andy press-ganging locals into carrying the big Zambezi Cowbell Trek banner, me walking regally - but with considerable embarrassment - before it and Talitha snapping away with her camera. It was a lot of fun and both Andy and I had pockets of Cowbell samples that we distributed to grinning children. I had my photograph taken with a toothless gentleman, called Talktime and when I asked him how he came to be saddled with the name, he said that his parents had given it to him. However, as Talktime - credit on a mobile phone - was a modern phenomenon and he was not, I told him, he was telling me fibs.

We both laughed uproariously, but the name was original so I forgave him his little deception. The morning was spent in light-hearted amusement and arriving back at the lodge, we were in excellent humour. Even an afternoon of fruitless fishing was enjoyable, but perhaps that was because of the beer.

I chatted at length to the staff and met Sean Mututwa, Charles' son who was running the lodge. He told me he had learned the hotel trade in England, but enjoyed life in Senanga. Well dressed and affable, Sean gave the appearance of being a typical hotel manager, but there was a helplessness about him that I don't think his British tutors would have sanctioned. At breakfast, despite my direct appeal to him, it had taken thirty minutes for two teacups to be produced and there were other annoying little problems that let the place down.

But the Safaris Lodge was comfortable, I didn't have a pack to carry and I was enjoying myself. Shortly after our arrival, I had been called to the reception desk and given an envelope containing my gloves, which I had left at Monde's house. With them was a note, addressed to 'David Lemon - Walker,' from the lady herself. In it, she reciprocated my enjoyment at our meeting and wished me God speed and a happy conclusion to my adventure.

It was a sweet note and added to my enjoyment of the weekend. While Andy was fishing and Talitha was doing whatever Talitha was doing, I chanced upon Charles Mututwa in the main building. I told him that I'd spent time with his cousin - which he knew - and that I was interested in learning more about his father and the other side of the Mututwa family. We arranged to get together that evening.

Later in the day, a vehicle drove past our chalets to the manager's house and a very old gentleman was lifted out, placed in a wheelchair and taken inside. It was Godfrey himself and I told my companions all I had learned about the Mututwa clan and their fiefdom in Senanga.

Shortly after the sun went down, Charles invited us to meet his father. The house itself was impressive and we sat in a vast room on splendid furniture. Godfrey Mututwa had been struck down by a stroke and sat huddled in a chair. His mind was still sharp however and his greeting was cordial. I asked Charles to tell me about Lozi tribal customs and he produced a projector on which he took us through the *Kuomboka* ceremony of a few years previously.

Kuomboka is the ceremonial passage of the *Litunga* when the Zambezi begins its annual encroachment on the plains and the Royal Palace has to be moved inland to Limilunga. This movement cannot take place until the royal drum *Mutango* is beaten and when the *Litunga* moves, he takes his possessions with him in the royal barge.

"I was privileged to be an oarsman on the royal barge, *Nalikwanda* that year," Charles told us and his eyes shone with pride. "It is the greatest honour any young Lozi man can aspire to and it was an occasion I shall never forget."

Charles had ambitions to get into Parliament, something he had already attempted, but seemed confident that he would manage on the next occasion. A big, heavy-set man, he oozed with that innate self confidence that is the prerequisite of every politician and I wished him luck when we parted.

"It was an honour to have you in my house, David Lemon," He said and I responded in kind, inwardly preening myself at the flattery. Mind you, Charles was a politician and they do tend to tell you what they think you want to hear.

I am being ungracious and it was a pleasant evening and one I will remember for a long time. Since my visit, Godfrey has died, but with strong characters like Charles and Monde to carry on, I feel sure that the Mututwa family will continue to prosper for a very long time.

Soon after leaving Senanga, the main road crossed the Zambezi, vehicles and pedestrians being carried on a pontoon ferry. Andy and Talitha were going on to Livingstone, so I rode with them to the ferry. On the opposite bank, we stopped in a field for an impromptu picnic, then I was on my way again. This was the area, pointed out to me on his phone by Gordon Hanna all those weeks before, so I knew there would be a path close to the river.

Setting my face toward the Zambezi, I found the path and moved east toward Livingstone some eight weeks away. My pack pulled hard on my shoulders and my legs soon felt rubbery, but I had an added incentive to keep going. Two of my grandchildren would be holidaying in Zambia and I was hoping they would be in Livingstone to meet me.

That prospect kept me going through eight long and arduous weeks.

*   *   *

I could hear them coming through the darkness, but there was nothing I could do. It had been an excellent day and I was camped in a grove of mango trees. The owner of the mangos had asked me not to make a fire as it would damage the leaves, so I had forsaken my evening drink but it didn't seem to matter.

The local headman had also paid a visit and we chatted at length about the problems of his area. They were problematical to him I suppose, but I envied him the organised normality of his existence. Other villagers called in from time to time and a fisherman called Laxson presented me with a bag of unshelled ground nuts, which made up for the lack of tea. All in all, it had been a pleasant day and I looked forward to a decent sleep among the mangoes.

But it was not to be. I didn't know who was approaching, but there were a number of them and they made no attempt to move quietly. That in itself was vaguely comforting, but I switched on my camping light, so they would know exactly where I was. The beam from a torch immediately came on and moments later, I was surrounded by young men. One of them announced that they were from the local army base and had received reports of a *mukuwa* camped in the area.

"You cannot sleep here," he told me politely. "It could be dangerous, so you must come back to our camp."

I had no intention of moving elsewhere. I told him so and the argument started. Some of the others joined in and it was pointed out that I could be eaten by hippopotamus or crocodile if I stayed where I was. I could even be assaulted and robbed by criminals. I knew they were showing concern for my safety, but it was nine o'clock at night and well past my bed time.

"Hippopotami are grazers," I responded sourly. "They eat grass and would not come in among the mango trees. Nor would crocodiles and as for wandering criminals, I have spoken to the local headman and he was happy for me to sleep here.

'As was the owner of these trees," I added as though that solved the problem. Then I had a brainwave and rummaged for Minister Lubinda's letter, which was studied in torchlight by two of my visitors, including the one who appeared to be in charge. While they read, I waved my cell phone.

"I have the minister's personal number on here," I spat. "Give him a ring and tell him that you are taking me away from my camp. You can even tell him that it is for my own safety, but he will not be pleased."

I had no idea whether Given Lubinda would have been cross or not, but I was gambling that these youngsters wouldn't dare make the call.

Fortunately perhaps, they didn't. After another few minutes of heated discussion among themselves, the letter was handed back to me and the leader bade me a courteous farewell. With the advent of higher authority in the form of a piece of government paper, his manner changed completely.

"I hope you will be safe Sir and enjoy a good night." With that, he and his band of military cut throats melted into the night. With a sigh of relief and a muttered thanks to Given Lubinda, I drifted off to sleep.

I had covered close to ten kilometres the following morning when I wandered through a village and was hailed by a villainous-looking fellow, repairing a fishing net. Dressed in trousers and a torn vest, he had a newspaper-wrapped cigarette dangling from one corner of his mouth, smoke curling into his eyes and making him squint - which heightened the impression of villainy. He called something around the cigarette, but I didn't catch what he said, so wandered across to him.

"Have you any spare hooks?" Was his question and I allowed that I had a few. He suggested that I spend the day with him and later on, we could go fishing on the river. It sounded good and that was how I made the acquaintance of Mola Kafuka.

The village was a large one and I soon had the usual audience of curious children, this time reinforced by a number of women. Food was prepared, a stool was produced for me to sit on and while we ate, Mola and I discussed the world in general. Our talk was in a curious mixture of English, Lozi, Luwale, Chilapalapa and sign language, but I think we managed to make ourselves understood. Mola was intensely curious about the world I lived in and confessed that although he had once been to Sesheke, he had otherwise spent his life in the confines of his village.

"I was born here; I was married here and I will die here," There was simple pride in his voice and I warmed to the man.

Our discussion was interrupted by a bout of wailing nearby and I looked up from my *nshima* to see a group of women running through the village, the one in front setting up a caterwauling that sent shivers up my spine.

"What is the matter with her?" I asked my host and he shrugged.

"Her teenage daughter died this morning," He told me. "She was preparing food and just fell into the fire, dead. I will take you to their village when we have finished eating."

I wasn't sure that I wanted to go, nor that my presence would be welcome, but Mola told me he was going and I meekly followed him to a nearby village. A dignified looking woman was greeting people, who streamed across the plain from every direction. A large, black and white duck followed proceedings with obvious interest.

"That is the grandmother," Mola indicated the woman. "She will organise everything, while the mother cries."

There was a great deal of weeping and wailing going on in a small area, enclosed by the usual grass fence. On entering the village, each man paid a visit to this enclosure, to be greeted by the dignified lady, then moved outside to sit in the sunshine, smoke and exchange greetings with other men. One or two elders were given chairs, but most sat on logs or the ground. The women stayed within the fence and howled their sorrow to the heavens. One lass, dressed in a Manchester United *chitenge* was so overcome by emotion that she had to be carried out and laid on the ground, some distance away.

The children also seemed caught up in the general hysteria and a number of them howled and wailed as they staggered around the village, their eyes rolled back in their heads and their faces drenched in tears. It was noisy and to the average Westerner would have seemed very strange and probably demeaning to everyone concerned. However, I have witnessed funerals all over Africa and never fail to find myself stirred by the obvious sorrow of everyone involved. While the men sit in stoic silence or talk quietly among themselves, the women and children give full vent to their feelings, ensuring that the deceased person has the best of send offs.

Food was served, but I was full of *nshima* already, so declined to take any more and shortly afterwards, Mola and I wandered back to his village, where we sat under a tree and did nothing for two or three hours.

Once again comparing the culture of rural Africa with the frenetic bustle so prevalent in the modern world was incredibly difficult. In Mola's village, time meant nothing and the day was there to be enjoyed. My western mind fretted to be doing something, but my host didn't need to occupy himself, except perhaps in thinking great thoughts. It is a difficult concept to grasp when one has been brought up in the West, but perhaps it is one reason why few African villagers suffer from heart attacks, stomach ulcers or cancer. None of them wear watches, but they always have time to spare and share with a stranger.

It was late afternoon when we took our rods down to the river where a couple of sturdy dugouts were tucked into a bank.

One Zambian shortage, I had not bargained for when planning my trip was that of pipe tobacco. Pipes were a forgotten part of the country's past and despite my pleas for a resupply of the precious stuff, my Cowbell sponsors had only been able to come up with a sack full of the coarse, local tobacco, normally wrapped in newspaper to be smoked as a rough cigarette. It tasted foul and had the kick of an angry zebra, so I used it sparingly but it came in handy for bribery or cajolement. When I lit my pipe with a little of my remaining good tobacco, Mola looked the question at me and with a sigh, I gave him some of my Zambian stuff. He was a heavy smoker, seldom without a bit of rolled newspaper hanging from his mouth and that little gift ensured that we would be friends for life.

We spent a happy hour or two fishing from dugouts in the river, but as so often happens when I am involved, we caught no fish. I don't know why it is, but I seldom catch them myself and seem to put a curse on those who fish with me. On this occasion, Mola did get a bite and a three-pronged lure, he had borrowed from me ended up with two of its hooks completely straightened.

"Big tigerfish," My companion muttered and while I did not think the fish had been particularly large, the damage to my lure showed the awesome power in the tigerfish's jaws.

Back in the village, Mola barked orders to his wife and moments later, a happily foraging chicken was caught, despatched and plucked by a little girl who was an obvious expert. That was supper, but before that I was cajoled into photographing the old ladies and children of the village. Then it was the turn of Mrs Mola and her mother, both of whom donned ornate headgear before posing and neither of whom would smile when I asked them to do so. Being photographed was obviously a more serious business than I had thought.

With bits of the deceased chicken inside me and a good night's sleep behind me, I set out early next morning. Mola accompanied me for the first few kilometres and even carried my pack. He had told me that to stay beside the river would mean long detours, so we took a dusty main road that wound its way between thickly wooded hills. Some way along this, my companion stopped, announced that he had things to do and left me to carry my own pack.

"Keep on this road until you reach Nangweshe," He advised. "There, you can go back to the river path and it will take you to Sesheke."

A cigarette still bobbing from the corner of his mouth, Mola smiled and was gone. He might have had a piratical air about him, but Mola Kafuka had a heart as big as Africa and I was proud to have become his friend.

I walked all through that day and in a town called Matabele - there had to be some historical reason for that - I was given more groundnuts by a retired school teacher called Julian. We chatted and he volunteered to accompany me to Sesheke, but I turned his offer down on the grounds that I did not want the added responsibility. He accepted that and we shook hands before I took the road again.

Mola had been right about Nangweshe. As I came into the dusty little centre, I spotted a path heading toward the river. I followed it and was soon lost as it twisted and turned between gardens. In a state of frustration, I had to ask the way, but found an exceptional camping site a few minutes later. It was close to the town, but on a small hill beside a bend in the river. Whichever way I looked, the mighty Zambezi could be seen, almost beaming as it purred its way to the Indian Ocean, still over two thousand kilometres away. This was the benevolent face of the watercourse I was coming to think of as 'My Zambezi' and I sat with my back against a big tree and enjoyed the moment.

Towards evening, a young herdsman spotted me and in a state of obvious panic, dived into the long grass. I called, but he didn't respond, so I walked towards him, murmuring idiocies in as soothing a voice as I could muster. When I was about ten metres from him, he stood upright, pointed his stick at me and yelled something that was obviously uncomplimentary. I carried on with my soothing tones and calmed him down enough to confirm that he had mistaken me for an evil spirit or perhaps someone from the Democratic Republic of Congo.

When I asked whether there had been troubles in the area with people from the DRC, he shook his head violently and made to run off again. I slowed him by handing over a couple of packets containing Cowbell milk powder and he told me he needed to put his cattle away for the night, but would come back and talk when that was done.

He must have told his friends about the *mukuwa*, camped by the river. Perhaps he told them I was an evil spirit, because as the evening was fading, I was surrounded by children and teenagers. They stayed fifty metres away and yelled what sounded like incantations into the gathering gloom. I stood up and signalled with my arms for them to come closer, but that caused them to flee with shrill shouts. I sat down again and they were soon back to shout some more. The noise was annoying and I struggled to keep my anger in check, but eventually it proved too much for me. Rising to my feet, I cupped palms around my mouth and bellowed with all the breath I could muster.

"Will you lot go away?"

They might not have understood the words, but it had the desired effect and suddenly there was silence. I stood where I was and none of my tormentors moved a muscle. We must have presented a strange evening tableau, but even as we stood there, darkness descended and I went back to my fire.

I heard and saw no more of my youthful audience, but they had spoiled my evening and I eventually dropped into a fretful sleep. Despite the lovely situation of my little camp, it had not been a particularly happy day.

*　　*　　*

As the kilometres fell away behind me, I seemed to be growing weaker, rather than stronger. Weight was still falling off me and when I took my shirt off, it was frightening to see how prominent my ribs had become. My shoulders still ached, despite the constant application of gel. I was struggling to sleep and kept falling over, even when there was no apparent reason to fall. Whenever I stood up, my vision blurred and I had to stand still for a minute or so before everything cleared and I could walk on.

To make matters worse, my front teeth were loose and I wondered whether they would last the distance.

My mind struggled to focus and I began to doubt whether I would complete the walk. It was illogical, because I had known from the start that it would be a massive challenge, but ever more often I felt that the doubters had been right. Perhaps I was too old.

But I was committed, so had to keep going.

A road was being built by the Chinese between Senanga and Sesheke and I walked parallel to this. At times I could hear the rumble of machinery and even shouts between workers on the road, so it would not have been difficult to ask for help, but

I was reluctant to do this. I had planned the walk for months and others - particularly Andy Taylor and Cowbell - had invested time, worry and money in my endeavours, so I had to keep going, no matter how hard things became.

My days had settled into a well-worn routine, but I wasn't enjoying myself. The villagers were as cheerful and friendly as ever, there were new sights to be seen and strangers to meet around every bend, but by mid morning, I would find myself looking for a patch of bush in which I could hide and wait out the afternoon, before surviving another night and hitting the road once more. I was going through the motions of walking the Zambezi at that stage and every day was another trial to get through.

On three occasions, I came across areas where forest had been cleared and land excavated, presumably to extract materiel for the road building. They were ugly scars on a beautiful landscape and I wondered whether the damage would ever be repaired.

Most men in the area seemed to work on the road, but their womenfolk were always friendly and children continued to follow me in wide-eyed bemusement. I was the first white person they had seen, so was probably a shock to their little systems. Few of them attended school and there were few schools for them along this stretch of river. I remembered the complaint of John Chipoya, who had eight children, six of them still very young. His wife Cleris nodded sadly as he spoke.

"I am a simple fisherman and catch merely enough to feed us all." It was a cry I had heard on many occasions. "I cannot afford school fees and the nearest school is twenty kilometres away. I can't make them walk that far every day."

It was a sad state of affairs and doesn't bode well for the future prosperity of Zambia. A generation will grow up illiterate and knowing nothing about the world around them. They might be able to follow their fathers into the fishing industry, but when the fish run out, as inevitably they must, what can they do?

It isn't only the school children who are likely to pose future problems. Throughout my walk, I had talked with groups of young men who hung around their villages with nothing to do. Many of them carried catapults and where these were in evidence, bird life was sparse. When I asked them why they didn't find work or start a business of their own, they were openly scornful.

"There is no need for that," A youth called Boniface told me. "We have maize delivered to our villages every month by NGOs and missionaries, so we will never starve. There is no work for us in any case, so what can we do but sit and talk?"

Wherever I went along the Zambezi, mango trees grew in abundance and when I asked villagers what happened to the fruit, I was told that most of it rotted in the hot sun. When I suggested to the ranks of unemployed young men that they should market the mangos, they shrugged my suggestion away. They didn't fancy the hard work involved and with everything laid on, who could really blame them?

Aid for Africa is big business in the western world, but I only wish donors could accompany me on my travels and see exactly how much of it is wasted and how sad an effect it has on ordinary lives. In every Zambian market, there are stalls full of clothing, donated by aid agencies and people for who it is intended are forced to buy it from unscrupulous traders. The middle men and entrepreneurs get ever richer and the poor folk get poorer, despite all the good will and largesse being sent in their direction.

Of course, not all young Zambians were on this sad little gravy train and I met a number of fine young men working their hearts out for little reward as carpenters or farmers, cultivating small crops of cassava, millet or ground nuts. However, such is the culture of rural Africa that farming is regarded as work for women and these lads were the exception rather than the rule.

Monde Mututwa and I had discussed the problem and she had visionary ideas as to what could be done to give the unemployed faith in themselves and a sense of purpose in life.

When I mentioned my idea about mangoes, she looked thoughtful.

"There are also cashew nuts, bananas, citrus fruit and other exotics being allowed to rot on the trees." She said sadly. "These could be utilized, packed and exported, but that will need investment from outside and although it is a success story in the context of modern Africa, Zambia has little to offer the investor."

Monde was undoubtedly correct, but Zambia needs more forward-thinking politicians and go-ahead people like her. I assumed that her vision, energy and hope for the future of her people came from her father, Maxwell and as I trudged toward Sioma, I couldn't help wishing I had met the man.

But Zambia's problems were dwarfed by my own along this stretch of the river. The walking was easy, with foot paths wending their way through thickly forested areas, but all too often I came across vast swathes of countryside where every tree had been hacked down or ring-barked. I know conservation is probably not a word ever encountered by the average Zambian villager, but it was sad to see so much woodland being destroyed. The burning of charcoal is a major industry in the country, but I didn't see any evidence of it along that stretch, so could only assume that the trees were being used as firewood for the workers or props for the building of the road.

There were cattle roaming the river area and as many of them carried bells around their necks and my walk was officially the Zambezi Cowbell Trek, I tried to photograph one with its bell displayed. I had vague ideas about a book cover, but not one of those contrary animals would cooperate. Time after time, they allowed me to approach, but as soon as I paused to take the photograph, the selected animal would run off, kicking its heels in obvious satisfaction at having outwitted me. I added to my distance covered with many a long detour after wildly jangling livestock and never managed a satisfactory photo.

It was a hot morning when I came into Sioma in search of the Sioma Ngonye Falls, which I had been told was an incredible sight. As I looked around for help, a battered truck pulled up and two men approached. The driver had his hand outstretched and a smile on his face.

"We saw you on television in Lusaka," He introduced himself as Stephen, "and we marvelled at any man doing what you are doing. Now I have met you, which is a great honour for me."

Flattering I suppose, but the countryside around me was flat, I was further from the river than I wanted to be and I needed to find the Sioma Falls before nightfall. Stephen and his mate, Mathew seemed nice fellows though, so I spent time talking to them and answering questions before venturing one of my own.

The answer was a depressing one.

"The waterfalls are five kilometres along this road," Mathew told me and dismay must have shown on my face. "Don't worry, we are junior consultants on the road building project, so we travel up and down. We will take you there because you look very tired."

I was very tired, but was soon in the cab of their vehicle as we drove toward the Sioma Ngonye Falls. This was a vast improvement on walking and my pack was in the back of the truck where it couldn't inflict any more pain on my tormented shoulders.

Perhaps I would complete my walk after all.

*   *   *

The Victoria Falls are rightfully famous throughout the world and visitors flock there in their thousands every year. Few of those visitors realise that a couple of hundred kilometres upstream is another waterfall that is every bit as spectacular.

Having been dropped off at the Sioma Ngonye visitors' centre, I waved farewell to my two new friends and wandered inside to see if there was anywhere I could camp. A tall Afrikaner studied me with interest.

"I have heard about you," He spoke quietly. "Your back up team came through a while ago."

A back up team - for me? It didn't sound likely, but then I remembered that Andy and Talitha would have passed this way after leaving me upstream. The Afrikaner, whose name was Flip Nel sent a guide to show me a camp site close to the falls. It was basic, but there was hot water provided and it suited me down to the ground. Although it wasn't in sight of the waterfall, there was a sandy beach leading down to the river and apart from the roar of nearby rapids, it was quiet enough to soothe my fretful senses and ease the ache in my shoulders. I didn't even have to build my own fire, as it was done for me and far better than I could have done it myself.

Flip occupied a wooden house in one corner of the site and when he returned from work that evening, he wandered across and invited me to supper. I had already enjoyed two cups of tea with biscuits, but I eagerly followed him across camp.

As evening faded into night, we sat by his fire and shared two beers and a load of stories - most of them about the 'good old days.' Flip was a year younger than me and had been a ranger in the Kruger Park for thirty years. Now he worked for the Peace Park Foundation who were building a Transfrontier Park, involving Zambia, Zimbabwe, Namibia, Botswana and Angola. It would take in the Sioma area and include a number of elephant corridors that would allow the great beasts to wander between countries as they would have done decades before.

"In fact, you will need to be careful a little further on," Flip told me. "The jumbo are already coming in from Namibia, so don't go camping in any of their corridors."

At one stage I commented to my companion that we were a typical pair of old codgers, sitting with our pipes and telling stories of the days when elephants roamed the land. He smiled gently.

"It is true though. You and I weren't around when the continent was opening up to the white man, but we have seen much that will never be seen again."

It was a sobering thought.

It was a lovely evening though and bully beef and baked bean hash with tomatoes and rice did me good. Back under my blanket, I looked up at the shimmering starscape, listened to the roar of tumbling water and reflected that life was not too bad.

The following morning, with a guide called Patrick, I wandered in awe struck bemusement around the area of the waterfalls. Livingstone when first seeing the Victoria Falls is said to have made a comment to the effect that 'sights so beautiful can only have been witnessed by Angels in their flight,' but that comment applied equally to Sioma. There are five waterfalls, set out in a great horseshoe of roaring, foaming water with towering columns of spray above them. The noise was terrific and Patrick told me that the name Ngonye refers to the booming sound of water rushing through rocks. Officially, these were the Ngonye Falls, but so many people refer to them as Sioma Falls that the names were put together and it became Sioma Ngonye.

Whatever one called it, the place was one of Nature's masterpieces and I spent the morning, admiring various views. Patrick and I sat on rocks, enjoying the cooling spray that drenched us, while he talked. He lived in the area and while he had been schooled in Lusaka and enjoyed boyhood dreams of doing well in the big city, he was a bush boy at heart and the Sioma area eventually drew him back.

"I am a farmer now," He told me proudly. "I grow cassava, maize and ground nuts, but only enough to feed my family and keep us going through the bad months. A number of us work as tourist guides here and I make more money from tips, given to me by visitors."

He and his fellow guides were employed by the local chief and received no wage for their services. "We do it because we enjoy it and because people in the outside need to know about these beautiful waterfalls."

It sounded like a rehearsed speech, but he was right about the beauty of the place. It was awesomely, spectacularly magnificent! I am being profligate with adjectives, but the Sioma Ngonye Falls should be listed among the wonders of the world and ought to be a must for every visitor to Zambia.

On the other hand, while money is undoubtedly needed, any influx of tourists to the place would mean alterations to the natural beauty and an inevitable deterioration which would officially be put down to 'progress.'

Perhaps, the Falls should be left in its pristine magnificence and allowed to remain a wonderful memory for those few folk who have been privileged to see the place.

Flip and I had discussed the future development of his little kingdom. It would be part of the new Transfrontier Park and he scoffed at my views on progress.

"Zambia needs foreign money," He told me. "This place ought to be a money spinner and once we have the area fenced off, I will bring in a few impala or zebra to give it the feeling of genuine Africa."

His plans made sense, but I forgot them when he invited me to enjoy a morning in the local game park. It would mean spending an extra night, but time wasn't an issue, although I kept having to remind myself that I wasn't in a hurry.

Sioma Ngwezi National Park is five hundred square kilometres in area and according to Flip contains approximately a thousand elephant, as well as a host of other species.

"The elephant come and go across the river," He told me, "but we have a central core that like to stay put. We even have lions at times, but they tend to stay close to the Namibian side of the park."

A strange anomaly of this haven for wild life was that to enter the park, we drove through a wide belt of hunting land. That did not make sense and when I raised my eyebrows at Flip, he shook his head.

"It is odd, but the animals soon learn where they are safe, so it seems to work."

I was not convinced, but forgot about it in the joys of being back in wild Africa. That probably sounds ridiculous, coming from a man who had walked over six hundred kilometres through some of the most remote countryside on earth, but there is a different atmosphere to a National Park. Humans become interlopers and wild animals rule the roost. Even the vegetation seems different, with trees getting their sustenance from forest pans and tinkling streams. It is all good for the soul - my soul at any rate.

We didn't see elephant on that enchanted morning, but we saw giraffe, banded mongoose, a solitary steenbok and a magnificent variety of birds. My weary muscles relaxed in the ambience of wild Africa and it was a lovely day. I was invited to have supper with Flip again that evening and once again, we two old codgers set the world - certainly the African side of it - to rights under a big moon.

I drifted off to sleep that night, feeling that I was privileged, not only to have seen the spectacular Sioma Falls, but also to have spent time with a man who loved the wild places as much as I did.

It is always nice to know that one is not alone in one's eccentricities.

*　　*　　*

I often wonder what human beings have against snakes. Normally sensible people will shudder visibly at the word and those few of us who enjoy the creatures are regarded as being crackpots.

Yet snakes are beautiful, they keep rats and other pests away from our homes and over ninety percent of them are harmless. Their brains are so tiny in relation to their bulk that they are incapable of aggression and even in Africa, few people ever see them.

I love handling snakes. They are cool, dry and incredibly sinuous. I have heard people describe them as slimy, but that is far from the case. Their skins are dry and smooth, cool to the touch and soothing to feel. My passion for the species has led me into a scrape or two over the years, but those are other stories, which I might share with the world one day.

A day or two after leaving the Ngonye Falls and its comfortable camp site I was sitting out the midday sun under a tree. The path I had been following ran past my feet and when I stretched my legs out, my boots rested on it. I was seated thus with my mind wandering when I spotted a snake slithering along the path toward me. As I was perfectly still, he hadn't picked up any vibrations to alarm him and seemed unaware of my presence. I watched with interest, wondering when he would detect me.

The snake was three foot long, dull grey in colour and had a coffin shaped head. There is only one species with a head like that and it is the black mamba - indisputably the most lethal reptile in Africa. Suddenly this was becoming serious. With less than three metres between us, I could frighten him with any sudden movement and in his fright he might bite me in self defence. On the other hand, if I didn't move, he would probably slither over my boots. It was not the ideal position to be in, but I had to do something.

Remaining perfectly still, I opened my mouth and said 'Boo' or something like that and the effect was remarkable. We have all seen people being given a fright and their contortions and facial expressions are sometimes fiendishly amusing. This little mamba was the same. Had he been able to, he would have clasped his hands on the top of his head and run. In the event, he reared up briefly, then shot to one side as though his life depended upon it. He probably thought it did and I don't think I have ever seen a snake move so quickly. Smiling to myself, I wondered whether anyone else could claim to having frightened a black mamba.

I think I joined a pretty exclusive club that afternoon.

A little further on, I was blundering down an intermittent path along the river bank, when I came face to face with a large hippopotamus, obviously making a late return to the river after a night on the town. For a few very long seconds, we stared at each other. We were metres apart and I had no time to think about the situation or get out of the way, but instinctively stood as still as possible. Obviously puzzled as to what I was, the hippo turned and crashed away through grass and reads, leaving me shaky in the knees but feeling immensely privileged to have been so close to a magnificent wild animal.

At that stage, I was sticking close to the river, where dark forests tumbled down the banks and the water was a deep blue, except where it hurled itself through rapids. I passed a few fishermen in their canoes and exchanged waves, but in general, there weren't many people to see. I skirted a massive quarry that must have covered four or five hectares of what had once been forest and there was an air of desolation about it. Rubbish and general detritus had been thrown everywhere and the fact that the area around the quarry was so beautiful, made it seem even more of a sacrilege. When will modern man realise that he is destroying the heritage of us all? I suppose 'never' is the answer to that, particularly where there is money involved.

Brooding on the destructive tendencies of my fellow humans, I walked into a wire fence that cut across the path. Muttering to myself, I followed it until I came to an open gate and a road into what appeared to be an incomplete camp. Men moved listlessly in the heat and there was a muted hammering coming from one building. Walking in, I made the acquaintance of Hilda Chipman Dunne.

Hilda was a lady of mixed race and an entertaining character indeed. She told me that both her grandfathers - one Scottish and one Canadian - were buried in the area, that she was married to an Irishman farming in Kabwe and that she had another lodge in Livingstone, where she ran her own botanical garden. Although she had been brought up in the area and spoke Lozi fluently, she professed dislike of the Lozi as people and spent much of her time bellowing at the men who worked for her. Yet at the same time, she shared her food with them and treated them with a kindness that was refreshing to see. For all her blustering exterior, Hilda was a sweet lady and when she suggested that I stay for a meal and spend the night, I was only too keen to agree.

The camp was on a high bank overlooking a vast white beach, spilling into the river, which at this point moved past in stately somnolence. It was an outlook to soothe the most troubled of souls and I felt myself relax as I sat in a comfortable chair and watched Hilda cook supper on an old wood stove, between shouting instructions at her staff. She had five men working for her and if they were bothered about working for a woman - not really the norm in rural Africa - who scolded them in their own language, while casting vigorously expressed aspersions on their ancestry, their brains and their ability to do anything correctly, they gave no sign of it.

In fact, from the sly smiles they exchanged when they didn't feel they were being watched, I think they rather enjoyed it.

With the onset of darkness, a fire was made and replete with pork stew and pasta, we sat beside it in companionable silence. A movement near my foot caught my eye and I looked down to see a large black scorpion scurrying for a pool of darker shadow where it could hide. I pointed it out to Hilda and she squeaked as she pulled her legs up beneath her. One of her staff ran over with a shovel and before I could stop him, he had bashed the scorpion over the head and deposited the still twitching corpse in the fire. I could feel shock flood through my system. Like snakes, scorpions are maligned creatures and seldom inflict their admittedly excruciating bites on people. The natural reaction is to kill them first and ask questions later, but the black ones are relatively harmless and very shy. This chap had just been passing through and hadn't deserved the summary justice meted out to him.

That was the only blot on my stay with Hilda Dunne and when we parted a day or two later, I walked on, feeling that I'd met another remarkable person. Big, brash and noisy, she was a lady of kindness and generosity. I had been privileged to meet her and offered a quiet prayer of thanks to whatever Deity was guiding my steps so benevolently.

Even now, I smile when I think of Hilda Chipman Dunne and lovely Kashavati Lodge beside the Zambezi. She told me of her plans for the place and I hope I will get back there when it is completed and be able to spend more time with a true African 'character.'

*   *   *

Village headmen on this stretch of the river called themselves n*dunas*, hinting again at some history between the Lozi people and the Matabele from further South. The riverside terrain became more difficult as I moved eastward, long grass spreading inshore and necessitating the use of hippo trails if I didn't want to get too close to the main Sesheke Road.

Hippo are nocturnal herbivores and with their bulk, they force their way through the toughest of countryside on their way to pasture. In the process, they make narrow tunnels through grass and reeds. These made for easier progress, but when walking my stooped way along them in the early mornings, my heart would thump at the prospect of meeting up with one of these behemoths on his way home. Fortunately it didn't happen and the hippo trails allowed me to make excellent progress.

There was elephant sign in abundance too and I could feel myself smiling inside at the prospect of seeing my favourite animals again. Locals warned me to be careful, but I was not particularly worried. Having spent much of my life among elephants, I felt I knew them well and would not be in any danger from them. When an n*duna* called Malindi told me he had been bothered by three hundred jumbo during the night, I hurried to the spot he indicated. There was sign and it was fresh, but there had probably been about eight elephants, rather than the huge herd he had indicated.

In another village, I sat with a group of elderly men and we set the world to rights, exchanging tales of elephants and other wild life. A bowl of soft *mealie* porridge was produced for me and the lady offering it, curtsied prettily and apologised because there was milk but no sugar.

The porridge was delicious and more so, because milk was rarely drunk in the riverine villages, despite the fact that every one had its own herd of wandering cattle. When I mentioned this to the elders, an order was barked out and a large bowl of warm, frothy milk was produced. I filled one of my water containers and drank the rest, feeling immediately replete and at peace. It seemed a pity that milk was so scarce along the road, but I supposed it had something to do with the importance of cattle in tribal culture.

Godfrey Mulelalabenga had promised to show me the path along the river and the day was getting on, so I said my farewells and shrugged my pack into place. As we prepared to leave, a young woman dashed out of a hut and ran toward me, three bananas in her hand.

"These are to keep you strong Sir," She told me breathlessly and I used both hands to accept her gift, feeling a surge of gratitude as I did so. These people had so little of their own, but were always pleased to share it with a wandering stranger. They made me feel very humble.

Godfrey set a cracking pace, despite being older than me. Sweat was soon pouring off me and my lungs were on fire, but with my usual stubborn pride, I forced myself to keep up with the long striding *nduna*. We had covered three kilometres, when he held up a hand and showed me which path to take at a fork in the road ahead of us. I thanked him profusely, but didn't mention that his pace had flattened me. He headed back the way we had come and as soon as he was out of sight, I slipped off the path and found a spot to camp beneath two trees with plenty of old elephant sign about. I could take Godfrey's path the following day.

In fact, the day began badly when I fell hard, climbing out of bed. With my right knee throbbing and my mind seething with mutinous plans to abandon the walk, I eventually got going, but later that morning, fell again - this time into glutinous, black mud. I was furious with my own clumsiness, but was forced to change my shorts and go back to the river for a laundry session, before walking on again.

That afternoon, I found myself wandering through what looked like perfect elephant habitat. Big trees were widely spaced and there was ample fodder between them for any self respecting pachyderm. From the broken branches, ripped vegetation and cannon balls of dung, it had to be one of the elephant corridors that Flip had mentioned, so I made camp beneath a big tree. The moon had been full the previous night, so even if the ellies arrived after dark, I would still be able to see them.

It was a pleasant evening and as daylight melted away, I stared into my fire and wondered whether I was going to be lucky. With stars glittering above my head, I went to bed, but despite wanting to stay awake in case of visitors, fell asleep almost immediately.

Shortly after eleven, I was woken by the crack of a branch breaking nearby. Without moving a muscle, I listened hard and the first sound was soon followed by others. I peered into the night, but in spite of the huge moon overhead, couldn't see any elephants. I could hear them though and thrilled to the sounds of foliage being ripped and chewed. Strangely, there did not seem to be the usual rumbling communication between the animals and I wondered at that. When elephants are together, they continually 'talk' to each other, sometimes with infrasonic sound, but more often with the gentle rumbling noises that for centuries were regarded as tummy rumbles. In fact, they come from nodules in the throat and the sounds are used by individuals to pin point their own location and assure their companions that all is well.

There was not a breath of wind, so it was not my presence that was keeping my visitors quiet. Something else was bothering them, but they continued feeding all around me.

I suppose it was inevitable that one elephant should decide to investigate my tree. I remained where I was, but slowly levered myself into a sitting position with my back against the trunk and smiled to myself as the huge shadow approached. In the moonlight, I could see that he was a young bull with small but thick tusks. Suddenly realising that there was something under the tree, he stopped ten metres away and I sat perfectly still, waiting to see what his reaction would be.

For long minutes - or so it seemed - that massive animal peered into the shadows, while I gazed back at him. His trunk came up to test the wind, then he cocked his head first to one side and then the other. There was nothing I could do but pray he didn't get a sudden fright and run over me in his panic, because he looked awfully large from where I sat.

At one stage that bull literally crouched down, almost falling to his knees in his efforts to see through the darkness and then suddenly, he realised what I was. There was a definite transition from puzzled pachyderm to responsible elephant. Raising himself to his full height, he took one last look at my shadowy shape, then moved purposefully into the darkness. There he must have told his companions of the man-thing, sitting beneath the tree and his tale caused instant consternation.

Moments after the bull disappeared, a family of cows with babies at heel came running past me, panic evident in their bodies. I could hear other animals crashing through trees and within two minutes of my silent confrontation with the bull, the entire area was eerily quiet. The elephants had gone and as I lay down again, I wondered what those great animals had suffered at the hands of mankind to make them so fearful of a wanderer in their midst.

Elephants are normally trusting, gentle animals and filled with natural curiosity. That this particular group had been persecuted in the past seemed obvious and not for the first time, I felt angry and upset with my own species.

It took me a long time to get back to sleep.

*　　*　　*

I was moving through rough countryside and on the advice of locals, moved away from the river and took the main road for a while. I didn't see any Chinese and local workers were as friendly as ever, but there were more of them and I soon tired of answering the same questions time and time again. After an hour or two of easy walking, I returned to the more difficult terrain of the river area.

One morning, I was pushing through very thick stuff and having my usual worries about water. Blood streamed from my arms and legs, I had lost any semblance of a path and passable gaps in the vegetation were few and far between. I wasn't far from the Zambezi, but to reach it would mean forcing my way up steep, heavily wooded banks. I wasn't sure I could take that.

As the sun grew hotter, my spirits fell deeper into my soul. I struggled to force my feet forward and hardly noticed when my face or arms were whipped by clinging vegetation. The water in my containers was going down at an alarming rate and I was not happy. With sweat streaming into my eyes, I was barely stumbling my way forward when I came across an inland pool and felt an immediate lightening of my spirit.

The pool was obviously used by cattle, elephant and whatever other wild and not so wild life there was in the area. The water was covered with a thick layer of scum, but I had purifying tablets in my pack and didn't care how it tasted. With a sigh of relief, I filled my containers and sat on the ground while the tablets took effect. I even contemplated a drink straight from the pond, but my stomach had been playing up and for once in my life, I decided not to tempt fate.

Once I had stored the precious water, I moved on, my eyes searching for a suitable camping spot. Two hundred metres beyond the pond, I saw a flash of green to my left and turning towards it, found myself on a lawn leading up to small, thatched buildings. I was at Chivumbo Lodge and with a feeling of relief, emptied my newly-filled water bottles on to the grass.

Chivumbo apparently meant 'thick bush' in Lozi and somehow it seemed apt indeed.

There were three people at the Lodge - David who managed the place, his wife Elizabeth and a general hand called Eric. They greeted me with wary enthusiasm and when I explained what I was doing, David showed me where I could have a hot shower, Elizabeth took my filthy clothing away to be washed and arrangements were made to make up a bed in the open air lounge. My protest that I could sleep on the decking was immediately overruled by David, who told me that 'it would not look good' for a guest to lie on the floor. As I was not paying for my accommodation, I wasn't sure that I could be classed as 'guest,' but David was insistent, so I didn't put up much of a fight.

It was Saturday and my three new friends were going off for the weekend, leaving me to the ministrations of a night watchman called Samuel who spoke only Portuguese and Lozi. I didn't care. I had no water worries, a comfortable place to sleep and even a kitchen in which to prepare my health gruel that evening.

It all seemed fairly typical of the topsy-turvy way my walk went from bad times to good times with nothing in between.

That morning, a stray branch had ripped the pocket of my bush jacket so that it gaped obscenely at my hip. I took the opportunity to cut it way and do some makeshift repairs with my sewing kit, but the end result still looked awful. There was nobody around to see it though, so I wasn't too worried. The lodge was perched on the bank of the Zambezi, so that evening I ceremonially cast a broken corncob pipe into the river and thanked it for all the pleasure it had given me. It turned out to be a mistake, as the very next day I was preparing an almost new cherrywood for my evening smoke when the stem broke in my hands, leaving me with just one pipe. I would need to be careful with that as my morning and evening interludes without something to puff on would lose much of their enjoyment.

Two days after Chivumbo, I walked into Kabuli Lodge, another pleasant establishment on the river and another place where I received an enthusiastic welcome. I enjoyed an afternoon, reading a cricket book in the lounge and what a pleasure that was, marred only slightly by a South African family who stared at me strangely, no doubt nonplussed to see a thin, scruffy-looking white man, lounging in such luxury.

The manager, Kenister had been disabled by polio as a boy, but hobbled around the place on an ornately carved stick and was happy for me to occupy a camping site for the night. It was bitterly cold and as I prepared for bed, Kenister told me that he had spoken to his boss on the telephone and he - the boss - had told him to allow me free use of a luxury chalet.

"He feels that after all you must have been through, you deserve some comfort."

I was tempted, but darkness had set in, my bed was prepared and kit that was lying around me in happy confusion would need to be gathered up and repacked. Reluctantly, I thanked Kenister for the offer and asked him to pass my gratitude on. I would stay where I was and be gone at first light the following day.

It turned out to be a bad mistake, firstly because I was surrounded by the fires of other campers and the smells of their cooking brought saliva to my mouth and heavy rumblings from my stomach. Secondly, the night was so cold that I had to break open my 'emergency blanket,' a wide sheet of silver foil that made a hideous amount of noise as I unfolded it. I didn't want to disturb my gently snoring neighbours, but for the rest of the night, every movement was accompanied with a crackling sound that must have been audible for kilometres around.

I moved on as planned, but the river banks were becoming more heavily forested and progress was slow. The nights were getting colder too and restful sleep was difficult. The only good thing about the drop in temperature was that mosquitoes didn't like it either.

*   *   *

I had no idea where I was. I had been walking for four hours, but had moved away from the river and suddenly, the countryside around me had changed drastically for the worse. Trees grew thickly together and I was forced to push my way through them. Thorns tore at my exposed skin, forcing me to stop repeatedly and free myself from their painful embrace. I probably covered three or four kilometres to make forward progress of one and it was frustrating as well as wearying. I was not enjoying myself.

Coming across a wide, open corridor between forested banks, I almost broke into a run, such was my joy at the relief it offered. Seconds later, I was up to my knees in cold, muddy water. Tiny insects rose in clouds with every step and I swatted at them in futile frustration. The swampy corridor was about sixty metres wide and travelled from north to south. I was moving east, so although I could have retraced my steps and found a way around it, I plodded glumly through the ooze, boots filling up and my clothing becoming ever dirtier and more saturated.

I reached the other side eventually, but as I was climbing a bank, I tripped over loose sticks and fell. As happened so often, the weight of my pack drove me forcefully downward and I felt breath coming out of me in a painful whoosh. I landed awkwardly and it took me a while to free myself from the pack and lever myself upright once more. When I regained my feet, I found blood on my hands and such were my assorted aches and pains that it took me a while to discover that a loose stick had carved a chunk out of my calf. It only started hurting when I found the wound, but then it made up for its previous reticence by hurting a great deal.

I had had enough. Sitting down on my pack, I used a filthy handkerchief to stem the flow of blood and wondered what to do. The countryside around me was unappetising to say the least and I wasn't sure where I was. The sun gave me a vague idea of direction, but in late morning, it could well be misleading. I had a compass, but in my despair, I squinted at the sky and wondered whether to use my satellite phone and call for help. After all, I could not be far from Sesheke, and the road from Senanga was a few kilometres away, so Andy's men should find me without much trouble.

I think it was only the prospect of getting my weary body to the main road that put me off. What I needed was not rescue, but a chance to bandage my leg properly and clean myself up. I was wet through, covered in dirty blood and very sorry for myself.

I am not sure how long I sat there, but had anyone offered me a lift out at that stage, I would have jumped at the opportunity. Fortunately, there was nobody available to make the offer and as I sat there, a faint, thumping sound intruded on my self-pity. Raising my head, I listened hard.

It sounded like an engine and seemed to be coming from the north, where the Zambezi flowed. Immediately, I felt better. Engines meant people and even though I was feeling decidedly anti social, people meant a chance to dry myself off, put a clean dressing on my leg and perhaps rest up for an hour or two. Using my walking pole as a crutch again, I hobbled in the direction of the sound.

Twenty minutes later, the bush opened up ahead of me, the thumping noise became recognisable as that of a generator or water pump and I staggered into a park-like area of huge trees and well tended green grass. A small swimming pool twinkled in the sunshine and a thatched building could be seen ahead. I soon found myself surrounded by concerned people.

This was Mutemwa Safari Camp and when I asked a small man who appeared to be in charge whether I could wash myself and rest for an hour or two, he told me that he would have to fetch 'the Madam.'

So I sat on my pack and waited for the 'Madam' to arrive. She turned out to be a petite and pretty woman with a smile that must have conquered many a male heart. Behind her were three younger versions and all four of them glanced a little warily at the unexpected and unprepossessing visitor.

Thus I came to meet Penny Johnson and her daughters, Shan, Kayla and Tammy. If it is possible for an old man to fall in love with four ladies simultaneously, I did and although I didn't realise it as I shook Penny's hand and introduced myself, I was about to enjoy three days of bliss that would have been unimaginable two hours previously.

CHAPTER SIX

(Comfort, Royalty and Rudeness)

What a joy it was to greet the dawn on a comfortable veranda with a warm blanket around me, rather than sitting uncomfortably beside my fire. I watched the rising sun turn watery mist a gentle pink colour and sighed at the beauty of the moment. I even had a pot of coffee brought to my tent. This was a far cry from the discomforts of life on the road.

Having listened to my story, Penny Johnson had ordered a tent to be made up for me. Not a little camping tent, but one of the luxury jobs I remembered from my son Graeme's safari camps. Water was heated for a shower and I was given tea and a plate of biscuits to keep me going till lunch time. Not chico biscuits either. There were custard creams, ginger nuts, shortbread and even some lemon creams. I struggled not to wolf them all down, but made a considerable dent in the supply. When I apologised to Penny for my greed, she laughed.

"You look as though you need it," She told me and I had to agree. One drawback to my tent was that it contained a large mirror and looking at my skeletal frame was not a pleasant experience. When I took my shirt off, ribs jutted from my skin and I didn't have a bottom any more. I had to make conscious efforts not to glance at that mirror in passing.

After lunch with the four ladies, Penny and I chatted for a while and when I innocently asked how far it was to Katima Mlilo where I might be able to buy pipe tobacco, she told me that her husband, Gavin was there and would get it for me. A phone call followed and Gavin duly returned with the tobacco and two tins of coffee - another commodity I was short on. Nor was I allowed to pay for it.

"Consider it our contribution to your adventure," I was told and there was no adequate way of expressing my gratitude.

I had heard of Gavin Johnson. A former South African rugby international, he had been part of the team that won the World Cup in 1995. A big, handsome man, he brushed aside my curiosity about his rugby career. He had put rugby behind him and was now committed to the people of Zambia and their problems.

The Johnsons were quietly devout Pentecostals and before every meal would gather in a circle, hold hands and pray for whatever they felt like at the time. It was a simple little ceremony and when Gavin thanked God for bringing me into their camp, I could feel emotion welling up in my throat. For the first time in weeks, I felt part of a family and before I went to bed, three of the ladies gave me a hug and a kiss to see me through the night. Little Tammy was too shy and possibly worried by my gaunt appearance, but the following morning, she greeted me with a huge smile and a hug that was very special. It seemed that I had 'arrived' in one little girl's affections and I felt ten feet tall.

Gavin went to Livingstone that second day and was forced through government bureaucracy to stay overnight, so I had the girls to myself and enjoyed a lovely day. Penny and I resumed our chatting, I wolfed my way through three good meals and spent the day reading and taking photographs. The food was delicious and the ambience of the camp was soothing. Mutemwa means 'big trees' and described the place to a tee. It was a magical spot and the Johnsons had been running it for sixteen years.

"Gavin grew up on a farm," Penny told me. "When injuries forced him out of rugby, he wanted to live in the bush. We heard about this place, came to see and immediately fell in love with it. In those days, it was a basic camp site, but we have built it up and I don't think it is too bad now."

"It is magical," I told her and I meant it.

A former teacher, Penny taught the girls herself and mornings were reserved for school. After lunch, I chatted with Shan and Kayla, the former picking my brains because she wanted to be a writer. I have never approved of home education, feeling that children need the company of their peers, but the Johnson girls were among the most well-balanced young people I have met. That was a credit, not only to their mother, but also to the loving atmosphere of the Johnson family unit.

My leg was causing me problems and Gavin's overnight absence gave me an excuse to stay another day, a few hours of which I spent exploring the area to see where I needed to go on leaving Mutemwa. The bush along the river was thick, so I decided to hit the main road and get a few easy kilometres under my belt. When I told Gavin, he volunteered to drive me to the road, as the track leading out of camp went through a wide expanse of water.

"We don't want you getting your feet wet," He grinned.

That evening, there were other people in camp and Gavin told me that he would be temporarily transferring operations to a fishing camp above Lukulu the following weekend.

"The money we make over a few weeks fishing keeps us going for the rest of the year," He said and I marvelled at man's enjoyment of what to me seems the most boring sport in the world. Having been part of the food chain myself, I always feel sorry for the fish.

We had an enjoyable supper and I was presented with a farewell gift from the girls. When I opened it, I found a woollen 'beanie' to keep my head warm during the freezing nights, a poem written by Shan and a vegetable-ivory key ring that I attached to my pack as a good luck charm.

"There was much discussion as to what wool should be used to give you maximum protection," Penny smiled, but I was too choked up to answer. I kissed them all and promised to wear the beanie whenever it was needed. As we were still in July, it was inevitably used a great deal over succeeding weeks and whenever I put it on, I remembered magical Mutemwa and smiled. It had been the most marvellous interlude and one I would never forget.

Friday the 13th was probably not the most auspicious day to restart my trek, but I needed to be moving on. After breakfast and a prayer for my safety, Gavin picked up my pack and slung it on to his back. Former Springbok or not, his legs buckled under the weight and he looked quizzically at me.

"That is heavy." He said simply and I could only agree, but after more kisses, hugs and handshakes, I was on the road again, the pack tugging at my shoulders but my heart singing. I felt privileged to have met the Johnsons and it had been wonderful to be part of their family, even for a short while.

Yet, it might never have been. The engine I had heard that led me to the camp was a water pump that was run for a couple of hours each day. When I spoke about it to Penny, she frowned.

"God is definitely looking after you," She said seriously. "We normally run the pump at four in the afternoon, so quite why it was on in the morning, I don't know. I am glad it was though."

So was I and even now, I shake my head in perplexity when I think about it. I have often been asked whether I feel God about me in the bush and there can be no question that there is often something guiding me along. There have been many occasions when I have survived only through what seemed divine intervention. The beauty and regal grandeur of the African bush also seems to indicate the presence of a Creator with wonderful aesthetic tastes and I am always overjoyed to accept His (Her's perhaps?) assistance, when I am in trouble.

Perhaps my meeting with the Johnson family was divinely organised, but I am profoundly grateful to whoever switched that generator on when they did.

*   *   *

Suddenly I was in a hurry. Mutemwa was fifty kilometres from Sesheke, but my ninety-day visa was running out and could only be renewed in the larger centre. I stuck to the road for two days, making good time and sharing my story with curious road workers.

At one stage, I was enjoying my morning pipe under a roadside tree when a familiar vehicle hove into view, towing a boat. Inside was the Johnson clan on their way to Katima Mlilo and we enjoyed an enthusiastic reunion.

"You have gone much further than we thought you could," Penny told me. "We have been looking out for you over the past eight or nine kays."

Gavin added that there was a path to the river less than a kilometre ahead and it would take me almost all the way to Sesheke, so after more hugs, they resumed their journey and I made my way back to the Mighty Zambezi.

The path was wide and the countryside was open, so I strode along, trying to ignore the pain in my shoulders. I was looking for the home of David and Jean Moir who had been recommended by the Johnsons as 'lovely people and very interesting.'

They were indeed. David was a retired bank official and they lived in a palatial riverside house with wide lawns rolling into the water. I enjoyed an afternoon discussing the Lozi people with David, who was an enthusiast on the subject and extremely knowledgeable about tribal history. We talked into the evening and a couple of whiskies before dinner made it all the more interesting. Like so many other River Folk, they made me welcome and I was sorry when the time came to move on. I had a date with immigration officials in Sesheke that could not be missed.

Sesheke itself is one of the oldest towns in Zambia and has a colourful history. David Livingstone wrote about the place and in those days, it would have been an important staging post for Zambezi explorers. Andy had sent me the phone number of a local entrepreneur, Maurice Mooli, who had offered to help with officialdom and once in the town, I wasted no time in contacting him. Maurice was a dapper little businessman and he booked me into a township lodge known as The Hometown House before we headed back to the border post.

"The Chief Immigration Officer is a friend of mine," Maurice assured me. "We won't have any trouble getting what you need."

But as so often happens with officialdom in Africa, it was not to prove as easy as that. The officer in charge was a big man called Simunje Minengo. Impeccably dressed, he peered at my tattered attire with visible scorn and seemed reluctant to assist.

"I can renew your permit for ninety days," He told me. "It will cost you four million kwacha."

That came to four hundred pounds sterling and I couldn't afford that. I produced Minister Lubinda's letter and pointed out the sentence wherein he asked all Zambians to give me whatever help I needed.

"I have the Honourable Minister's telephone number," I told Simunje wearily. "Would you like to ring him and tell him my Zambezi Trek is over and that is entirely due to the Immigration Department."

His manner softened and having read through the letter, he phoned Head Office in Lusaka. Maurice and I sat in uncomfortable wooden chairs and listened to one half of the conversation. Two hours later, we were still waiting for a decision to be made, but at last the big man took another call, then turned to me with a smile.

"The Deputy Director has agreed to bend the rules in your case," He told me. "I can issue you with the permit we usually give to truck drivers. It will allow you to travel in and out of Zambia for six months, but will cost two million kwacha."

I hesitated before replying. Would Cowbell fork out that much? I didn't know and reluctantly took leave of the immigration chief with the promise that I would contact my sponsors and let him know the following morning.

Once again, Andy Taylor and Cowbell came up trumps. Three million kwacha was promptly transferred to me via the post office at Sesheke and when I collected the cash, the lady behind the counter, glanced at the paperwork, then looked hard at me.

"You look so much younger than your actual age," She told me and I could have hugged the lass. At long last, someone had said something complimentary about my appearance.

With the cash in my hand, Maurice and I made our way back to the border post and I left there a few hours later, the proud possessor of a red booklet, allowing me to wander around Zambia for the next six months. To celebrate, I took Maurice to a restaurant, where we ate roast chicken with rice and washed it down with warm beer. Later I explored the market and enjoyed being the centre of attention. At one stage, I was hailed by a white lady, who jumped from her Land rover and asked me if I was me. I allowed that I was and she introduced herself as Rosemary Stapleton.

"I am David Moir's sister and have heard all about you," She said. "I am so pleased to have met you now."

While we chatted, we were joined by her husband Mike, but he was somewhat negative about my chances of getting much further.

"There are a lot of flood plains to cross before you get to Livingstone," I felt my spirits sink. "They won't be passable before September."

As we were only half way through July, that was bad news, but it had been nice of them to stop and I tried to banish my worries. I would cross bridges as and when I came to them and nothing could be as difficult as crossing the Luena Plain. I knew I could get through anything after that, but the prospect of wading through more leech-infested waters did nothing for my peace of mind.

When I set out from Sesheke the next morning, I was comfortably replete with morning coffee and a handful of biscuits. I had slept well, but for some inexplicable reason, I went in the wrong direction. Instead of going east, I walked back toward the Immigration Post. I have no idea why I did that, but the end result was to get myself hopelessly lost, endure two more falls in rough countryside and - horror of horrors - lose my last pipe. It must have dropped out of my pocket when I fell and there was no way I could go back and find it.

It was late morning when I limped disconsolately back to the Hometown House, where I booked in for another night. My hostess made no comment on my mud-spattered appearance, nor the fact that I had so unexpectedly returned, but it caused hilarity among the older men I chatted with later in the day.

I consoled myself with the thought that 'There in no hurry in Africa' but it didn't really help.

*   *   *

Since leaving Senanga, I had eaten relatively well. Monde Mututwa started it by feeding me on fish, potatoes and salad, but there had been steak and boerewors with Andy and Talitha, delicious bush meals with Flip Nel and Hilda Dunne and days of pampering at Mutemwa. One particular lunch of pork chops, mashed potatoes and peas, swimming in delicious gravy lived on in my mind for days and a chicken soup that Jean Moir produced was also memorable. I had even dined well on successive meals of roast chicken and rice in Sesheke, yet still the weight was falling off me.

As I wandered down the side of the Zambezi, I could feel myself weakening and adding to my troubles was a big toe, gashed on a piece of wood and cracked heels that were proving ever more difficult to walk on. Dizzy spells were commonplace and the early morning chill made my blood ache. I was a mess, but I set my sights firmly on the little town of Mwandi and pushed on.

I didn't have any alternative. Mwandi was the home of Chief iNyambo Yeta, senior chief of the Lozi and a man I had been advised to see. Flip had mentioned him as an authority in the Peace Parks Foundation and he had recently been elected to the board of that organisation.

"He is the guiding light behind our trans frontier park," Flip told me. "He has big ideas for wild life in this country and you'll like him."

David Moir described the chief as 'a fascinating man,' although he warned that I would have to be vetted by the chief's ndunas before I would be allowed in.

"That is an interesting experience," he assured, "but you won't have any difficulty. Just be patient and smile."

So I was looking forward to meeting the chief, but Mwandi was over a hundred kilometres from Sesheke, so I had a long way to go.

The countryside was open at first and teeming with cattle, many of which had cowbells dangling from their necks. I spent more fruitless hours, trying to photograph them but the *mombies* weren't keen and the pictures I did get were hardly suitable for a book cover. One night, I slept beneath a tree, surrounded by cattle and inevitably one with a bell kept tossing its head for much of the night, so I didn't get much sleep.

One of the joys of walking along an African river is that with the dawn, mist collects in hollows around the countryside and as the sun rises, it turns orange then pink before disappearing in the blink of an eye. It made for a spectacular start to my days and my only regret was that the morning air was so cold.

Despite my injuries, general weakness and lack of sleep, the kilometres fell away and I began to feel quite excited about meeting the chief. I had met three of them already, but iNyambo sounded like a colourful character and I was interested in picking his brain, not only about the Peace Parks, but also on the Barotseland issue.

In one village, I exchanged greetings with a number of people and a dignified looking elder gestured to me to approach.

"You look weary My Friend," He introduced himself as Reuben Mwananyambo. "Come, sit and have breakfast with me. You cannot be in a hurry here."

He was right of course and I spent hours with Reuben and his wife Beatrice - a pretty girl, who wore designer jeans beneath her *chitenge*. No I was not peeping! She happened to loosen the outer garment to take something from a pocket of her jeans. We ate *nshima* and fish, with vegetables for breakfast and I wolfed it down, even though I am known for my dislike of culinary greenery. *Nshima* and fish was on the menu again for a late lunch and Reuben told me he had eaten nothing different for as long as he could remember.

He appeared to be a proficient fisherman, did Reuben Mwananyambo and I watched as the morning catch was freed from the nets and placed in separate piles for marketing. Some of the smaller fish were discarded, but Reuben assured me that they would be used as food for the family.

He seemed as fascinated by my life as I was with his and questioned me closely about my trip and the reasons for it. I had no answer to the 'why' and merely shrugged the question away with a smile. At one stage, Mine Host produced a cell phone and asked whether he could take my photograph. It was my turn to ask why and he looked vaguely embarrassed.

"Tomorrow I will take it in to Sesheke and have the photograph blown up to poster size," He smiled. "Then I will be able to show it to my grandchildren as proof that David Lemon visited my house. You will be famous My Friend."

I doubted that, but the explanation was so sincere that it touched my heart and I smiled dutifully for Reuben and his camera. I wonder if he ever did get it printed.

The countryside kept changing as I wandered down the river. One moment, I would be on my hands and knees, struggling to push through tangled undergrowth, the next I would be wandering through wide-spaced forest, almost like English parkland. I passed a number of riverside lodges, but saw no sign of tourists. A big man called Watson was in charge of building a particularly spectacular lodge for a well known Zambian politician.

"It will cost him lots of money," Watson told me over tea and biscuits. "There will be twelve chalets, so how he can afford that, I do not know. I don't think the people he represents will enjoy the way he is spending the money, even if it has been earned legitimately."

Another grand edifice was occupied by a former officer in the police Drug Squad and Watson shook his head in bemusement.

"These people take money from all sides," He said. "Then they are forced to build their mansions in remote places, so nobody can see how rich they are."

I don't want to cast aspersions on politicians or policemen, but it seems that human venality is the same everywhere.

On another morning, I was directed by villagers to a path that would lead me to Mwandi. Four hours later, I was struggling along and feeling desperately tired, when a farmer called Lawrence pulled up in a Scotch cart. When I told him where I was going, he shook his head in amusement.

"Either those people were trying to get you lost or they were too stupid to understand what you were asking," He said of the villagers. "You are moving further from the river and your best way is to put your pack in my cart and come with me to Mahondo. From there, you can take the road to Mwandi.

Thus it was that I walked twelve kilometres, chatting with Lawrence, my shoulders free and the pack bouncing in the cart ahead of us. It was relaxing and most enjoyable, although Mahondo itself was on the main Livingstone road and a long way from the river.

The name means 'late in the evening' and it was when we arrived. Bidding farewell to my rescuer, I started walking disconsolately eastward, but was hailed from a roadside village.

Another Lawrence, this one with an unpronounceable surname was sitting by a fire, drinking traditional beer. He invited me to stay overnight and share his food and his drink. I took a tentative sip of the latter and then decided that as Lawrence was a nice man, I would join him in a tipple, but it would be from my emergency hip flask. He informed me that I was his first visitor in ten years, so that had to be worth celebrating.

Lawrence had eight children and most of them were daughters. They stared at me, but their curiosity was friendly and after a minute or two, three of the girls broke away and ran laughing into the bush.

"They are building a new toilet block at the school," Lawrence told me. "The girls have gone to collect wood to be used in the construction."

When I watched them marching off to school the following morning, each with a hefty tree on one shoulder, I couldn't help wondering how English children would react to an assignment like that. The thought made me smile.

But I was ten kilometres from Mwandi and wanted to reach it in a day, so I bade Lawrence an early farewell and hit the road. I didn't like walking along main thoroughfares, but I had little choice, so strode along, trying to ignore the curious stares of fellow travellers. Motorists stopped to ask whether I wanted a lift, but the day was warm and clear, so I strode out and made good time. I would find myself a room when I reached Mwandi and see the ndunas in the morning.

I wasn't sure what I would do if the Great Man wasn't in residence, but would worry about that if it happened.

*   *   *

As a former policeman, I am familiar with courtrooms, but I had to come to Mwandi in Western Zambia to discover how it felt to be sitting in the dock. Despite my age and experience, I felt decidedly nervous as I faced my inquisitors.

Everyone who wants to see iNyambo Yeta, Senior Chief of the Lozi, has first to be vetted by a panel of ndunas, each of them a leader in his own right. Unlike other supplicants, I was given a chair to sit on, but that was the only concession to my age, colour or dignity. I was facing a row of ndunas on chairs with padded seats, covered in royal purple, while behind me was the court interpreter, who whispered translations into my ear and took notes of the proceedings.

My chief interrogator was a big man, younger than his colleagues and he laid into me about my ideas on wild life.

"What will you do when you are face to face with a lion?" He asked, but that was easy.

"Stand still and wait for the lion to move off."

I must have been in that courtroom for half an hour and all the ndunas had something to ask, but at last I was told to wait outside for their decision. Back in the sunshine, I felt wrung out and fretful, so don't know how I would react if I was being tried for some crime.

Ten minutes later, the young nduna reappeared with a paper in his hand. His manner had changed from the formality of the court and with a shy smile, he asked me to accompany him. We entered a lavish garden around the Royal Palace, where he gave me a brief lecture on princely etiquette.

"Bow when I do and when the chief tells us something, we must both clap gently." He demonstrated with a soft double clap of his palms, but when iNyambo Yeta arrived, I forgot about my lesson.

Senior Chief iNyambo Yeta was an ascetic looking man, wearing spectacles like mine and colourfully dressed in a tracksuit and beanie, the ensemble topped off with a pair of yellow plastic gloves. The bowing and clapping from my companion increased in volume, but I was too busy studying the chief to take notice. I was in the presence of Zambian royalty and determined to take in every detail.

Chief iNyambo was the second son of a former Litunga, Ilute Yeta IV and David Moir had told me that the chief had been disappointed not to be made Litunga when the last incumbent died. Nevertheless, he had been Vice President to Kenneth Kaunda and held the position of Minister for Home Affairs as well. We discussed his plans for the Trans Frontier Park and his enthusiasm was palpable.

"The Kavango Zambezi Park will span the borders of five countries and share the resources of the Okavango and Zambezi River basins," He had obviously made the speech before. "It will bring hope and prosperity to my Sesheke chiefdom and the Barotse people, who at present occupy Zambia's poorest and least developed area."

When I asked him how it had come about, he went on.

"On the 18th August 2011 at a summit of the Southern African Development Community in Luanda, the presidents of Angola, Botswana, Namibia, Zambia and Zimbabwe signed a treaty that established the Kavango Zambezi Transfrontier Conservation Area. This will cover an area fifteen times larger than Tanzania's Serengeti ecosystem and similar in size to Sweden. Yes it is an ambitious concept, but this cross-border sanctuary will be magnificent. It will amalgamate thirty-six national parks, game reserves, forest reserves, community conservancies and game-management areas into a single ecological unit. It will restore ancient migration patterns to a quarter of a million elephants and sustainably manage the ecosystem for the socio-economic well being of the local people.

'When I was young," iNyambo Yeta went on. "My grandfather used to talk to me about the old Barotseland, a place flowing with milk and honey where wildlife was plentiful and the forests were thick. Hunger was never a factor in the lives of people. Today there is a complete disconnect between people and their natural resources. There is no wildlife, and they are surviving simply on a hand-to-mouth basis. This has to change and my people must strike a balance between what they take from the environment and what they put into it.

'Like Martin Luther King, I have a dream that we can fight poverty and we can defeat it. We must get the local community involved in conservation of resources. I want to bring back the animals that were once here, but this time we are going to look after them better than we did before."

I pointed out that for the proposed conservation area to be a success, a huge education programme would need to be carried out among local people so that they looked upon wild life as a national asset rather than food on the hoof. He frowned thoughtfully.

"That is true and you will have noticed that in Zambia - even in the area of the proposed park - we still carry out professional hunting. I know that hunters are conservationists in their own right, but at the moment, we do not have the natural resources for this to continue."

I had been allotted twenty minutes for the meeting, but it was nearly two hours later that the chief brought it all to an end. Having given me his phone number and email address, he pointed to my companion.

"Nduna Lubinda will be in charge of the project, so if you have any questions, address them to him. Now I must go, but I wish you luck in your Zambezi venture and hope to hear from you fairly soon."

When I stood up to leave The Presence, iNyambo Yeta stretched out his arms and gave me a brief hug, much to the horror of Nduna Lubinda and twenty minutes later, I was back in Mwandi. Going over my meeting with the chief in my mind, I decided that if he can bring half his dreams to fruition, he will be doing a wonderful thing, not only for his people, but for Africa as a whole. Wild life is the heritage of us all, not only we Africans, but everyone in this increasingly heartless and ever more developed world.

Somehow, we have to protect it and keep it safe from the dangers posed by 'progress.' The world needs more visionaries like Senior Chief iNyambo Yeta and I reflected that I was honoured to have met the man and listened to his ideas.

Back in my room in the Home Sweet Home Lodge - it had electricity, but no running water - I wondered what I could do to help and determined that I would do something, even if it merely meant writing about Chief iNyambo Yeta and his dreams for 'my' elephants.

*   *   *

Soon after leaving Mwandi, I found myself facing a familiar and forbidding landscape. Around me a vast expanse of yellow grass stretched into distant horizons. There would be water beneath the grass and I felt nervousness curdle in my stomach at what might lie ahead of me.

But the plain had to be crossed so I pushed on and slowly relaxed as the ground underfoot remained dry. But relaxation is never a good thing when walking in Africa. It must have been mid morning and my mind had switched off when I realised that my boots were sinking into a glutinous ooze. Black and foul-smelling, it covered my socks and was half way up my calves before I realised what was happening.

Circling around muddy spots, I made tortuous progress across that grassy sea, but breathed a sigh of relief when I was hailed by a young man driving a 'twin-engined' scotch cart. He had a pair of oxen in the front and behind them were two donkeys, but he seemed a cheerful soul and I was happy to throw my pack into the cart and walk beside him.

His name was Hakim, which sounds very Muslim, but he told me he was a devout Christian and went to church whenever he could. We stopped in numerous villages, where logs were unloaded and it seemed that Hakim was an itinerant wood merchant.

"People pay me to collect their firewood," He told me. "I don't make much money, but I enjoy myself."

Which seemed as good a reason as any for doing it.

Hakim told me that I was on the edge of the Simalaha Plain and although there was a lot of water lying around, I should be able to get around the difficult places.

"Your only problem will be the Sifo River," He said. "I will find someone to ferry you across."

The Sifo was a broad tributary running into the Zambezi and when Hakim hailed a canoe and bade me farewell, I was only too pleased to sit back and be carried.

Across the river was a fishing village, where I was handed over to Kingston, who told me that he had two wives and five sons. Although I was beginning to feel like a relay baton being passed from one person to another, I followed Kingston on a four kilometre march in which he strode ahead, chattering about his cleverness in leaving his wives and family to work in Lusaka, while he enjoyed the life of a fisherman on Simalaha.

Nevertheless, Kingston was a pleasant soul and I was grateful for his guidance as there were few landmarks to show me where I was going. Another village loomed out of midday haze and the baton (Me) was passed on to a fisherman called Lackson and his pretty wife, Alice. Kingston harangued them at length and from what I could follow, he told them I was an important person and my safe passage was necessary for the future well being of all Zambians. They therefore had a duty to look after me and ensure that I went safely on my way the next morning.

Lackson looked unimpressed and went off to do something with his boat, while Alice provided a meal for Kingston and I. When the talkative one finally left us, Alice made scones in a pit oven and I watched with interest. Zambian scones are not as sweet as their equivalent in the West and more like unleavened rolls. They are very popular though and Alice sold hers in the village shop. Probably noticing the way my nose twitched at the baking smells and my eyes followed the scones as they were removed from the oven, she gave me three to eat and they were delicious. What they would taste like with butter and jam, I could only imagine, but the thought brought saliva flooding to my mouth. She gave me two to take with me the following day and I clapped my hands in gratitude.

I slept in the open and it was bitterly cold but I was on my way early, this time without an escort although Lackson had shown me the path to take. The grass underfoot was tangled and I stumbled repeatedly, but I made excellent progress. The sun was shining and the sky was blue, but there was an icy wind howling across that barren plain and I did not enjoy that.

Slowly, I worked my way eastward and it must have been late afternoon when I stumbled into a noisy little village where most of the male population appeared to be drunk. Finding a party of elders, I asked whether there was anywhere I could spend the night, but when one man asked how much I would pay for that doubtful privilege, I thanked them and walked on. As I was leaving, two men suggested that I accompany them to another village where people would be more accommodating. I was tired and the other village was two kilometres away, but I had little choice.

Through his son Rodwick, I was introduced to the eighty-seven year old headman of the village. He was also Rodwick and the family name was Ilema, so when I told them that I was Lemon, there was much hilarity among the villagers. I was given a hut for the night, with Rodwick Junior promising to escort me to his brother's house the following day.

"You will need a boat to get you across the Sifo River," He told me and I wondered how many more Sifo Rivers there were. It seemed as though I would be crossing a river I had already crossed, but didn't suppose it made much difference and enjoyed a good night for once. I was out of that freezing wind and although the hut was home to a variety of creepy-crawlies, it was warm and the floor was level, so I was reasonably comfortable.

The following morning I walked with Rodwick to the village of his brother Webby. There we enjoyed breakfast of tea and fritters, which was followed by the 'full Zambian' of fish and *nshima*.

Webby didn't seem keen to take me across the water, which I learned was not the Sifo, but an area of flooded plain. He asked for twenty pin to make his journey worthwhile and with the thought of those horrible leeches in mind, I was happy to part with the money. It turned out to be blatant extortion as the canoe journey covered less than a kilometre, but I suppose it was worth it because I kept my feet dry - well almost.

I was left on an inhospitable piece of plain and my companion pointed out conical rooftops on the horizon.

"That is where you must go," I was told. "That village is on the edge of the Zambezi."

It probably was, but I never reached it. The going across that bleak and awful plain was horrendously difficult. Much of it was burnt, but even where the grass was down to charred stumps, the earth underfoot was so soft that it was virtually impassable. In other places, I was forced to wade through swathes of scummy water and as the day wore on, I was becoming ever more fed up with my lot. The village did not appear to be getting closer and when different huts appeared to my left, I took a chance and went toward them. Webby had warned me not to walk across the plain itself, but with the new village much closer, it seemed worth the risk.

I was lucky and although I still had wading to do, managed to avoid most of the standing water and lurched my way into the village in early afternoon.

Situated a hundred metres from the Zambezi and separated from it by grassy lagoons and sandbanks, Simusisi was a birdwatcher's paradise. Herons, egrets, storks and a variety of other water birds teemed in the area below the village and even though I was tired, my eyes were wide as I took in the sights and listened to the avian clamour.

I was met by a young lady called Marjorie who brought a chair for me to sit on. This is one of those wonderful Zambian customs, wherein visitors are provided with the best chair to be had. If there was a seated headman present, he would remain where he was, but even village elders would give up their chairs and sit on inferior models to allow the visitor the best that was available.

Marjorie had obviously sent word of my arrival, as we were soon approached by a group of men, led by a dignified fellow who introduced himself as Horence Mufaladi, son of the headman. Horence barked at Marjorie to provide me with food and move my pack out of the sun. I could see her knees buckle as she hefted it onto thin shoulders and protested to Horence that not only did I not need food, but could carry my own luggage. He waved my protests aside, but said something else to Marjorie and a bowl of rice, rather than the usual fish and *nshima* was produced for me. It was to be eaten with milk and sugar, but I horrified my rapt audience by asking for salt instead. This was obviously unheard of and many quiet comments passed among watching villagers as I struggled to get the food down.

Horence insisted that I stay the night and I did not take much persuasion, but when he pointed out a small bell tent and suggested that I share it with him, I demurred.

"It will be too hot for me, Horence," I told him. "I usually sleep in the open and need the fresh air."

Pointing out a thatched shelter that was used as a washroom, I suggested that it made a perfect bedroom, but was told that I would 'die of cold' there. Eventually, a mattress was produced and laid beside the cooking fire. As it looked out over the river, I was happy with this and the provision of pillows and two thick blankets made it all the more luxurious. A younger man, called Goula had appointed himself - or perhaps been appointed by Horence - my mentor and he set up my bedding, found a comfortable chair and told everyone who would listen about this marvellous *mukuwa* who was walking even further than had David Livingstone.

One of the village matrons spent time rummaging in a hut that was obviously used as a storeroom and emerged, waving an old and tattered newspaper. Shyly, she showed it to me.

It was the Solwezi Daily Mail of 28th April and there was I on the front page, looking fatter and healthier than I did now. A hugely flattering article accompanied the picture and when he read it, Gaula insisted that we do an evening tour of the village, displaying the newspaper to all and sundry. It was embarrassing, but quite enjoyable, although folk at the far end of the village hid their faces and didn't want anything to do with me.

When we returned to the kitchen, I discovered why. The headman, James had returned and he told me there had been other visitors to the village that afternoon.

"They saw you walking across the plain," he chortled, "and told the villagers that a ghostly spirit was approaching. Some of our people are still very backward."

Everybody laughed and I felt strangely pleased with myself, but that was not to last.

It must have been about eleven that night and everyone was asleep when my battered system rebelled and my body threatened to erupt. I was woken by the most violent attack of wind I have ever experienced and then it was a sudden rush with my toilet roll into that dark and inhospitable plain. Few Lozi villages have proper toilets and I stumbled into that vast expanse of tangled grass, feeling that my life was about to end.

It didn't, but in a few violent seconds, I got rid of most of the food I had eaten over the previous few days and that first 'visit' was followed by three more at hourly intervals. It was a horrible night and when daylight arrived, I felt washed out and feverish. Gaula was the first awake and he took one look at my sweaty face and hurried to find James and Horence. The former decided that I must stay abed as I was obviously ill and I felt too weak to argue. I spent a few hours tucked up in my blankets, but as the temperature rose, levered myself on to the chair and made sure the toilet roll was close at hand.

Further trips to the plain followed at regular intervals and although it was easier to move when I could see where I was going, daylight added to my embarrassment as there were always villagers looking to see what I was doing. I had no choice however and it proved to be a long and uncomfortable day. Feeling that drastic measures were necessary, I broke into a course of antibiotics, prescribed by my lovely dentist, Sue Browse and hoped they would clear things up.

That evening, we gathered around the fire again and for a while my soul was soothed by the sound of singing. This came from a lass, married to another of James' sons and she sang to God and to the sky. Her voice was so sweet and true that it brought shivers to my spine and a deep ache to my heart.

That second night was not as difficult as the first, but my sleep was again interrupted and in the morning, although I was feeling better, it was felt by my hosts that I should stay for another day and even another one after that.

"I will escort you to Ngwezi myself," James decided. "I have business to attend to there, so we can go together."

Once again, I provided little argument and enjoyed another peaceful day of bird watching.

There were a number of black egrets performing below my chair and I couldn't help chuckling as the little fellows spread their wings over their heads and peered beneath then, looking for fish. I have always called them 'umbrella birds' and it was lovely to see them again. Huge flocks of storks flew westward every morning and returned in the evening, while throughout the day, a wide variety of bird life performed and cavorted for my benefit.

There were pelicans, crowned cranes, saddle-billed storks and skimmers everywhere. A variety of kingfishers thrilled me with their colours and there was even a pygmy kingfisher, a species I had not encountered before.

It was a lovely experience to sit there watching them and I repeatedly thanked the *Nkosi Pezulu,* not only for easing my stomach gripes, but also for turning me toward Simusisi, when I had been heading for a different village.

Perhaps Somebody up There really was guiding my footsteps.

*   *   *

Despite the trauma of a viciously upset stomach and no loo available for the necessary, Simusisi provided a refreshing interlude in my journey. Between them, Horence and Gaula laundered my clothing - even my hat - and the result was considerably better than anything I could have done.

My days were spent in gentle bird watching and during the evening, we sat around the fire while Gaula prepared food and our conversations were wide ranging and interesting. At one stage, James asked whether my 'First Born' had built me a house yet. I assured him that it was an unlikely eventuality and he explained that in tribal tradition, Lozi children were honour-bound to build for elderly parents and provide them with food well into their dotage. I pointed out that I wasn't really old yet - I didn't think so at any rate - but assured him that I would explain the principle to Brian when I saw him again.

At one stage, I mentioned my meeting with Chief iNyambo, but my hosts were unimpressed.

"He worries more about animals than he does about his people," Horence muttered scornfully. "His wife is a government minister and she tries to help us, but iNyambo is forever taking trips to other countries, while his people struggle."

A little to my surprise, they were great admirers of the current Litunga, who I had found to be popular among white Zambians but not so well loved by the black population.

"Ah, but that is a good man," James told me. "Under his guidance, the Lozi nation will never go wrong."

It seems that even in Africa, there are sharply divided loyalties when it comes to politicians.

One afternoon, Gaula told me his story. He had a wife and children in Livingstone, but finding it difficult to support his family, had come to do some fishing in Simusisi.

And was it going according to plan? He shook his head sadly.

"No; I have nets of my own, but no boat, so have to rely on others to take me out. Many of them don't want to work hard, so I am not making enough money and my wife keeps scolding me. She thinks I am having fun, but I am trying very hard."

The misunderstandings of matrimony were having their effect, even in this remotely idyllic spot.

Gaula also explained the various methods of fishing with nets.

"First and most common is '*malalika,*' which is the process of laying the nets in one place and checking them at daily intervals, but there is also '*lukuka,* which is when nets are allowed to drift with the river or are towed behind canoes to collect the fish. Sometimes the nets are set in a circle to surround a spot where there are known to be fish and this is called '*letua.*'

Then there are times when fish are chased into the nets and this is called '*kutumpula*.'

I didn't suppose the information would prove of much use to me, but promised to include it in any writing I might do after my journey.

"That way I will be remembered, whatever happens," Gaula said wistfully.

The one drawback to my comfortable bedroom was that James' chickens roosted ten metres away and like cockerels everywhere, they were early and exceedingly noisy risers. Wrung out and exhausted, I would stagger in from one of my enforced visits to the plain, fall wearily on my mattress and snuggle into those lovely warm blankets, only to be awoken shortly afterwards by raucously derisive crowing.

I woke up on my last morning at Simusisi to discover that one of my sandals was missing. It was something I could not afford to lose, but the village dogs prowled at nights and one of them must have picked up my footwear. In some despair, I wandered around, searching for it before being hailed by Hope, another of James' sons and husband to the lady with the wonderful voice. When I explained the problem, he laughed.

"I will find it for you," He promised and the sandal was returned with only minor teeth marks, while Hope wandered off, whistling cheerfully.

Shortly afterward, there was drama in the village. I heard a lot of shouting and barking of dogs. Hope rushed out of his hut, brandishing a spear and I could see a number of people running around on the plain.

"What is happening?" I asked Horence.

"They are chasing a fox," was his explanation, but I was bewildered. The only African fox is the cute little bat-eared variety and I didn't think they would be found on the swampy plain. Alternatives rushed through my mind, but none of them made sense until Hope marched back, a magnificent otter impaled on the spear, its head having been bashed in with a paddle.

I felt sick and it was nothing to do with my ravaged digestive system. Otters are ever rarer in Africa and like the proverbial hens' teeth in rural Zambia. This one had been in the wrong place at the wrong time and had paid with its life. I couldn't really blame Hope or the other villagers, because they were natural hunters, but this sort of wanton killing was what I envisaged as the biggest problem facing iNyambo Yeta and his Peace Park colleagues.

"What will you do with the carcass," I asked Horence and he shrugged. "We won't eat it ourselves," he told me, "but the dogs might eat it."

It seemed a terrible waste of one precious life and I turned away so that Horence couldn't see how I felt. It wasn't his fault. It was merely the culture of his people and it would take many decades to eradicate it. It was a sad end to my stay at Simusisi.

True to his promise, James escorted me to Ngwezi, where he seemed to be quite a personality in the area. I spent a fascinating half hour watching a boat builder working on a dugout canoe and he told me that prices for the craft ranged from three hundred to nine hundred pin. It seemed cheap for such sturdy vessels, but he explained that people bought boats as investments.

"They take them across to Namibia," He explained. "They exchange them for cattle. The beasts are brought back here, sold for a profit and then they buy more canoes.'

A little like a rural stock exchange I supposed.

Having said goodbye to James, the road to Mambovu was pointed out to me and as it went directly inland, I had two of my water containers filled. Walking out of the village, I stopped when my shoulders became suspiciously wet. A two-litre container had split across the top and the precious liquid was pouring into my pack. It was a bitter blow and I wondered if I would have enough to cope if water became scarce.

That night, I camped in *mopani* forest and dared to hope that I was finally away from those dreadful plains. This was the sort of countryside I love and I stared into my fire that evening, reflecting on the trip and what lay ahead.

For all the trying times, it had been a great experience and I had spent time with some truly special people. Ahead of me was Livingstone and the Victoria Falls, which I hadn't seen in fifty years, but before that I had to get through Mambovu and Kazangula. The former was the seat of Chief Sekute and although I wanted to see him, I had been repeatedly warned that the town was a hotbed of criminality - a sort of Crooks' Corner of the modern age.

I would worry about that when I got there, but the following day, while walking through a desolate piece of countryside, with no sign that humans had been there in decades, I was surprised to meet a taxi, heading the other way. It was a smart looking vehicle, but crept along what was no more than a footpath at less than five kilometres an hour. The passengers waved and I returned the gesture, but went on, shaking my head in wonderment. Where on earth were they going and why didn't they take an easier road?

Truly, there are strange things that can happen only in Africa. Which I suppose is why I love the place.

*   *   *

I don't know whether it was the tales of skulduggery making me paranoid, but I didn't like Mambovu. As befitted the site of a royal presence, it was larger than most settlements in the area, but there was an air of decay about the place that was disturbing. I wanted to see Chief Sekute, but when I asked a youth where I could find him, he laughed and pointed to the sun.

"At this time of day, he will be drunk," He told me cheerfully and his lack of respect for the chief was obvious. This seemed such a contrast to the fawning adulation - or so it seems to western eyes - meted out to most tribal chieftains in Zambia.

Nevertheless, the young man guided me to a large wooden house on stilts that he told me was the royal palace. I hesitated at the gate. The only person I could see inside the surrounding fence was an old crone, sweeping idly at the dust. Yellow sand billowed from her broom and she paid me no attention. Suddenly I decided that I needed to move on. It was irrational, but the ambience of Mambovu was not a pleasant one. I felt relieved when I wandered back toward the river.

Kazangula was the next stop and it wasn't a great deal better, but feeling the need for a bit of comfort - my internal problems were still grumbling, despite the antibiotics - I booked into a riverside lodge and wandered around the town for a while. This was where Zambia, Zimbabwe and Botswana met across the Zambezi and I had been looking forward to seeing the place, but it was a disappointment. Dry and dusty, the most notable feature of Kazangula was a queue of lorries waiting to get through border formalities. The queue stretched for kilometres inland and most of the drivers seemed content to make little homes underneath their vehicles. I chatted to a few of them and they chuckled when I asked if they were ever bored in such places.

"There is no hurry here," A Zimbabwean driver called Henry Ndhlovu told me. "These fellows" (the border officials) "must have their fun, so we wait."

I admired his fortitude, but decided that despite my lorry driver's permit, I could never be as patient as these drivers.

A few kilometres out of town, I was hailed by a well dressed chap, going the other way. He introduced himself as Isaac Musa and told me that he would love to stop and talk, but was on his way into Kazangula for a 'stakeholders' meeting.' Apparently the subject up for discussion was 'gender equality in the rural areas' and that made me smile inwardly.

Somehow I could not imagine that gaining much credence in rural Barotseland.

Isaac gave me detailed instructions as to how I would recognise his village when I came to it. I did too and paused to speak with a family man who occupied huts at the end of Musa village. As always, a chair was produced for me - on this occasion, a blue plastic job that looked terribly ornate in those surroundings and Josaphat Kalani yelled to his wife for food.

Moments later, he turned somewhat apologetically to me.

"I can only offer you *nshima*," He said sadly. "The fishing has been bad and we have no vegetables for relish."

Rummaging in my pack, I found a packet of vegetable soup that Mrs Kalani made into a more than passable relish. The shared meal tasted good and did no additional harm to my ravaged system. After we had eaten, Josaphat suggested that I make camp under a large tree near the village and offered me the use of his chair while I was in the area. So it was that I camped in splendour. No lolling around on logs or sitting on a backpack for this hedonistic wanderer. I sat grandly in my blue plastic chair and contemplated the countryside, feeling very pleased with the luxury. My camp area was even cleaned out and enthusiastically swept by Josaphat's children, who brought me enough firewood to last a week.

My only visitor that afternoon was a man called Chica, which apparently meant mortar and pestle. We chatted and later on, were joined by Josaphat. I sat in my chair like the Lord of Linoleum, while Josaphat who owned the ruddy thing, squatted contentedly at my feet. It didn't seem right, but I wasn't complaining.

That evening, we were joined by Isaac Musa, the dapper fellow I had met along the road that morning. He asked whether I would like a cup of tea and although I accepted eagerly, I wondered what it would be like. Rural Lozi seldom drank tea or coffee - in one village, I had to explain the use of a tea bag - but twenty minutes later, Isaac returned, a tray of tea things in his hand and an elderly woman following him with another plastic chair. This one was a bilious yellow.

Wonder of wonders, Isaac had even brought a few chico biscuits and we sat in that wild and remote spot, setting the world to rights over tea and biscuits.

I was less than thirty-five kilometres from Livingstone and going too fast. I was a week ahead of schedule, so my arrival in

Livingstone could prove a problem, but I was having difficulty in contacting Andy and found myself eaten up with frustration when I was supposed to be enjoying myself.

I had to slow down, but that was never easy. Hilda Dunne had invited me to stay with her in Livingstone, but she had been good to me already and I did not want to push my luck with any one person. So I loitered. I spent a day beside the Katombora Rapids, which were splendid, joined an early morning beer drink beside the first road I had seen in ages and walked for a while with a teenager called Nathan, who made my day by listening to my story and hitting me with the biggest conversational gem of my entire trip.

"Will you be going all that way on your own feet, Sir?" He asked with absolute sincerity and the mental image of walking along on somebody else's booted toes made me smile. Biting back the obvious retort, I assured him that I would be using my own feet and nobody else's.

One Sunday morning, I came upon a middle-aged couple, cooking beside the road, so stopped for a chat. He was Cosmos and she was Justina and in a pot at their feet, fritters bubbled and hissed in boiling oil. Cosmos invited me to taste one and it was delicious, so I tried to buy some for my breakfast, but this lovely couple gave me a packet of five fritters to take with me. I am ashamed to say that I ate them all within twenty minutes.

Later that morning, I was hailed from a village.

"Grandfather, Grandfather - where are you going?"

A young woman came running out and beamed from ear to ear when I tried to explain my venture. Her name was Bridget and I defy anyone of even my advanced age to refrain from loquacity when being questioned by an admiring and very pretty young woman. When I came to a halt in my explanation, she smiled and told me to stand still. Then she planted a big kiss on each of my cheeks and hugged me firmly to her bosom.

"You are a great man," She told me. "But I need you to take my photograph please."

I readily agreed and she ran back to the village, emerging moments later with two young boys.

"My sons," She explained and with the photograph taken, I went on my way, wondering anew at the kindliness and good humour of these Zambian people. Bridget would never see her photograph, but it is contained in the screensaver of my computer now and every so often, I am reminded of a very special Sunday morning by the picture of a smiling young woman and her two little boys.

*   *   *

After Katambora, I seemed to be in lodge country. From the Royal Chundu Lodge - presumably they had the backing of the local chief - onwards, I passed sign after sign announcing the presence of some riverside establishment. I gave them all a wide berth, although I did get lost one Sunday morning and ended up having delicious coffee and toast in a lodge whose young manager was more interested in tales of England than tales of my walk.

"My wife and I come from South Africa," I won't mention his name in case he hasn't moved yet, "but we have had enough of Africa and went to look at England last year. We enjoyed it so much that we will probably go there for good."

He was enthusiastic, so I refrained from pointing out that living in a place was vastly different from visiting as a tourist and nowhere in the United Kingdom was he likely to experience as nice a life as he had on the Zambezi.

The going was relatively easy along this stretch. There was always a footpath to follow and occasionally, I came across dusty roads running parallel to the Zambezi. The only problem with the paths was that all too often, they divided into two, giving me a horrible choice as to which fork to take. I would take the one that seemed to head for the river, but usually managed to select the wrong one, leaving me with a difficult bit of bush to plough through. Locals often indicated the 'road' to take and in response to my queries would assure me that 'it goes straight,' but I knew from bitter experience that they were merely trying to be helpful and give me the answer I wanted.

The nights were also frustrating. The opposite shore was Zimbabwe and obviously part of a game reserve. Every night, I heard the rumbling, squealing and happy flatulence of elephants, the manic howling of hyena and a host of other familiarly evocative sounds. It felt lovely to be back in proper Africa, but on my side of the river, the only sounds that disturbed the night came from barking dogs, sleepless cockerels and the occasional wild party.

One such party went on all night and when I walked through the village the following morning, was still in full swing. Drummers gave vent to their feelings, music blared from loudspeakers and village ladies danced with enthusiastic abandon. I approached a group of elders, sitting quietly over mugs of beer and was told that the celebration was being held in honour of a young woman who was ready for marriage. They were too inebriated to be clear, but I decided it was probably to celebrate a young girl's first menstrual cycle - often a source of ceremony in rural Africa.

Whatever the case, it was a lot of fun for all concerned and I allowed my face to be daubed with white powder that seemed to be a mixture of ash and talc, because it smelt extremely sweet. I wandered among the celebrants for a while and with their permission, took a few photographs, but when a tipsy young woman wanted payment for posing, I moved on.

I could only presume that it was proximity to the tourist fleshpots of Livingstone and the lodges that tempered the attitude of the people I walked among. They wanted money for the most minor of favours. On two occasions, I was approached by headmen, demanding payment for sleeping near their particular village and on the only occasion anyone offered to carry my pack, the young man concerned wondered what I would pay him. Like the headmen, he learned that I had no intention of parting with my money unless it was earned.

Another problem with this last leg before the Falls was that I was still going too fast. I was running out of food however, so the longer I remained on the road, the less chance I had of my supplies lasting. It was difficult to cope with, but eventually I decided that I must keep going and hope I could contact my sponsors and tell them I was going to be early. With luck, Andy would suggest somewhere for me to stay.

Despite the proximity to civilisation, this was one of those stretches in Zambia where phone reception was poor and I was reluctant to use the satellite phone, so I plodded on, hoping for the best. Lodges gave way to farmland and according to my GPS, I was but a day or two from Livingstone. Excitement and worry mingled in my chest and I found it difficult to sleep at night.

I was excited at the prospect of seeing my Bratlets and whenever I thought about it, my eyes filled with happy tears. I have never been much of a family man, but find being a grandfather easier than being a Dad, so really give it my all. The thought of seeing those beloved faces and giving them both a huge hug brought a definite spring to my step.

Early one morning, I spotted a phone mast on the horizon and managed to send off a text, explaining where I was and when I would arrive. Reception lasted but a minute or two, but it was enough for the message to be delivered and I walked on, feeling better. Despite the fact that the nights were still bone-achingly cold, the daytime sunshine was warm and invigorating, so apart from the pain in my shoulders and the fact that my body was still skeletal, I felt fit and capable of almost anything.

I was walking through commercial farmland, twenty kilometres out of Livingstone when I ran out of path again. The going had been easy till then, but it seemed I would have to take a turn away from the river and continue along the main Livingstone road - not something that appealed to me. I had passed a farmhouse twenty minutes previously, so made my way back to ask for directions.

A white man in shorts and sandals came out at my call. I told him that I had lost my way, but he did not seem impressed.

"You are on private land," He told me brusquely. "Go back to the main road and hitch a lift."

I felt distinctly nonplussed and not particularly pleased. For three months, I had met with courtesy and help from local people, yet here was this man not even bothering to ask where I was going. Trying not to show my disappointment at his attitude, I thanked him politely and made my way back to the path. As I reached the man's gate, my phone buzzed in my pocket and it was a message from Andy, telling me that a lady called Karen was looking out for me and had baked a strawberry cake in my honour.

Apparently she lived on a farm twenty kilometres from Livingstone and I wondered whether the said Karen lived in the house I had just left. In which case, it seemed obvious that the cake could be forgotten. There was no point in going back to ask the farmer if he knew a Karen in the area, so I walked on. Andy had given me a phone number for Karen, but I could not get a signal and I certainly wasn't going to ask the grumpy one for the use of his telephone.

The road was wide and dusty, but at a crossroads I saw people, obviously waiting for transport. One chap was chattering into a cell phone and when I asked if I could borrow it, he was only too pleased to hand it over.

"It has just been filled with talktime, Sir," He told me, "so you can speak for as long as you wish."

I assured him that I would not take much time, but couldn't help contrasting his helpful attitude with that of the farmer I had just left. Truly people make me cross at times.

'Karen' turned out to be Karien and she did indeed live in the area in which I found myself. She gave me directions to Waterberry Farm, told me how much she was looking forward to meeting me and ended by telling me that the farm was five kilometres from where I was.

"It is quite a long way to walk," She added cheerfully. "But for you, it will only be a stroll."

I forbore from pointing out that the day was hellishly hot and I already had twelve kays or so under my belt. With a sigh and effusive thanks, I handed the phone back to its owner, hoisted that horrible pack on to my shoulders and set off in the direction I had been told. My legs ached and I was still smarting at the reception I had received from the farmer, but all I could do was plod on. Five kays would take me an hour and a half, so I shut my mind to everything else and concentrated on walking.

I passed elephant sign along the road and some of it was fresh, but nary a jumbo did I see. They probably had more sense than me and were dozing contentedly in whatever shade they could find in that arid bit of countryside.

It was not a pleasant walk, but the thought of a bed for the night and a slice or three of strawberry cake kept me going.

CHAPTER SEVEN

(Trouble in the Gorges)

Livingstone was roughly halfway between source and sea on my Zambezi walk. With over twelve hundred kilometres behind me, I was finally out of those vast, depressing plains, so felt extremely proud of myself on reaching the place.

Karien Kermer turned out to be a blonde Dutch lady with a bustling manner and an infectious smile. Shaking my hand, she inadvertently shattered my euphoria by telling me that Andy was away, but would send his Lusaka team down the following week to resupply me.

This was desperate news. I had been so looking forward to seeing Nicholas and Zara that I had pushed myself for days and was far too early for the planned resupply. Trying to hide my disappointment, I followed Karien into her house on the river. The garden led down to the water and I could feel tension ease from my shoulders as I looked out across 'my' Zambezi.

"Of course, you will stay here until your Cowbell people arrive," Karien told me sternly. "You look in need of fattening up."

I didn't want to foist myself on anyone for a whole week, but she brushed my objections aside.

"Don't be silly," She produced tea and cake, swimming in strawberry sauce. "My husband is in Johannesburg and this is the perfect place for you to rest."

I decided that I would enjoy a couple of days in that enchanted spot before moving on and camping closer to town. I knew there was a line of lodges along that stretch but felt sure I could find somewhere suitable. In the meantime, there was strawberry cake to enjoy.

Later that day, I weighed myself and the result was a shock. I had started the trip weighing ninety-three kilograms. A lot of it had been centred around my middle, but my weight was now down to seventy-one kgs. I had lost almost three and a half stone during my wanderings. No wonder I felt bad at times.

My face - never pretty - was lined and gaunt, bones standing out like buttresses above my cheeks. My collar bones jutted obscenely and my ribs made a washboard pattern on either side of my chest. As for the lower half of me - I had known my hips were prominent, but to see them was horrifying. My bottom had disappeared and while I had heard of bedsores, I wondered if I could start a new fashion with bed bruises, sustained where bones made contact with hard ground for night after night.

Karien smiled grimly when she heard how much weight I had lost.

"I will fatten you up," She said firmly. "You can relax here and read in the sunshine, but you will eat at least three meals a day, with plenty of snacks in between."

She was as good as her word, the lovely Mrs Kermer and when I moved on, I had regained nearly five of the lost kilograms - which isn't bad for an eight day stay.

My hostess asked if I needed anything from South Africa and I hesitated. Deborah had promised to send another pipe with the children, but after my shock at not seeing them, I wasn't sure it would arrive.

"I do need another pipe," I said doubtfully and it was arranged. When Peter Kermer arrived with their son, Munene two days later, he brought with him a brand new pipe and four packets of proper tobacco. After having done without for nearly four weeks, I was overjoyed and when Deborah's pipe also arrived, I had an abundance of riches.

I had lived in Livingstone as a boy and it didn't look to have changed much, but that was an illusion. The sleepy hollow of my boyhood had metamorphosed into a thriving metropolis with supermarkets, restaurants and even a traffic light. Mind you, the locals agreed that traffic flowed better on the frequent occasions that the light broke down.

Although the Kermers had a spare truck, I preferred to go into town with Karien in the mornings. After weeks on end without seeing a vehicle, I didn't trust myself to drive and Livingstone traffic seemed hectic to my jaundiced eye. In town, I wandered the streets and watched people. Karien and I lunched together most days and she kept a severe eye on my plate to ensure that it was well filled and duly emptied. I did not find it difficult to comply and even ate between meals by treating myself to chicken and mushroom pies at the supermarket close to her office.

I spoke to Livingstone residents and spent hours discussing the woes of the world with roadside stall holders and street kids. Most of them found it difficult to imagine the Livingstone of my youth – a town without tourists.

The one disappointment was the Victoria Falls themselves. As a boy, I would spend hours on the bridge, staring in awed wonderment at that majestic display of falling water, but one couldn't do that anymore. There were wooden footways everywhere, railings and a long line of taxis waiting for tourists wanting to go back into town. Tickets had to be purchased to enter an enclosure surrounding the Falls and shabby stores offered cheap curios, while a gaudily apparelled 'witch doctor' plied his trade for gawping tourists. The waterfall was as magnificent as ever, but what passes for progress in this tawdry modern world has cheapened one of the most wonderful natural sights to be seen on the planet.

The Cowbell team of Victor and Martin, reinforced by David from the Ndola office arrived and I went through the obligatory photo shoot with the Falls behind me, but quickly went back to town with the chaps and found a bar where modernity did not seem so out of place.

Among the items they brought me was a letter from Zara, which inevitably had me bawling again. She told me that even though she always complained, she was 'missing my bear hugs.' How could any geriatric wanderer not cry at that?

One high spot of that Livingstone sojourn was lunch with Joe McGregor Brookes, an eighty-five year old youngster who had been a Tsetse Control Officer at Sinazongwe fifty years previously. I asked Joe the best way to go from Livingstone as I was worried about the gorges below the Falls. He frowned and took a sip from his rock shandy.

"If you go through the main gorges," He said slowly, "you won't make it. The cliffs are too steep and with a heavy pack on your back, you are bound to fall and break something."

It was a prospect that scared me witless. Even with a satellite phone with which to call for help, breaking a leg in the gorges would almost inevitably mean a slow and painful death.

"The only way you can get through," Joe went on, "is to head East to the Kalomo River and follow that to the Zambezi. You will still be in the gorges and the going will be hard, but that route will give you a chance."

Joe was known as *Siatwinde* (Great Hunter) among the Tonga people and had a wealth of experience of bush travel, so I took his advice and it worked. We were to meet again later on but there was a great deal of hardship, pain and suffering to experience before then.

There were other fine people in Livingstone apart from the Kermers. I enjoyed breakfast with Sandy Dankwerth, a farmer's wife from Choma and was invited to stay for a night or two at The Waterfront - very much the trendy place among younger visitors. In the event, I never got there, because it seemed easier to remain at Waterberry Farm.

A young Italian named Enrico Dela Pieta was also staying there and we chatted long into one evening. Enrico worked for Davidoff cigars and gave me one to take along 'for a special occasion.' That great big cigar travelled with me for the rest of the journey. There were occasions when I longed to puff at it, but somehow just having it there gave me a weird sort of comfort.

"How would you like to ride an elephant?" Karien asked me one day and although my initial reaction was one of horror, it was too good an opportunity to miss.

As a self-proclaimed 'elephant man,' I abhor the way these gentle and dignified animals are used for the entertainment of man. Elephants are wild creatures and human beings do not have the right to 'tame' them and make them act as our inferiors.

But that is my personal view and thanks to Karien, I was being given the chance to see it from the other side. So it was that I made my way to the Riverside Lodge, where both elephant riding and walking with lions was on offer.

Gerald Chibanda was a burly young Zimbabwean who immediately disarmed my prickly hostility to his endeavours by telling me that he had read my book, **Never Quite a Soldier** and very much enjoyed it. He had been schooled at Prince Edward in Harare and we had a number of mutual acquaintances, so inevitably got on well. He showed me to my quarters for the night, a cell-like room in a nearby house, obviously adapted for the purpose.

"The work here is carried out by volunteers from all over the world," Gerald told me. "They pay for the privilege and we put them up in this house and another one down the road. You will find it spartan but comfortable.

'Mind you, we have been invited to supper at the Lodge," He added with a twinkle in his eye. "The food there will definitely be better."

It was and I went to bed that evening, feeling replete and sleepy. The following day was going to be a momentous one in the life of this crumpled scribbler. I was going to do the tourist thing and ride one of my beloved elephants.

The morning was cold and crisp, but instead of having to haul my pack on to my shoulders and set off along a dusty track, I was able to wrap my palms around a mug of hot coffee and listen to Gerald as he told assembled tourists what they were going to do. The visitors looked a motley crew and

I wondered what they would get out of sitting on such a noble creation as an elephant. Despite the coffee and biscuits, I was not a happy man as the elephants were led into a mounting area by their handlers.

"They are content here," Gerald had explained to me over dinner the previous evening. "They lead a good life and enjoy the work. Sometimes wild elephant come through the estate, but even though they are free, ours are seldom distracted. In fact..."

He told me how one female had gone off with a wild herd a few years previously, but that episode had ended unexpectedly.

"She came back nearly a year later," Gerald beamed, "and settled back into routine as though nothing had happened. Much to our amazement, we discovered that she was pregnant."

He pointed to a young elephant, wandering among those to be ridden. "That is the baby and both he and mother are happy and contented now."

It was a strange and heartening tale that seemed to bear out his contention that the elephants enjoyed their lives. While the tourists went on a leisurely safari atop their gigantic steeds, Gerald and I walked with them, chatting quietly and enjoying the morning air. He offered to get me a walk with lions as well, but I have no real interest in the big cats, so I declined. Elephants are my passion and I had mixed emotions as I walked among these great beasts. There was no sign of fractiousness and each animal behaved with quiet dignity, posing for photographs when required and occasionally reaching a trunk up to assure the 'mahout' that all was well.

The tourists were also worth studying and each and every one of them had an expression of awed reverence as they rocked gently in their seats. I didn't need to be told that this was the high spot of their holidays. It was obvious by the expressions on their faces. I had a great deal of confusion in my heart as we wandered back into camp.

Once everyone was back on the ground, more coffee was served and Gerald introduced me to the tourists, many of whom had been studying me with as much curiosity as I had been studying them. I was asked a few questions and posed for photographs, then Gerald asked whether I would like a ride.

"Go on," He urged. "If you are to write about this, you have to try it."

He was right of course and minutes later I was up on Danny, senior bull in the small herd. We didn't go far, but I had to admit that it was comfortable and I would not have missed the opportunity for the world. Danny fondled my neck with his trunk when we posed for more photographs, me sitting on his extended foreleg. It felt strange, but the huge elephant didn't turn a hair.

When I bade my genial host and his charges farewell, I had decidedly ambivalent feelings about wild elephants being taught tricks for tourists.

*   *   *

I was sorry to leave Livingstone and the lovely Kermer family, but I had a river to walk.

Karien's cooking and generous TLC had built my strength up again and loose stitching on one boot had been sorted out in the local township - at the princely price of one pin. I had given the cobbler a five pin note and told him to keep it because he hadn't tried to rip me off and his work was excellent, with only the most basic tools at his disposal.

Yes, the place had been good to me and as I started out again, I could still feel the bristly hair of those wonderful elephants against my palms. I have spent much of my life in close proximity to ellies, but this was the first time I had actually touched live specimens and despite my misgivings, it had been a thrill.

Following the advice of Joe Brookes, I decided to head across country until I reached the Kalomo River and follow that down to the Zambezi.

"It should be dry now," Joe had assured me. "The going will be hard, but there will be pools in the river where you can fish if necessary. Get yourself a guide from one of the villages. Those blokes know the area and will keep you out of trouble."

It was sound advice from a man who knew, but I was sorry to say goodbye to Karien at Eastwood Farm. She had driven me there one morning and after coffee with the family, I hugged my little Dutch benefactor and in company with a farm worker called David Milupi, headed East toward Chuunga Village and the wild Kalomo River.

David set a cracking pace and I was glad he hadn't been with me before my sojourn in Livingstone. I was stronger now - thanks to Karien - but I struggled to keep up. We stopped at his home village of Nderere and after eight days of delicious western food, I was back to *nshima* - this time with vegetables. At one stage, David indicated a path heading south and suggested that he take me down to the Zambezi itself. It would have meant cutting through the bush and bypassing the Kalomo, but Joe Brookes' warning loomed large in my mind. I felt fit and strong, but with the Livingstone resupply, my pack was back to its thirty kilogram weight. David told me that the way he would take me, although shorter than the Kalomo route, necessitated a fair amount of climbing.

I decided to stick to the original plan and my companion cheerfully agreed to take me through to Viyali village, a few kilometres further on.

"From there, it is not far to Chuunga," He told me. "The headman at Viyali will give you somewhere to sleep tonight."

I preferred to sleep in the bush, but David looked horrified at the thought. Humouring him, I promised to talk with the headman and on we went, arriving in Viyali late in the afternoon.

This was spectacular countryside, with rocky hills and sweeping valleys visible in every direction. The village extended over a wide area and inevitably, we had to walk right through it before arriving at the headman's house. He immediately put a damper on my day.

"You will die if you walk down the Kalomo," He told me witheringly. "It cannot be done, even now that the rain has gone."

I tried to convince him that I was perfectly capable by telling him about my crossing of the flood plains, but he was dismissive.

"That was just water. The Kalomo is very dangerous."

A meeting was called with his senior villagers and there was much 'oohing' and 'ahing' with repeated shaking of heads until I was fed up with the rigmarole and the headman's negativity. Turning to David, who had been acting as interpreter, I thanked him for his guidance, slipped him twenty pin for escorting me and marched back to the 'road' we had come in on. I had no intention of retracing my footsteps, so I was going to walk down the Kalomo even if it was dangerous.

I didn't bother with the formal farewells that are customary in rural Zambia and ignored the headman and his negatively-minded elders.

At Chuunga village, I was enthusiastically welcomed by the people. A young man named Kennedy took me under his wing, introduced me to the headman and had a dilapidated shelter swept out for me to use as a bedroom. When I flopped on to my mat that evening, my night was disturbed by cattle and pigs feeding around me, but I was too weary to bother about them.

There were a surprising number of young men in Chuunga and my shelter became the hub of the village for a while. We discussed everything from religion to crocodiles and the previous rainy season. At one stage, bibles were produced and my young friends read out passages from the Good Book to me and each other. We ate together and a veritable feast of *nshima*, fish and vegetables was soon demolished by youthful appetites.

Soon after lunch, another man approached our gathering to say that I was wanted by the former headman, Patrick Kambizi. Four of my companions volunteered to accompany me and we made a cheerful party as we wandered through the bush. As I approached Kambizi's village, I sensed that all was not as it should be.

Patrick was a wrinkled fellow, possibly older than me and very drunk. The men around him were also inebriated and I was regarded with obvious hostility by some of them. The headman, whose name was Thadeus (he pronounced it Tedious) was present, but he sat quietly and listened to Patrick who obviously felt himself to be the most important personage in the village. There were a number of empty beer bottles lying around, but bloodshot eyes and stumbling speech indicated that most of the imbibers were on the stronger local brew.

A chair was produced for me and I sat patiently waiting to be 'interviewed.' Patrick's questions were hostile and delivered in a challenging monotone that made my hackles rise.

Why was I - a white man - walking through 'his' area? Where was I going? Did I have permission from Chief Makuni? If so, where was his letter?

Karien had tried to arrange a meeting with the chief in Livingstone, but he had been away so it hadn't happened. I explained this to Patrick and produced my letter from Minister Lubinda, but he waved it away.

"I don't want words from some government lackey," He shouted. "Makuni is the chief of this area, so only he can allow you to proceed. If you don't have a letter from him, you cannot go on. I will not allow it."

There were mutterings of agreement from his tipsy cronies and I looked to Thadeus for support. He was the headman. Why was he allowing this aged cretin to usurp his position?

But Thadeus was avoiding my gaze so I turned my attention back to Patrick.

"I am going on to the Kalomo River," I told him quietly. "From there I will walk down to the Zambezi and continue my journey."

"You will not." He shouted. "This is my village and you will go back to Livingstone and see Chief Makuni."

Others were shouting now and the clamour made my senses spin. I turned to Thadeus.

"I thought you were the headman," I said as politely as I could. "Why are you allowing this old fool to make decisions for you and will you please ask these drunks to speak one at a time instead of shouting together?"

Kennedy was acting as my interpreter and there was apprehension in the glance he shot at me. I think he translated properly however as Thadeus looked suitably abashed. A well-dressed younger man, less inebriated than his fellows spoke quietly to the throng. He was obviously a figure of authority as the rest listened attentively.

Kennedy whispered in my ear.

"He is the village secretary and an educated man. He is suggesting that a note is sent to the senior headman of this area and he can decide whether you are allowed to go on."

Eventually the hubbub died down and I addressed Patrick, who seemed considerably put out by the usurpation of his authority.

"'It sounds a good idea to me," I told him. It didn't and would mean further delay, but I was forcing myself to be polite. "You are too drunk to make decisions and in any case, you are not the headman, so let us approach someone who can think. Send the messenger back to my hut and I will give him my ministerial letter and a note from myself explaining things."

With that, I left the gathering, once again not bothering with farewells. It was rude of me, but I was trembling with anger and did not want it to show. My Zambezi Walk was in jeopardy through the rantings of a drunken old sot and I did not want to go all the way back to Livingstone.

The messenger would not go to the senior headman till the following day, so it meant another night at Chuunga, where I felt I had probably outstayed my welcome. Feeling thoroughly disgruntled, I sat down on my pack and tried to calm down.

The process was helped by Thadeus' wife, Eleanor who shyly approached to ask whether I wanted food. I told her I didn't and needing someone to talk to, explained my problems with the former headman.

"Ah," She nodded wisely. "Was he drinking beer?"

She told me that Patrick Kambizi was a nice man when he was sober, but inclined to be 'harsh' when in his cups. That was the reason he had been deposed as village headman, but it didn't help me.

Eleanor was a sweet lady and tried to cheer me up with a cup of *'mahewu'* - a non alcoholic drink made from maize, water and sugar. I had enjoyed it in a number of villages despite the fact that scraps of maize stuck in my teeth and I needed to spend ages picking the morsels out.

I didn't sleep well that night and when daylight arrived, I was scratchy-eyed and more irritable than ever. A thick-set cyclist called James announced that he would take my letters to the senior headman and rode off with a cheerful wave. Once he had disappeared into the trees, I settled down to what was likely to prove a very long day.

*   *   *

Well into the twenty-first century, the remote villages of Zambia exist in a time warp. Chuungu was ten kilometres from Viyale, but it was situated in wild, inhospitable countryside, so had a feeling of isolation that was soothing to my senses. From my tattered little shelter, I studied day to day routine and found myself envying the villagers the relaxed tenor of their lives.

At first light, women would sleepily emerge from their huts, wander off into the bush - presumably for a pee - then return to prepare cooking fires from the ashes of the night before. Once the fire was blazing - and even on cold mornings, the flame was kept low - they would either stand, warming their hands and bottoms or start on the daily chores by enthusiastically sweeping the dusty ground around their living quarters. Although at first glance, an African village appears untidy and littered, they are spotlessly clean and much care goes into keeping them so.

Once the fires were going, men would emerge from their quarters and walk to what I thought of as the 'talking hut' - a thatched shelter where they would gather to chat, think great thoughts and dream. Invariably, the first act for most of them was the preparation of newspaper-rolled cigarettes which were lit from the fire and smoked with obvious enjoyment. Although I have never been a cigarette smoker, I am not against the practice and wish the do-gooders of the western world could see how much enjoyment rural folk in Africa get from smoking.

Breakfast in the village is prepared around eight o'clock by the women and served initially to their menfolk. Even children wait for the men to satisfy themselves. By modern thinking it is sexist and misogynistic, but it works and few African women rebel against the system. Even Monde Mututwa had ensured that I was full before having her own meals and Monde was a modern woman who had dined in some of the best restaurants in the world.

I was surprised to see Thadeus staggering around that Saturday morning. His eyes were bloodshot and I could smell stale beer on his breath, but he seemed friendly. He invited me to Patrick Kambizi's huts for more beer, but I declined on the grounds that it was far too early for me. It was just after seven and when he had gone in search of further libations, I wearily told my dictaphone diary that it was 'no wonder these bloody people can't make any decisions.'

That wasn't really fair, as it was only a small coterie of elders who were involved in the drinking. I was soon surrounded by friendly faces again and Eleanor appeared with a bowl of mealie porridge and milk. My refusal to eat the previous evening had obviously worried her. Mealie porridge is best eaten with sugar, so I mixed a couple of sweetening tablets with the milk and enjoyed my breakfast.

Chickens jumped in and out of the village grain store, to be chased away by whoever happened to spot them and I spent ten minutes smiling at the caution of a ground squirrel doing the same thing. The little brute spent minutes on reconnaissance before scrambling up the ladder to the grain bin, filling the pouches in his cheeks, checking again for approaching trouble and scrambling down. He obviously wasn't worried about me as he ignored my presence.

Feeling fretful about my uncertain situation, I went for a walk during the morning. The countryside was arid, but hauntingly beautiful with massive hills and outbreaks of rock stretching away on all sides. Feeling the need to practice with my GPS - apart from reading the mileage covered, I still didn't know how to use it - I switched it on to discover I was heading due south instead of due north. Sitting on a fallen tree, I wondered whether to follow my always shaky instincts or rely on the instrument.

In the event, I relied on technology and found my way back to Chuunga, wondering where I would have ended up without GPS. It was a salutary lesson. I am alright when wandering along the course of a river or relying on sun or shadows, but in deep bush, I am as likely to get myself lost as any newcomer to Africa.

Eleanor appeared again at lunch time, on this occasion presenting me with *nshima* and beans, a dish that I didn't want but eventually wolfed down as it was delicious. One 'modern' bit of equipment in Chuunga was a hand-driven grinding machine to crush the maize kernels into meal. In most villages, women still pounded away with mortar and pestle, but here it was a matter of putting kernels into the machine and winding a handle. I tried it for a while and it was hard work, but Eleanor and her female cronies seemed pleased with this example of modern technology.

It was late in the day and a new moon was high in the sky when James returned with Martin, who had spoken on my behalf the previous day. Martin's English was excellent and he told me the senior headman was only too pleased for me to continue my journey, particularly as it was being done 'for all Zambians.' He insisted however that I took two guides from the village with me.

"James and I will accompany you to the Zambezi confluence," He finished off and that was fine by me apart from one small problem.

"I can't pay you much," I warned, wondering how many kwacha I had left in my wallet.

Martin waved that objection aside and told me that they would accept whatever I could afford. However, the next day was Sunday and they wanted to attend church, so he asked whether I could delay my departure till the evening. That thought did not appeal as I had no wish to be walking in the dark, so I decided to have another day of idleness and depart early on Monday morning.

Preparing for bed, I wondered whether travelling with an escort was a good idea. When on my own, there was nobody to witness my occasional ineptitude or moments of fear and desperation, but with two companions, these could not be hidden.

I didn't have much choice however, so spent Sunday in a relaxed overhaul of my kit, watching villagers in their finery heading off to church and generally allowing the kinks to ease from my body. The extra day of rest did me good, but that evening, I had a huge attack of doubt as to my capability to complete the trip. I had heard so many horror stories about the difficult terrain ahead that I was genuinely scared and wondered with maudlin self-pity whether I would ever see my nearest and dearest again.

I did not sleep well, but was up early to wait for my guides. Martin had promised to be there by six, but inevitably he was late and I struggled to stifle my impatience.

After all, there is no hurry in Africa.

*　　*　　*

It was primeval countryside and I felt a sense of awe as I gazed around me.

I was sitting with my feet in a pool of hot water that bubbled gently from rocks and above me, massive crags and boulders seemed to thrust themselves toward the sky. To my right was the Kalomo River, apparently carving a vast chasm through the countryside. The landscape made me feel small and insignificant and I would not have been at all surprised had a dinosaur lumbered down to drink at one of the pools that were all that remained of the river.

The silence was all enveloping. It seemed to press down on my shoulders and while not oppressive, it gave me a definite feeling of inadequacy.

We had eventually started out that morning after stopping for breakfast at James' little home in the hills. He cheerfully told me that he wanted ten children to see him through his old age, but his wife was such a tiny thing that I couldn't see that happening. Mind you, he already had five, so was halfway there.

Initially our journey to the Kalomo had taken us over mountainous countryside and the scenery was spectacular. Vast folds in the earth stretched in all directions. The bush was dry and inhospitable, but the views made up for that. I stopped repeatedly to take photographs and without the sound of our footsteps on the hard earth, the only noise to break a brooding silence was the occasional bark of a distant baboon or the mournful 'woo - woo - woo' of the emerald spotted wood dove - that lovely little chap who sounds so unhappy but to me, is always a sign that I am back in wild Africa.

For three hours we walked through those massive hills and at times, the path would have been baulked at by any self-respecting goat. More often than not, it was merely a scar on the earth and without my walking pole I would probably have fallen to my death from those precipitous walkways.

My companions walked ahead of me and I envied the easy familiarity with which they tackled the climbs and almost vertical descents. We made good progress until we came to what proved to be the very last lap to the Kalomo. I found myself on the smallest and most precipitous path yet and was forced to descend very slowly, taking care to bring the toe of one boot to the heel of the other before entrusting my weight to either leg. On my left, we skirted a vertical cliff that towered above us and to the right, the landscape dropped away in a fall of about fifty, totally sheer metres. The Kalomo was visible way below me, but keeping my footing on that tiny path required all the concentration I could muster, so I kept my eyes on the way ahead. Even my companions were moving slowly and there was nothing I could do but follow them.

How long it took to get down that final slope, I have no idea, but it seemed like a lifetime to my tormented mind. Sweat streamed down my face and the pack tugged at my shoulders, but I didn't dare shrug it into a more comfortable position. I needed every iota of my concentration or I would fall and break my neck - if I was lucky.

Both Martin and James kept an anxious eye on my progress and I blessed them for their concern. Mind you, they must have worried as to how they would get me out of that remote spot if I did fall. I think we were all relieved when the path began to level out and the vegetation around us became thicker and more riverine.

Almost without warning, we were down. There was water trickling cheerfully to one side and Martin gestured at it.

"Hot spring," He said laconically. "Always good for a bath."

I wasn't interested in bathing, but the spring fascinated me. It trickled down in a tiny stream until it widened into a metre-square pool, surrounded by algae-covered rocks. A *mopani* tree lent shade to this enchanted spot and I wasted no time in getting boots off to bathe my feet in hot water.

There was a fisherman camped nearby and we chatted with him. An old man in ragged clothing, he told us that he had been there for the past four months, but wasn't catching more than he could eat. I envied him the peacefulness of his existence, but don't think I could have survived on his diet of dried fish and nothing else, as he had long since run out of mealie meal.

"Now we walk," Martin told me cheerfully. "In maybe two and a half days, we will reach the Zambezi."

It seemed a daunting prospect, but Martin's estimate was right and for two and a half days, I looked upon myself as privileged to be wandering through an incredible landscape. The fact that I was the first white man to walk there since Joe Brookes fifty years previously made it all the more memorable.

*　　*　　*

The silence was almost tangible. It pressed down on me like a physical presence and the rocky crags made me feel small and insignificant. People talk about silence in the African bush, but it is usually a misnomer. There is always some sort of sound, even if it is just the rustle of an insect pushing its way through the grass. In the Kalomo, silence meant silence.

The complete absence of sound was nerve-wracking, but thrilling at the same time. I sat away from my companions, enjoying an evening pipe at the side of a pool and try as I might, I could not hear a thing.

As the rocks dissolved into darkness, I decided that I was uniquely privileged to have been allowed to experience such a spot. It was a place where the soul was free and the constraints and frustrations of modern life were absent. It was a place where only survival mattered and where tomorrow would take care of itself. Nature could be savoured to the full and I felt the strains of the day ebbing from my muscles. I knew I would sleep well that night.

And boy, there had been strains during the day. At one stage, we had left the Kalomo and taken to the hills, where once again, steep and heart-stoppingly dangerous paths were the norm. I fell a couple of times and ended up badly grazed, but knew I had been lucky. A fall in those circumstances could easily lead to a broken neck.

Seeing my difficulties, Martin offered to swop packs with me, but while his was lighter than mine, it didn't have wide shoulder straps and I had to carry it with lengths of cord hitched over my shoulders. These dug into my skin and I ended up padding them with my jacket - uncomfortable but vaguely effective. When we finally returned to the river, I stared across at what appeared to be a totally featureless hillside towering sixty metres into the air.

"Did we really come down that?" I asked plaintively and my companions smiled. Martin pointed out the route we had taken and when I eventually managed to discern a tiny line through harsh yellow grass, I was appalled. Even baboons would surely avoid a track like that.

Yet we had done it and I was still in one piece. Sitting contentedly beside a small fire, we dined on *nshima* and grilled barbel. White people generally avoid eating barbel, but in those awe-inspiring surroundings, it tasted delicious.

We were on the road early the following morning, although Martin and James insisted on having breakfast - yet more *nshima* and fish. I contented myself with coffee and a few slivers of dried fruit. The going was hard and progress was slow, but at one point, we detoured again to climb a steep bank where footholds were few and rocks tumbled below us, giving due notice of what would happen if we fell. I wasn't sure what we were doing in those rocky heights, but James explained that Martin's father had been killed by a snake there and they were looking for his grave.

"It was a green mamba," He explained, but the green mamba is an arboreal snake and there weren't any tall trees on those slopes. The offending snake was more likely to have been a black mamba, many specimens of which are a dull green colour.

Whatever the case, the old man was buried in a beautiful spot.

We didn't find the grave and an hour or two later, were plodding along the river again. This necessitated a lot of rock climbing and my legs ached from the strain. In places, the river sand was covered in salt, but when I asked my companions why, they just shrugged.

"Nobody knows," was James' laconic answer. "It is just there."

Early in the afternoon, Martin put a hand on my arm.

"We are approaching the *dagga* farms," He told me quietly. "Please don't ask too many questions or take photographs."

'*Dagga*' is cannabis or marijuana and I had been warned many years previously that there was a lucrative, international trade in the substance at the western end of Lake Kariba. My informant was a senior member of the Zimbabwe Republic Police, but it seemed that he might have had his locations wrong.

There were plantations of cannabis growing on both sides of the river and they showed a bright, emerald green against the dusty backdrop of the bush. Elaborate systems of irrigation had been built and men working among the plants looked up warily at our approach. James and Martin were greeted politely, but questions were hurled at them from all sides and from the way I was being studied by the *dagga* farmers, these obviously centred on my presence.

At last I was accepted and we sat down on the ground for a chat. Newspaper-wrapped cigarettes were passed around, the sickly-sweet smell making it obvious how they were filled. I contented myself with a pipe and managed to take a few surreptitious photographs without causing undue offence. At last I had a chance to question the farmers myself and a little to my surprise, was given a tour of the 'farm' by a wizened old chap who told me his name was Frederico.

It was certainly a well run business. Workers were picking the ripe cannabis leaves and laying them on drying racks where the sun could do its work. From there, they were packed into bags, which were loaded onto sledges for the journey to the Zambezi.

"At the river, it is taken by the Zimbabweans," Frederico told me, "and they pay us in US dollars."

But wasn't he worried about the Zambian police? After all - I gestured around me - everything was in the open, so what would happen if a patrol came along, as we had.

Frederico's laugh was scornful.

"There are no roads here," He scoffed. "Policemen in Zambia won't go anywhere without their vehicles, so we are safe. It is only the occasional fisherman who walks this way. And you..." He made a gesture with his hands that seemed to indicate an inability to describe what I was and I smiled reassuringly.

I am an avowed critic of drugs and drug dealing, but I had to admire the efficiency and organisational ability of the Kalomo *dagga* farmers. In a land where so many young men were unemployed, these fellows had set up their own venture and were obviously making a success of it.

We passed two more *dagga* farms in the Kalomo and they were as casually efficient as the first. I couldn't help hoping that they would continue to get away with their criminal activities and do well for a long time to come. I know that was remiss of me, but I had liked Frederico and he made it all sound so simple.

But it was another long day and I was deeply asleep before darkness set in. I woke at one stage to hear Martin and James quietly discussing whether to wake me for food, but I grunted that I didn't need anything and was soon asleep again.

It was approaching noon on the third day that the sand underfoot changed colour. It had been a dull uniform brown, but suddenly it was sparkling white, much as it had been in the reaches of the river before Livingstone. Martin grinned at my surprise.

"Zambezi sand," He explained. "We are almost there."

We were and after a quick meal, I laid my bed in an empty fishing camp, which Martin told me had been used as a staging post for guerillas in the Zimbabwe liberation war. I had learned that Chuunga had been a training ground for Joshua Nkomo's fighters during that awful conflict and it gave me macabre satisfaction that I was using the same places for more innocent purposes.

We chatted for a while and my companions made preparations to depart. Without me to hold them back, they reckoned to get home in two days, rather than three and after I had paid them what I could afford, they disappeared upstream, often turning to wave as they went. I knew I would miss them, as not only were they excellent company, but they had saved me many unnecessary kilometres with their short cuts, precipitously dangerous though some of those had been.

Feeling unaccountably anxious, I spent that evening watching the Mighty Zambezi as it rushed past the mouth of the Kalomo. Cliffs towered above me, but they were well forested and fish eagles screamed sardonic welcome as they watched from riverside trees.

I didn't know it but I was about to embark upon the most difficult section of my walk. The magnificently lonely Kalomo was behind me, but now I had the gorges to contend with and they would tax me to my limits.

*   *   *

The Zambezi is nearly two kilometres wide when it plunges over a hundred-and-eight metre cliff to form the Victoria Falls. It is an awesome spot, but even more awesome is the fact that all that immense volume of water is funnelled into a series of narrow gorges, through which it rushes toward the distant sea.

After the scenic excitement of the Kalomo, I rejoined the gorges fifty kilometres downstream. The river was still narrow and very rough as it surged past the mouth of the Kalomo, but I started out on 23rd August feeling confident I had bypassed the worst of the gorges. I was being naive again.

It was my wedding anniversary and to her surprise (I don't usually remember) I used the satellite phone to ring Lace and wish her Happy Anniversary. That was the only good part of the day.

Martin and James had told me that walking the gorges would be easier than walking the Kalomo, because I would only have 'little rocks' to cope with. The rocks were certainly smaller than the massive crags and buttresses we had climbed over for three days, but there were more of them and after four hours, my GPS told me I had covered less than three kilometres.

Although the walls of the gorge weren't as steep as those immediately below the Falls, they towered above me and ended at the river in massive heaps of rock, sitting at an angle of forty-five degrees. The rocks were of various sizes, many of them loose and walking across them was exhausting and dangerous. Every step had to be considered beforehand and I had to test the footing before entrusting my weight to the rocks. I fell three times in those first few hours and my muscles screamed for rest, while sweat cascaded down my face and saturated my shirt.

For all the discomfort and danger it was a magnificent bit of Africa. The silence was broken only by the sound of rushing water and the occasional cry of fish eagles, but apart from the birds I could have been alone in the world. Martin had explained that villages in the area were on top of the cliffs and supplied with water by pumps and boreholes, so there would only be the occasional fisherman along the way. He added a warning.

"Do not go into these villages, Sir," His tone was serious. "There are bad people there. They are smugglers and thieves, who in recent months have shot a policeman and a white cattle dealer."

I was never able to confirm that story and soon forgot the warning in the effort of getting across the rocks, but the uncanny quiet of my surroundings was disturbing at times.

I had started before seven that morning, but by midday, my legs were shaky, I was covered in blood and sweat, dizzy spells were back and I frequently had to stop and wait for my head to clear. The river hurtled hungrily a few metres below me and I knew that if I fell again, I was likely to find myself in serious trouble.

Late in the morning, I spotted a small area of sand high above my head, so climbed laboriously up to it and made an uncomfortable camp among the rocks where I spent the rest of the day feeling sorry for myself and trying to read. I had covered only a few kilometres and longed for the cheerful company of my guides, but they would be well on their way back to Chuunga, so I was alone in the wilderness.

I had at least forty kilometres of this terrain to get over and at my present rate that was likely to take me a fortnight. As I bathed and disinfected the grazes on my legs and arms, I felt it would be a long fortnight indeed. I had to keep going and pray I wouldn't seriously injure myself on those dreadful rocks.

Despite feeling unutterably weary, I did not sleep well. It had been a wedding anniversary to remember, but not for good reasons.

*   *   *

Suddenly, much of the pleasure had gone from my trip. I was exhausted, making little progress and no longer enjoying myself. After three weeks of constant company, I was lonely. I have always enjoyed my own company, particularly in the sort of spectacular surroundings in which I now found myself, but those rocks were affecting my soul as well as my body.

The river didn't help. The stately lady that had been the Zambezi above the Falls had been transformed into a viciously grumbling harridan, swirling among rocky outcrops and telling me in no uncertain terms that she was willing me to fall and end up in her depths.

I was dirty too and while that doesn't normally worry me, I longed for clean, freshly ironed clothing and a hot bath, neither of which were likely in the Zambezi gorges. I had always tried to keep myself relatively clean, but I was too exhausted to spend time washing.

In short, I had had enough and wanted to go home. Not that there was any chance of that. I had the satellite phone for emergencies and this probably ranked in that category, but who could I phone? Andy was in Cape Town and I didn't know where I was. I spent hours inwardly wrestling the problem, but the only solution was to keep going and hope the torment would ease before my mind and body gave up on me.

According to my map, I was about forty-five kilometres from Devils Gorge at the western end of Lake Kariba. In normal circumstances, that would take me five days – but these were hardly normal circumstances.

Progress was desperately slow and although I started out at first light, I was making less than one kilometre per hour and managing a maximum of four hours before trembling muscles and a pounding heart would bring me to a halt for the day. Suitable camping sites were difficult to find among the rocks and one memorable day, I made camp in a patch of sand that was barely a metre square. My sleeping area was so small, I was forced to coil my legs beneath me when I went to bed, yet I enjoyed a good eight hours of sleep to refresh me for the following day.

But that – apart from the magnificence of my surroundings – was the only time I felt at home in those gorges. Walking was difficult and debilitating, I fell frequently and my spirits plummeted ever further. The muscle in my calf that had given trouble in gentler times began to act up again and some of my cuts and grazes went septic, forcing me to stop for numerous 'clinic' sessions.

Not that there was much I could do apart from apply liberal splodges of antiseptic cream to the affected spots, but I suppose it helped my wandering mind. My dizzy spells were getting worse and worrying me. One day when I took my boots off to cool my feet, I found my socks matted with fresh blood and realised that my heels, split before Livingstone were considerably worse and they too required lashings of antiseptic cream. It seemed my entire system was joining the rest of my body in rebelling against the harsh treatment and the rocks we were being forced to fight against.

I passed the occasional fisherman along the way and we exchanged greetings, but – perhaps it was the way

I looked – none of them expressed any interest in where I was going or what I was doing.

An exception was an old fellow (probably ten years younger than me!) whose name was Nelson. He was camped in a gulley above the river and sat with me for a while, anxious to hear my story. I obliged to an extent, but rather than regale him with my woes, I tried to remain cheerful about my progress. That evening, he reappeared with a freshly caught bream that he presented for my supper. I wasn't hungry and didn't want the hassle of cooking, but the bream would have taken him hours to catch and the gesture was a generous one. I ate the fish half cooked, but for a while my faith in human nature was restored and Nelson made things even better by taking me to a spot where a path led away from the river and up into the forested slope above.

"That will take you for five kilometres," He told me gravely. "It will cut off a big bend in the river and save you time."

For me, that little path became Nelson's Road and I blessed him for his kindness. It gave me one day of reasonable walking despite being steep and rocky in places. I covered the five kilometres in a couple of hours and as Nelson had told me I would, came out at a village beside an inlet, where I was hoping to rest for a day or two.

The village was clean and well-maintained, but deserted. I made myself tea in the shade of a hut and wondered which building would make for the most comfortable night. My musings were interrupted by the arrival of a youth called Richard. He eyed me warily and told me that the village inhabitants had gone back into the hills, but the place seemed too clean for that to be true. I told him I intended to stay there for the day and he looked a little uncertain, but while I was drinking my tea, I saw him running into the bush, obviously heading into the hills.

With Martin Chabilani's warning about this being 'bandit alley' ringing in my ears, I reluctantly decided that he had gone to warn others as to my presence and it behoved me to move on. It was not an easy decision as it was late morning, the sun was fiendishly hot and there was little chance of finding a more comfortable spot.

Nevertheless, I set off again, moving as quickly as I could to put distance between myself and the empty village. At one stage, I had another fall and managed to lose the new pipe that Deborah had sent out. I still had the one from South Africa, but knew that unless I wanted another spell of tobacco starvation, I would have to be careful with that.

How I longed to be back on the flatlands above the Falls, where the locals were friendly and walking was relatively easy.

I had forgotten all about the sweat, toil and terrors of those vast flood plains. How easily the human mind discards bad memories.

*   *   *

Something had woken me and I lay still, trying to see what it was. The night was very quiet and a meagre moon did nothing to illuminate my surroundings.

Nevertheless, I felt sure there was someone very close to me and my eyes began to ache as I peered through the darkness. Whoever or whatever it was, seemed to be close to a large rock, two metres from where I lay. I couldn't see anything, no matter how hard I strained my eyes.

I should have been scared I suppose. After all, I was still in 'Bandit Alley,' lying on the ground with nothing to hand with which to defend myself. My heart ought to have been pounding as adrenalin rushed through my system, but it wasn't like that.

I felt only a deep sense of peace and tranquillity. If there was anything out there, it was not going to harm me, of that I was certain. I felt what can only be termed a sense of companionship toward my unknown visitor and was reminded of a similar feeling during my kayaking adventure, three years previously. On that occasion, I had been wandering through the lion-infested, Matusadona bush during the night - cold, frightened and sure I would die before daybreak. It is a long story and

I will leave it for another time, but I should not have survived and that I did, can only be put down to blind luck and perhaps the fact that 'Somebody up There' was looking after me.

At one stage during that terrible night, I had been aware of a presence very close to me. I was trying to get warm under a bush when I felt 'someone' beside me. I spoke aloud to whoever it was, but of course there was nobody there. Nevertheless, the feeling of a presence and an air of loving care had been strong and for a while, I followed blindly, not knowing who I was with or where I was going. Somehow I survived till daylight, even though I had blundered through the darkness for over twelve hours in one of the wildest parks in Africa. I couldn't explain it, even to myself.

When I had described the incident to friends, some suggested the presence of my Guardian Angel, but I was never convinced. Although educated by Jesuits and brought up by a devoutly Catholic mother, a long policing career had disillusioned me. My belief in a Deity was always there but I had become cynical about religion and those who embraced it.

During that night in the gorges, the feeling of a presence was again very strong. Even when I sat up and shone my light around – there was nothing to be seen but rocks – I was aware of something almost tangible.

Wryly wondering what was happening to me, I made a fire and put water on for coffee, but while I sat waiting for it to boil, I was aware that the tension and frustrations of days had seeped out of my mind and body. I felt totally relaxed and knew I was not going to die in the gorges and would reach Lake Kariba in due course. After the traumas of the previous days, it was a heady feeling and I didn't know how to explain it.

Writing this many months later, I still don't have an answer but whatever it was in my camp, I wish I could have made some sort of contact with it/her/him. When I retired to bed that evening, I had been in a desperate state of mind, yet when I walked on the next morning, all seemed right with my world.

Perhaps I was in the process of losing what few marbles I had left. I will never know, but that 'presence' was very real to me at the time.

I was moving east and one disadvantage was that it meant walking into the early morning sun. It took a couple of hours to rise above the rim of the gorge, but when it did, it blinded me and made my rock hopping ever more difficult and dangerous. By mid morning, it was fiendishly hot and I was forced to keep changing my shirt to keep comfortable. I would have liked to discard my bush jacket as this added to my discomfort, but although it was tattered and filthy, it contained too many well-used pockets and I didn't want to put any more weight into my pack.

So it was a question of plodding carefully on and making slow progress across successive piles of rocks. In some areas, these were interspersed with sandy patches, but the soft sand sucked at my boots and tore painfully at overtaxed calf muscles.

Two nights after that strange 'visitation,' two porcupines visited my camp in the early hours, but they were easy to recognise. Snuffling and grunting, they examined my kit, paying particular attention to my cooking pot, doubtless still smelling of my hot tea nightcap. It was when one of them started pawing at the bag, containing tea, coffee and everything else that I was forced to chase them away. They were still huffing indignantly through the bush half an hour later and I was pleased that there was still a bit of wild life in Zambia.

It was difficult to see what the cliffs were like on my side of the river, but on the Zimbabwean side, they were huge, steep and impossibly rocky. Vast crags and buttresses showed amidst thick vegetation and baboons shouted their raucous challenges across the river. They must have wondered what sort of animal I was and occasionally, I yelled back at them, feeling foolish as I did so.

Occasionally I climbed above the rocks in search of a path like Nelson's Road that would offer easier passage, but these were few and far between. One disadvantage to leaving the rocks was the proliferation of *wag n bietjie* thorn in the undergrowth and I would end my exploratory forays with my arms and legs bleeding badly.

The days were hard, but even though I was averaging less than four kilometres per five-hour day, I began to feel I was making progress. It was difficult to explain this new found optimism, but it had started with that strange midnight experience.

*   *   *

My 'bed bruises' were adding to my physical difficulties. Like most people, I like sleeping on one side or the other, but with the bruising, this was difficult. I tried sleeping on my back and it was comfortable, but once I drifted into dreamland, I would turn over and be woken by sharp pains shooting up from whichever sorely afflicted hip had made contact with the ground. There was nothing I could do about it except put on more weight – an unlikely eventuality in the circumstances.

My days degenerated into hours of painfully slow progress in ever increasing heat and a haze of sweaty, swearing scrambling over those horrible rocks. In fact, 'scrambling' is hardly the correct verb. I was crawling – sometimes literally - and any day during which I covered more than three kilometres was a good one. I couldn't help thinking back to days when twenty-kilometre days were almost the norm.

One afternoon, I was carving *biltong* into chewable chunks with the blade on my Leatherman. It had to be cut thus as my teeth were becoming looser by the day. When the meal was done, I slipped the Leatherman into its sheath on my belt and settled down for a snooze, but a while later, I needed the implement for something else and it was no longer in place.

Panic surged in my chest. I could do without many things, but that Leatherman was my toolkit, my carving knife and my life support. There were few days when I didn't use the implement and the thought of continuing without it was horrific.

I searched among the rocks, through my kit, even in the thick bush that ended metres above the place where I had been sitting. I didn't find it and grew ever more worried and upset. Time and again I told myself to sit and think it out, but within moments I was scrabbling again for that missing Leatherman. It had to be found.

Forty-five minutes after beginning my frantic search, I found it – in the back pocket of my shorts. I had somehow missed the sheath when I was putting it away and it had fallen into my open pocket. The incident and my subsequent panic were indicative of a very troubled state of mind.

Another near casualty was my camera. I had been photographing two fishermen who told me the gorges would end after seven more bends in the river and I would be able to walk on flat ground. They were wrong, but I didn't know that and when I got back to my camp, my camera had gone. I frequently dropped the ruddy thing, but it had a number of precious photographs on it, so I went back along my tracks to search for it.

Three quarters of an hour later, I had just about given up when I stopped to drink from the river. The world around me seemed to creak in afternoon heat and as I turned to resume the search, a flash of something caught the corner of my eye.

There was the camera, half hidden beneath a rock and I offered up a fervent prayer of thanks to whoever was looking after me from above. These frights, although they seem minor from this distance were gnawing holes in my self confidence and not doing me any good at all.

Another weird experience was being attacked in a very human way by a troop of baboons. I heard them barking from the cliff above me and when their calls became irksome, yelled at them to shut up. My shout provoked a brief spell of quiet and then they started again. The cliff was rocky and stones were obviously loose, as I heard a number of small landslides filter down. I was taken by surprise when a single rock landed in the middle of my camping area to fly on down the bank below me.

This was followed by another rock and then another until I could have no doubt that the *bobbos* were pelting me with stones. I have been charged by buffalo and elephant, scared witless by the close proximity of lions and hit hard in a boat by a hippo bull, but this was the first time I had been attacked – and there is no other word for it – by the humble *bobbo*.

The siege lasted but a few minutes, but I was forced to put everything breakable underneath my pack for safety.

I should have been enjoying myself. I was alone in one of the most magnificent parts of Africa I had ever seen. The scenery was breathtaking in its lonely beauty and I knew that I was privileged to be where I was. Although a few intrepid tourists passed through these gorges in rubber rafts during the season and a couple of even more intrepid kayakers had gone through in their flimsy strips of fibreglass, I was the first white man in many decades to walk that way.

But I was always so weary that it was difficult to take in my surroundings. Blood dripped constantly from my heels, my legs seemed permanently rubbery and giddy spells robbed me of balance for minutes at a time. My teeth rattled in my mouth and my loss of weight played havoc with my stamina. Repeated falls among the rocks left me with painful grazes and walking into a stray branch inflicted a deep cut on my scalp that made me bleed like the proverbial stuck pig.

When I fell badly and sprained my left ankle, I felt an overwhelming urge to sit down and cry my eyes out. It had to be the end of my dream and I knew I could not go on.

*   *   *

It was 28th August and my daughter Deborah's birthday. When I woke up, I was horrified to see that my ankle was blue and very swollen. It was difficult to put any weight on it and for the first hour, I hobbled slowly, using my walking pole as a crutch. The only sounds in that rocky gorge were the murmur of the river and the laboured rasp of my breathing, sometimes interrupted by a gasp of pain or stifled sob when my ankle turned on a rock. My heart pounded, but it was more from fear than exertion. For days, I had been scared of breaking a bone, but now that possibility was doubled and I wondered how long it would be before I went down.

Once again, baboons were in fine voice, but I ignored them. A solitary fisherman looked up at my limping approach, then looked away as if embarrassed by my presence. I suppose I must have presented an odd picture to these lonely occupants of the gorges. They came from inland villages and would spend weeks and sometimes months on their own, fishing with hand lines and living off what they caught until they had accumulated enough dried fish to take back and sell. Then they would live off the proceeds and when their money ran out, return to the gorges and start again. It was a hard and lonely existence for these men, but in a weirdly masochistic way, I envied them. I was enjoying the wild solitude – as much as I could enjoy anything with my aches and pains - but I would return to civilisation and have the comforts and amenities of the modern world. They were stuck in their own particular rut for the rest of their lives and I don't suppose they appreciated the magnificence of their surroundings as much as I did.

It was mid morning when I came upon a sandy bank flanking the river. A fig tree spread shade across the sand and although it was too early to make camp for the day, I lay down with considerable relief. For once, there was plenty of soft ground and a quick glance showed oodles of firewood lying around, so with the pain from my ankle becoming ever more intense, I decided to give myself a day off to rest.

Once I had made myself comfortable, I set up the satellite phone and rang Deborah. It was lovely to hear her chirpy tones, but of course the contact brought floods of tears as I tried to explain the difficulties I was facing. At one point, I told her my teeth were loose and she immediately interrupted.

"That sounds like scurvy Dad," She opined and I could hear concern in her voice. "You are killing yourself, so stay where you are and I will get help and medicine to you."

It was a tempting offer, but of course it was impractical.

"I don't know where I am Babe," I explained. "Even if I did, there is no point staying here till someone finds me. There are no roads and getting a boat or helicopter would cost a fortune. I will be okay, I promise."

But she is a difficult one to convince, my daughter.

"Promise me you will stay where you are and rest until your ankle feels better," I had explained my comfortable camp. "Andy can bring you some *muti* (medicine) on the next resupply. I will tell him you are in trouble."

I didn't want that, but asked her to arrange for the resupply to be in Sinazongwe, rather than the planned stop at Siavonga. Sinazongwe was a hundred kilometres closer and with the slow progress I was making, I didn't think my food stocks would last till Siavonga.

Not wanting to waste precious air time, I broke off the conversation as soon as I could and sat under my tree, sniffling pathetically after listening to a beloved voice. I had promised rest, but knew in my heart that if I remained where I was, the effect on my mental strength would do more harm than continuing on my injured ankle. I had to keep going and get the gorges behind me.

By the following day, I had had enough. It was nice to sit on the sand and not worry about those horrible rocks, but I was bored. The atmosphere in the gorges was more impressive than the scenery, because staying in one place meant that I enjoyed only one narrow view. Opposite me, a steep hillside rose into the heavens and half way up, I could see a gigantic rock crag, but nothing changed and looking at that for hours on end was hardly inspiring.

So I packed my kit and set off again, despite the day being fiendishly hot. A young fisherman called a greeting and I asked him whether there was a path that would get me off the rocks for a while. He smilingly assured me that he would show me just such a 'road' and was as good as his word. It meant a steep and difficult climb, but despite my ankle, I managed to cover over two kilometres in a couple of hours and that felt marvellous. The young man made it all the better by telling me that the part of the river I had just come through was known to be 'very dangerous' and many fishermen had broken bones in falls among the loose rocks.

He left me with a cheery wave and I plodded on, feeling better about life and wishing I hadn't wasted my birthday call to Deborah by snivelling like a baby through most of it.

*   *   *

It was like an oasis in the desert and I spotted it from a long way off. At first, it was merely a pale smudge beneath a towering cliff where the river took a turn to the south, but as I drew closer, I could see that it was flat land with sand and grass, interspersed with a couple of straggly trees.

The last few hundred metres to this haven seemed particularly hard, but that was probably because I was in a hurry to get there and enjoy more comfortable conditions than I had experienced for many a long day. Soft sand tore at my calf muscles, but gritting my teeth I ploughed on, my ankle shrieking in protest. It was mid morning and the sun was high overhead, so my body streamed with sweat, despite the night before having been particularly cold.

My little oasis was situated at the mouth of a gap in the hills that seemed to lead inland. I could see no sign of a riverbed, so it was just a fissure in the hills caused by geological upheavals many millennia previously. Whatever the case, I didn't mind and I felt supremely happy as I explored what had to be my camp for the night.

Soft grass was everywhere and in the sand, I noticed spoor of hippopotami and duiker. Birds clamoured cheerfully and as I scattered my kit around, I was able to watch in rapt fascination as a baboon on the opposite bank was dive bombed by two angry plovers.

The 'bobbo' had obviously strayed close to the plovers' nest and they were driving her away with a great deal of screaming invective and a series of steep dives that ended centimetres above her head. At times the baboon – a young female, so what she was doing away from the troop was unclear – would raise herself on her hind legs and slap with her forepaws at the shrieking attackers, but she was fighting a losing battle.

Eventually, the birds left her alone, so I presumed she was far enough from the nest not to pose a danger any longer. Smiling to myself, I prepared a fire for tea and felt my muscles relax as I sprawled out on the grass and let my mind drift.

The hills on the Zimbabwe side of the river were lower than they had been and much further away from the river itself. There too, was a vast meadow of green grass, interspersed with palm trees and I dared to hope I was getting to the end of the gorges. I knew from experience that it was too early to count chickens, but I faced the rest of the day with more equanimity than I had felt in ages.

And it was a good day. Hippos grunted through the afternoon, fish eagles shrieked raucously to the heavens and as evening enveloped the land, flocks of birds hurtled overhead, obviously on their way to roosting areas upstream. Every time they went over, the sound of thousands of beating wings was loud in the stillness. I didn't know what species they were and not for the first time, regretted not having bird book or binoculars with me. It had been a difficult decision to make before I started, but even the smallest of books and lightest of binos would have been more to carry and I was weary enough with what I had.

I ate well that evening and went to bed feeling pleased with myself. Peering downstream, the cliffs were definitely less awesome than they had been in previous days and although I still had rock banks to get across, I could see areas of white sand between the stones, so hopefully, the going would be easier the following morning.

My sleep patterns had changed during my nights in the gorges. I would go to bed with the onset of darkness and usually had little difficulty in dropping off to sleep, but after an hour of light slumber, I would be awake again. I seemed to manage an hour at a time of this half sleep until midnight and then I would drop into deeper sleep, but still only for an hour. It felt very strange, but I must have been getting enough sleep to keep me going.

It didn't feel like it though.

On this particular night, the grass and soft sand was balm to my tortured hips and I slept reasonably well – or would have had not a hippo made a lot of noise from the opposite bank. I had watched him approach during the evening and hoped he would come and feed on my bank, but just before darkness fell, I saw him lumbering ashore in Zimbabwe. He spent much of the night, snorting and chuckling to himself, whether at my presence or not, I had no way of knowing, but it did not help my sleep.

A distant hyena added his voice to the night and I loved that. They might not be the prettiest of animals, but the sound of those whooping calls always reassures me that I am back in wild Africa, where I belong.

Just before the dawn, I could hear something moving around on my side of the river, but the moon had gone and I couldn't see what it was. Nevertheless, the sound was comforting and my final sleep of the night was a deep one indeed. I was up before the dawn and couldn't help reflecting that if anyone could see the way I wobbled at daybreak, they would be amazed that I had managed to get as far as I had. My back ached abominably in the mornings and my legs took time to sort themselves out, so that I staggered around like a drunk for the first ten minutes of the day. Then everything seemed to settle back into its allotted space and I could get on with things.

My first task was to make myself a cup of tea or coffee – depending on how I felt – and that was usually drunk in bed while I watched daylight creep across the landscape. Never wanting to waste water, a second cup would follow and then it was a question of a leisurely clean up and careful distribution of the various items in my pack. Once it was light and I could see that I wasn't leaving anything behind, the pack would be slung on to my back – usually accompanied by a woof of expelled breath as the weight hit me – and off I would go.

During the early weeks of my walk, I had managed over four kilometres in my first hour, but through the gorges, I rarely managed four kilometres a day. The early mornings were quite enjoyable though as the pain, weariness and frustrations of the day hadn't yet had time to take effect.

I have to confess that when I left what I fondly remember as my 'oasis camp,' I was full of confidence that I was coming to the end of the gorges and even managed to whistle before it became necessary to conserve my breath.

It was a lovely start after an excellent twenty hours, but as I picked my way through the first rock bank, I cautioned myself not to become too cocky.

There was a long way to go and I knew from bitter experience how the Zambezi could build me up and then knock me down again just as quickly and with far more effect.

* * *

I don't suppose many people ever think about how life would be without a bum, but such thoughts were ever present in my mind. One's bottom is such an essential part of the anatomy, but mine had disappeared and as my usual seat was a rock or fallen tree, the act of sitting down was becoming ever more painful. I was literally sitting on bones and it hurt.

But I was making progress again and it was a wonderful feeling. I was still deep in the gorges, but the slopes on either side of the river no longer towered vertically above me, but were gentler and more varied. Although I still had masses of rocks to get over, they were loosely spread, so I was able to pick my way through them.

In the three weeks since I had left Livingstone, I had covered under eighty kilometres, so progress had been slow, but on the day after making camp in my 'oasis,' I did my first five-kilometre day in what seemed a long time. My heels still bled profusely and my heart hammered in my chest with the exertion, but I had regained a bit of confidence and pushed on, feeling that all was not yet lost.

After days on end without seeing people, villages began to appear and in one of them I met a cheerful soul called David, who told me that the going ahead was relatively easy. David was on his way to a neighbouring village to collect milk and invited me to accompany him, but I did not have the strength to keep up, so waved him on his way. I had asked him about the path ahead as I was terrified of taking wrong turns and he left large arrows in the sand to show me exactly where to go. It was so typical of these gentle, helpful Toka Rea people and when we met up again at the next village, I thanked him profusely.

I met two Zimbabwean fishermen, Joe and Pirie among the rocks and they told me that they lived in Hwange, but found it easier to fish on the Zambian side of the river.

"People are friendlier here and the police don't hassle us as they do at home," Joe told me and I shared an excellent breakfast with them. I even tried what Pirie referred to as 'bottlefish caviar,' which was the roe of a bottlenose. I didn't like it much, but then I have never been partial to caviar. Both my companions roared with laughter when I made a face.

I had been following a fairly distinct path just before I met the Zimbabweans, but when it turned and headed directly inland, I left it to keep as close to the river as I could. Pirie told me that the path would have cut off a wide bend in the river, so I went back and tried to find it. All I managed was to get lost and find myself in a deep gulley, full of loose rocks and *wag n'bietjie* thorn. Cursing my own stupidity, I followed this back to the river and made a reasonable camp, even though two hours of exhausting, blundering progress had taken me but a couple of hundred metres downstream. It was frustrating, but I was at least making progress.

On 2nd September, I decided that I was not going to make it through Mozambique and would have to call a halt before I reached the border. The sensible option was to stop right then and there, calling for help through my satellite phone. My GPS – how I cursed all this technology – would give my exact global position and there had to be a road somewhere, even if it was twenty kays away. My problem was that I still felt that I could salvage something from the trip if I carried on until I had a thousand miles (sixteen hundred kilometres) and six months under my belt. That would mean going on past Sinazongwe, but I reckoned that even if I managed five kays a day, I could reach Siavonga by the end of October, which would achieve both goals and make me the first person to walk right around Lake Kariba.

It was a difficult decision, but once it was made, I felt better. I would tell Andy and beg his forgiveness when I could, but in the meantime, I determined to enjoy the rest of the walk, no matter what it cost me in pain, hunger and weariness.

Deka Drum came and went on the Zimbabwean side and I looked longingly across at the buildings and wondered whether anyone would spot me and come across to see what I was doing. Visions of a good meal filled my mind and I could even smell something cooking. However, nobody came across and I trudged on, feeling distinctly dissatisfied with life.

A couple of mornings later, I was forced inland by a tributary that seemed to stretch for kilometres. Eventually, I removed my boots and waded across, but found myself caught in thick bush, liberally interspersed with the dreaded *wag n' bietjie*. I have probably explained them before in this narrative, but *wag n'bietjie* is a creeper-like bush with cruelly hooked thorns that tug and tear at whatever comes into contact with them. As this was usually my skin, I was left a bleeding hulk when I escaped from their clutches and finding myself back at the river, I mopped at my lacerated arms and legs with a torn and tatty handkerchief.

A movement caught my eye and I paused to see what it was. I have never been a great admirer of goats, but on this occasion they were a welcome sight. Goats meant a village and I soon found a path that I followed through dense *mopani* forest before coming out at a fishing village.

The headman, John Marimbo eyed my bleeding limbs with obvious concern and called for his wife, Bettina to minister to me. Hot water was produced and a big bottle of Betadine antiseptic. I protested that I had antiseptic cream in my pack and that they should save theirs for genuine emergency, but John – who spoke Dutch and German as well as English and Chitonga – was not having that.

"You are not in good condition Sir," He told me. "It is our honour to treat your wounds."

"I suppose you are going to McDonalds," he added and the thought of one of those massive red and gold 'M' signs in this wildly remote part of Darkest Africa made me double up with laughter. The sheer incongruity of it tickled my somewhat warped sense of humour.

I wondered what he was talking about.

The Lozi paddle standing up

The Tonga sit down

River market at Mongu

They made bathing interesting

Mola preparing for our fishing expedition

'My' Zambezi

Posing with Martin and David - and the banner - in front of
the Victoria Falls. Photograph by Victor Mwansa

Martin Chabilani (carrying my pack, bless him) and James
lead me down the wild Kalomo

Showing the strain

Posing with the Cowbell banner

A genuine cowbell at last

Lilayi orphan Zambezi knows what is good for him.
Photograph by Andy Taylor.

CHAPTER EIGHT

(An Unofficial Official)

Of course, there was no burger sign in the bush and 'MacDonalds' turned out to be the cliff top home of Mac and Alma MacDonald. I spotted the house from the river and wondered whether to call in or keep going, but the prospect of shelter and food won out – as it always did.

It was a steep climb to the property and near the top I crossed a bush airstrip that reminded me of something Karien Kermer had said. She had been talking about possible resting places below the Falls and mentioned an elderly missionary couple who flew their own aircraft.

"I think they are Canadian," she told me, "but I know nothing about them."

In fact, he was from New Zealand, she was Australian and they weren't missionaries. They ran a game farm called Tiger Mile in the hills. Mac was still a strapping man at eighty and had been a pilot all his life.

"I love flying," he told me, "and have built a couple of light aircraft that I use from time to time."

Mac's elder brother Joe was visiting from New Zealand and had I dropped in the previous day, the place would have been empty as they were driving back from Lusaka. Once again, Lemon's Luck had brought me to the right place at the right time.

The house – a thatched dwelling with the darkly cool interior that typifies old houses in hot countries – overlooked the Zambezi and upstream was a gaunt canyon that made my tummy tighten as I remembered clambering over its rocks.

Closer to hand, hippos grunted from the water and I could see impala frolicking beside a tributary. Canyon aside, it was a view to soothe the most tormented of souls.

I spent two delightful days with the MacDonalds and for much of the time, was left on my own to rest, drink tea and read. They had a catholic collection of books and I was put in a garden chalet, so I sat in the shade and devoured book after book. My aches and pains seemed to ease as tension drained from my body.

Mac proudly showed me the aircraft he was building and we went on a drive around the farm, which was stocked with kudu, impala and other specimens of plains game. Alma and I sat in the open back of the vehicle and bumps were hard on my wasted bottom, but it was nice being with a lady again. I had seen few people over preceding weeks and I enjoyed Alma's company.

As with everyone else I had met along the way, the MacDonalds did their best to feed me up, but it was beginning to seem a lost cause. My chalet had a mirror on one wall and after one glimpse of my skeletal reflection, I turned it to the wall so that I would not have to see myself. I was even scaring me at that stage.

Downstream, I could see more rock banks and the thought of crossing those did not appeal.

"That lot don't last long," Mac said when I mentioned my concern. "My man Charles can arrange a guide for you, but how on earth are you going to get through Devils Gorge? You'll have to hitch a lift in a canoe or you will struggle on those cliffs."

Although I airily shrugged off his concerns, it was a worry that had occurred to me. Devils Gorge did not get its name for nothing and I had rowed it in my dinghy, Hobo many years before. I remembered the steep cliffs, craggy faces covered with clinging bush and the thought of climbing through there was not a pleasant one.

However, that was still a few days away and I concentrated on enjoying the hospitality and friendship of three very nice people. The night before I left, Alma told me to check the freezer before I went.

"We won't be up," She smiled, "But I have prepared a few snacks for you to take."

The snacks were fish cakes and hard boiled eggs, a gesture that was truly kind and inevitably brought tears to my eyes.

I kissed her goodbye and shook hands firmly with Mac and Joe. The three of them had provided me with a lovely rest and I was grateful, but I still had a long way to go.

The feelings of confidence, enhanced by my stay with the lovely MacDonalds were soon to ebb away. Back on the river, my body and spirit began to suffer again under the relentless battering being handed out by the Zambezi.

*   *   *

Mac MacDonald's right hand man was a Tonga called Charles, who was self-educated and had gone on to make himself indispensable as a general handyman. He could service a truck, build an aeroplane and sort out any of the difficulties associated with living in the African bush. Be it fixing a plumbing problem or finding flowers for Alma's garden, Charles was the man everyone turned to.

"He really is a great chap," Mac told me enthusiastically. "I am not sure I could manage this place without him."

Charles and I spent time looking for a suitable guide to take me through the next lot of gorges and found an old boy called Nicholas who offered to do the job for five US dollars. I was happy with that and Nicholas promised to collect me early the following morning.

"Nicholas is our local hero," Charles told me. "Some months ago, we had a robber in the area and Nicholas took a loaded AK rifle off him, before taking him to the police in Livingstone."

He must have seen the look on my face as he smiled.

"He didn't walk like you did," He went on. "The Boss took him to the main road and he took the bus, but nobody offered him a reward and nor has he received any government recognition of his courage."

That seemed a shame and I gave Charles the phone number I had for Minister Lubinda. I hope that in due course Nicholas' bravery will be recognised.

At five the next morning, I was up and waiting, but as always, we were going by Tonga time and eventually set off at a quarter past six. It wasn't Nicholas escorting me either, but one of his sons, a cheerful soul called Katora. I had been looking forward to hearing more about the episode with the armed robber, but Katora talked only about himself. After months of silent walking, it was difficult to concentrate on my footing as well my loquacious companion.

We made steady progress along a faintly defined track that overlooked the river. It was hard going, but Katora pointed out a camp site at Msuna Mouth from which I could distinctly smell bacon frying and then the actual opening of the Msuna River a kilometre further downstream. At midday, our progress was halted by a wide tributary, but Katora sat down and gestured for me to do the same.

"They will come to fetch us," He said and ten minutes later, a large canoe nosed out from the opposite bank. The boat had room for both of us and my pack, but Katora whispered that I was expected to pay the boatman for his kindness.

He put us down on the edge of a village and I handed over a couple of thousand kwacha, which were gratefully received. A group of elders looked up in surprise when I appeared in their midst. Katora explained my presence in rapid Chitonga and a chair was produced for me to sit on.

"You must be tired Sir," The bearer of the chair told me and he was right.

Katora told me that he had to be home before dark and held his hand out for the promised five dollars. As he disappeared, I felt a sudden sense of abandonment that was unusual. I had been in hundreds of similar villages and spoken with many groups of elders, but this lot obviously looked at me with considerable suspicion.

They continued talking among themselves, but eventually a powerfully built fellow approached me.

"I am Shadreck," He announced. "I will take you to my village where you can sleep tonight."

It is difficult to estimate age among the Tonga, but Shadreck must have been well into his fifties. Nevertheless, he set a brisk pace through rocky hills and I struggled to keep up. The path we were following was narrow and in places only suitable for mountain goats, but I forced myself on. I wasn't sure whether Shadreck was testing my stamina, but he kept the pace going and when he paused to ask whether he could help with my pack, I was surprised to hear myself turn down his offer.

I was not going to show weakness in front of the man.

We must have walked for an hour in sweltering heat before dropping down a precipitous slope among the rocks and arriving at Kanjeza village on the edge of the Zambezi.

It was a beautiful spot and I walked to the river to get my breath back after that punishing walk.

"This is my house," Shadreck pointed out a basic Tonga hut. "You can sleep in there if you like."

It was a generous offer from a man whose unsmiling countenance belied a kindly nature, but I told him I preferred sleeping in the open and laid my bed beneath an orange tree, unfortunately devoid of fruit.

I gave Shadreck some of my tobacco, while he prepared food and he told me he had set up the village in 1997 and was happy to see out his life in Kanjeza.

"There were few of us then," He said proudly. "Now we are a big village and catch lots of fish. None of us are rich, but we live well."

It seemed there was a road on the hills behind the camp and when I asked Shadreck about Devils Gorge, he advised me to take that road.

"It is rough country in the gorge," He warned. "If you fall, you will die."

His warning supplemented Mac McDonald's and I wondered whether to ask for a ride through the gorge in his canoe. I did not want to burden anyone else with my difficulties however and felt that if I was going to walk this ruddy river, I had to do it on my own. Climbing up to the road was a daunting prospect and I was not sure I could manage it.

"I will escort you to Makongo tomorrow," Shadreck promised. "From there, it is easier to reach the road."

I spent a disturbed night wondering what to do.

$$* \qquad * \qquad *$$

Suddenly I knew how a fly feels when it is caught in a spider's web. With only two hours of daylight left, I was perched helplessly on a steep cliff face and pinned to the stone by clinging vegetation. *Wag 'n bietjie* and other thorns tore at my arms and legs and although I was trying to cut my way through matted branches, the blades on my Leatherman were too puny to do much good.

Four metres below, the Zambezi flowed malevolently past and brown water seemed to leer up, telling me what would happen if I fell from my precarious position. I would drown. There could be no question about that. The weight of my pack would drag me down and death would at least be swift. As if to emphasise the morbid thought, a crocodile slid silently into the current below me.

I was making tortuous progress. Many of the rocks were loose and every centimetre of forward movement had to be tested before I could entrust my weight to the cliff. I had to concentrate and ensure my weight was evenly distributed or the pack would drag me backward with probably fatal results.

I had woken that morning to the sound of singing and a fisherman telling the world what a successful night he had enjoyed.

"I am the greatest fisherman in Zambia," He wasn't speaking quietly. "If I keep going in this way, the river Zambezi will lose all its fish. I am just too clever."

That was how a smiling Shadreck interpreted the diatribe for me and judging by the expression on the man's face, I'm sure it was accurate.

With full daylight, Shadreck led me up another steep path, but I seemed to have proved myself and he didn't set nearly as brisk a pace as he had the day before.

We arrived at Makongo village where another meeting was taking place. This time it was the village committee setting the world to rights and they had a secretary taking minutes. Shadreck handed me over to the headman, Ignatius who arranged breakfast of *nshima* and hippo meat. When Shadreck explained my intentions, Ignatius frowned.

"It will be dangerous," He warned. "You must take the road to Namesu fishing camp."

But the warnings were having a negative effect and I became ever more determined to take the gorge. I knew I was being foolish, but was determined to prove them all wrong.

It was midday when I moved on and fiendishly hot. I should probably have stayed at Makongo overnight, but having gone against all reasonable advice, I almost felt obliged to move off so that nobody could witness my embarrassment should things go wrong.

I had been walking – 'scrambling' is a better description – for forty minutes when the rocks disappeared under a blanket of thick vegetation. I tried climbing over this then moved further up the cliff in the hopes that it would thin out a little.

It didn't. Creepers that had been relatively light on the lower slopes seemed to thicken and become more clinging. Thorny scrub appeared between the branches and I had to hack my way to make progress. I was in the direct rays of the sun and sweat poured down my body. I was moving less than two metres every half hour and wondered what I would do if I was still on that dreadful cliff when night fell. It was an appalling thought and although I knew I could survive, the prospect was terrifying.

Thorns ripped at my exposed skin and blood poured down my body. I heard my shirt tear and the flowing blood was matched by flowing tears. I was stuck on that dreadful cliff and would probably have to die there. I should have listened to all the well-intentioned advice, but had been too stubborn to do so. Nightfall was drawing closer and to spend a night on a thorny cliff in an upright position was going to make life very difficult.

"Are you alright, Sir?"

I thought I had dreamed the voice and shook my head in irritation, but it came again.

"Are you alright?"

There was nobody else on the cliff, but when I managed to look downward, I saw a battered 'banana boat' with three occupants peering up at me.

"No I am not alright. I am stuck on this bloody cliff."

I had to sound gruff or I would have burst into tears.

"If you can climb down here, Sir, we will give you a lift to Namesu," My unexpected benefactor called hesitantly. "Or my friends can climb up and bring your bag down."

I assured him I would get down under my own steam, but once again I was being foolishly stubborn. A ten metre descent took me half an hour, but eventually, I perched precariously on rocks beside the boat and swung that horrible pack across. My rescuer smiled at me.

"They told us at Makongo that you were walking this way," He said happily. "We thought you might need help, so have been looking out for you.

'My name is Linda Evans," He added and I felt too despondent to query it. With a feeling of despair, I climbed into the boat.

*   *   *

Even with three men paddling, it took an hour to get through the gorge and looking up at those cliffs, I reckoned would have taken me three days – if I made it at all.

The banana boat was heavily laden with four adults, my pack and six bags of hippo meat, so my time was spent baling out water, steadily rising around my feet.

Linda Evans – that was his real name – was buying hippo meat to sell at his home in Choma. He told me that a hippo had recently died in the area, but we both knew he was lying. I had heard that a purge on the animals was taking place and been served with a lot of hippo over the preceding week. It was sad, but people had to eat.

Linda Evans kept glancing at me in obvious concern and when I asked what was bothering him, he pointed to my legs and the blood-reddened water lapping about my ankles.

"You have lost much blood," He pointed out. "We should land, so you can clean it off and put bandages."

But now that I was in the relative comfort of a boat, I had no intention of going near those unforgiving cliffs and I waved him on, assuring him that my wounds were skin deep and would heal.

It was dark when lights appeared ahead and when I asked Linda (he called himself Evans) where they came from, he said we were approaching Mlibizi at the top of Lake Kariba.

For me, it was a thrilling moment in spite of the circumstances. I was almost back on the lake that has been part of my life for decades. I was coming home and it felt good.

But we were still an hour from Namesu and when my companions finally shipped their paddles, I staggered ashore like a drunk. My legs were rubbery and my vision blurred, but I tottered toward the light of a fire, while Evans carried my pack. Feeling weak and sick, I laid out my bedroll beneath a tree. I didn't feel like making conversation and within moments, had fallen into a deep sleep.

'Namesu' means jellyfish in Chitonga and in daylight, it turned out to be a sprawling camp beside the lake with the buildings of Mlibizi visible across the water. Shortly after dawn, Evans appeared with an elder called Maxwell and both were concerned for my welfare.

"We have been talking about your journey," He told me gravely. "We can see that you are not well, so we will take you to Mlibizi in a canoe. The Kariba Ferry leaves there today, so you will be safe until you reach Kariba."

It was a lovely offer and typical of these friendly Tonga folk, but I still had a walk to complete. I assured them that although I probably didn't look too good, I was in fine form and would move on down the lakeshore the following day.

Maxwell was horrified.

His English wasn't as good as Evans' but the younger man translated a torrent of rapid Chitonga.

"We have prepared a sleeping hut for you, so you must stay for some days and rest your body. The way ahead is hard and you need to build up your strength. We have fish and *nshima*, so we can feed you up."

I assured them I had food of my own but would be pleased to spend another day with them in Namesu. That seemed to satisfy everyone and I enjoyed the day in a typical lakeside fishing camp. The routine was similar to that of the riverside establishments, but the fishermen operated in wider and wilder waters. They seemed graver and more serious than their counterparts upstream, but they were just as hospitable. Maxwell and I spent the morning in desultory conversation, while he repaired nets and after cleaning up my kit and applying antiseptic to my grazes, I sat near him, reading from my Kindle.

Technology of that sort was a novelty in Tonga society and I soon had a number of curious fishermen around me, asking me how it worked and reading aloud when I opened pages. To an onlooker, it would have been a marvellous study of the new world meeting the old in the twenty-first century. Throughout the day, small deputations – many of them women and children - would shyly approach and ask to see 'the book.' They were fascinated by this example of technology from a world they would never experience and I didn't know whether to be sad that they didn't have access to such wonders or envious of the simplicity of their lives.

Martin Sims was Namesu's football fanatic and regaled me with stories about '*Chipolopolo*,' the National football side who in 2011 had become Champions of Africa. He knew the names of each player and followed all their matches. Zambia were due to play Uganda the following day and Martin told me that he would watch the game on television. Apparently, there was a school twenty-seven kilometres inland and he was going to walk there. The fact that he would then have to walk back didn't worry him.

"If they win, I shall be happy," He grinned at me. "If they lose, I won't care how far I must walk."

A simple philosophy, but one typical of these inhabitants of rural Africa. In every village I visited, I found myself humbled by the accepting natures and smiling enthusiasm of its residents.

"Will you come to dinner with me?"

Martin asked the question and for a moment, I was taken aback. Nobody had ever given me such a formal invitation in the course of my African travels, but my footballing friend was genuine and I was pleased to accept. Dinner was scheduled for seven that evening and I wandered across the village to Martin's house and was made welcome. A wooden stool was produced and I sat on that while he prepared the meal – inevitably *nshima* and fish, but I didn't mind.

I have been to dinner in many grand houses and eaten in restaurants all over the world, but that simple meal in a mud hut at Namesu was so genuinely offered and so innocently prepared that it will live long in my memory.

As I settled down to sleep that night, I reflected that I would never truly understand the Tonga people, but they had to be among the nicest and most genuine folk in the world.

*   *   *

Linda Evans had decided to see me off the following morning, but it was Maxwell – whose name turned out to be Emmanuelle Madina - who appeared from the gloom.

"I will escort you," He said simply. "It is a long walk, so let's go."

And go we did. He might have looked an old man, but Maxwell was in his early forties and the pace he set was too brisk for me. I dropped further and further behind as we wandered along a path through *mopani* scrub and I wondered how far we were getting from the lake. I could feel the familiar water worries welling up in my chest.

We must have covered two kilometres before Maxwell noticed that I had dropped back. He offered to carry my pack and I readily agreed. Walking without it was a treat, particularly through countryside that was fascinating in its forbidding barrenness. A small snake slithered across the path and Maxwell gave chase for a metre or two before the weight of the pack proved too much for him. I laughed, but felt a sense of relief that it had escaped.

"Ah, but this is too heavy," My guide complained. "I am too old to carry loads like this."

"Huh!" I scoffed. "I am twice your age and have carried it for many months. How do you think I feel?"

"Ah but all *wazungu* are mad," He told me frankly. "You are madder than most because you walk when you could ride in a truck or take a boat. As for this," he gestured toward the pack on his back, "why do you not pay a young man to carry it for you?"

Why not indeed? But the thought of having constant company was too much for me.

"I will pay you then Maxwell," I grinned. "How much would you want to escort me to Siavonga – and carry my pack of course?"

The look on his face said it all. There was no way that a senior fisherman like Maxwell would be caught dead carrying 'luggage' like some village woman. With a contemptuous spit in the dust, he shook his head and resumed walking.

It was nearly an hour before we returned to the lake. A small canoe rested among reeds and a youth greeted us cheerfully.

"I will leave you here," Maxwell gave me a rare smile that was probably engendered by relief at being able to hand the pack back. "This young man will take you to the village of Evans."

The 'village of Evans' was a collection of five huts perched on a hillside and the man himself was there to greet me.

"I would have collected you at Namesu," He told me. "But Maxwell wanted to escort you himself."

That was nice and I smiled at the thought that behind Maxwell's crotchety exterior, there was a kind man. Linda Evans was wearing a white shirt over jeans, the ensemble rounded off by a pair of gleaming white shoes. I wondered where he was going in such smart clothes, but he seemed to have taken responsibility for my welfare and twenty minutes later, was walking ahead of me, my pack sitting comfortably on his shoulders.

Again, we walked inland, but I had learned that locals knew the paths so although it seemed the wrong direction, I followed meekly in his wake.

This time, it was a hard walk as my young guide set a cruel pace, despite the weight on his shoulders. We climbed into hills and by the time we reached the crest of a ridge, the sun was well up and I was drenched in sweat. The countryside was arid mopani scrub and there were few signs of life apart from the occasional cooing of a dove or the mellifluous chatter of a bulbul – or toppie as they were colloquially known.

At last, we came down again and wandered through the outskirts of a large fishing camp.

"We will see the chairman and he will direct us onward," Evans told me and I wondered how long my Choma friend intended to escort me. Not that I minded. Although not a large man, he was strong enough to carry the pack without showing distress and I was happy for him to continue with it as long as he liked.

The chairman – for some reason I didn't record his name or the name of the camp – was a young man and had returned the previous day from a shopping trip to Mlibizi. We were served breakfast of bread and peanut butter, washed down with sweet tea that even had milk in it. What a treat that was. I had to stop myself from eating too much. The villagers' needs were greater than mine. As I ate, my every move was studied with rapt attention by the village ladies and their offspring. At the start of my walk it would have unnerved me, but I ignored them and got on with my repast.

After breakfast, the chairman shook my hand and spoke in rapid Chitonga to my companion. Linda Evans turned to me with a smile on his face.

"I have told him you are employed by the government," I was aghast. "There is talk about closing fishing camps from December to March and I have said you are looking into the problems."

"But why?" I protested. "That will make me an enemy to everyone."

Evans shook his head.

"No, you will find that everyone will want to look after you and tell you their stories while they escort you from camp to camp. I will take you to Twabani which is not far and hand you over to the chairman who will take you on.

'You will see."

It sounded fraught with difficulty, but I followed meekly to Twabani fishing camp, where I bade farewell to my strangely-named young friend, who after a conversation with the village chairman, told me not to worry.

"You will be okay," He sounded confident. "Just don't talk much and look as though you are paying attention to your surroundings when you get into a camp. Each chairman will escort you onward and hand you over to the next one."

It was not an ideal arrangement. I needed time on my own and preferred sleeping beneath the stars to sleeping under shelter, but Linda Evans was so enthusiastic that I didn't have the heart to tell him so. There was nothing for it but to go along with his plans.

At least I wouldn't get lost for a while.

*　　　*　　　*

What worried me most about my newly acquired status as an unofficial official was that I would be questioned and not have answers. Evans had brushed my doubts aside.

"These Tonga people are too polite to question you," He opined. "They will be nice to you and hope you will help them with the government."

It seemed an underhand way of getting help from people who had looked after me whenever they could, but I had little choice in the matter.

The chairman at Twabani was another Shadreck, but he was a giant of a man who looked far too heavy to paddle a dugout canoe. He insisted that I stay the night and take advantage of Twabani hospitality.

Wandering around that afternoon, I stopped to chat with a youngster carrying a vervet monkey by its hands. The dead animal looked sad and Christopher told me he had shot it with his catapult. When I asked what he intended to do with it, he smiled at my naiveté.

"I shall eat it," He said with enthusiasm. "Monkeys are good meat. Do you want to share it with me?"

Although it seemed like cannibalism and there couldn't be much meat on a monkey, it was an opportunity to try something new, so I accompanied him to his hut and we sat in the shade, while his wife prepared the meal.

It was delicious, despite my misgivings. The meat was white and tender, the flavour a delicate one that lingered on my palate for hours. I felt sorry for the monkey, but I hadn't been responsible for its demise, so banished my scruples and enjoyed the meal.

We made a late start the following morning, but Shadreck strode through the bush as though he owned it all.

"These are my people," He announced as we passed a group of women with their children. "They look to me to provide and I am their father, but if the camps are closed for four months, we will all starve."

It was the first direct reference I had received to my supposed role as a government agent and I hummed and ha'd without saying anything that might lead to misunderstandings. Shadreck seemed to forget the matter entirely and greeted everyone we passed with roaring salutations. I trudged morosely behind him, wondering what trouble I had been dropped in by Linda Evans who had only been trying to help.

The next camp was Chavuma and we had a tributary to cross before reaching it. Shadreck found a leaky canoe in some reeds and despite his bulk, hopped into this and indicated that I should sit in the bow with my pack. I looked somewhat askance at the flimsy craft, but with Shadreck paddling, we shot across the water. I didn't have time to bale and when we nosed into the opposite bank, found myself sitting in six inches of water. Fortunately, the hot sun soon dried everything.

Chavuma contained over fifty residents and I was a solemn spectator at an inter-camp draughts match between Shadreck and the Chavuma chairman, a muscular fellow, introduced to me as Cholo, although his name was Sidney Kalongo. The game was played with bottle tops on a home-made board and they played with fierce intensity. I am not sure who won, but honours were probably even as both men were smiling when they finished. Another meal was produced and at the end of it, Shadreck bade me farewell and jumped into the leaky canoe.

He headed across the river with a final wave and I was left with Sidney, who told me that he was not a Tonga, but a Bemba from further north.

"When the lake was first built," He mused. "The Tonga people were farmers and had to be taught how to fish, so my grandparents were brought down from the Kafue area to teach them. They stayed on and here I am, but Chibemba is spoken in my camp."

He showed me around the camp, which was remarkable for two reasons. Firstly, there was an all-woman fishing crew, led by Sidney's wife, Rose and secondly, I met a man called Douglas who was eighty-three years old and still fishing. I had been pleased with my own performance of walking a long way at sixty-seven, but if I can still cope with the harsh life of a Kariba fisherman when I reach eighty, I really will be proud. Douglas was a sprightly man with a big smile and laughed bashfully when I complimented him on his stamina at such a ripe age.

"Work is good for us, Sir," He said proudly. "I can only work as a fisherman as I don't know any other life."

The female crew was even more unique. There were three of them and in misogynistic Tonga society, I could only imagine what difficulties they must have faced to set themselves up. They used a banana boat and did their own repairs, smilingly assuring me that they were more successful than many of the male crews. Talking to them, I could well believe it.

Chavuma had a wide beach fronting the lake and in the middle of this was a small tree surrounded by grass, where I determined to make my camp for the night.

Sidney was horrified.

"We can put you in a house," He exclaimed when I told him my intentions. "My wife will cook for you and you won't be annoyed by mosquitoes."

But I wanted to sleep outside and shrugged his arguments aside. As the sun tumbled toward the horizon, I set up my bedding and hung my mosquito net from a convenient branch. The water was calm and as I made coffee over a small fire, I reflected that this would be my first night alone beside the lake in a very long time.

I was determined to enjoy it.

*   *   *

I reckoned to reach Siavonga and the dam wall in six weeks and gazing at the stars through my mosquito net, I pondered on the problem with which I had become so unwittingly associated. Fish stocks throughout the lake could not last forever, so the government scheme to ban fishing for four months of the year was a good one. It would give the fish a chance to regroup, but would spell disaster for fishing villages like Chavuma. They relied on fish for their income and without money, entire villages would find it difficult to survive.

It was an insurmountable problem, but despite my new and uncomfortable role as government official, it wasn't mine. Linda Evans' inspired bit of trickery would probably make life easier over the next few days, but I wondered how I would get out of being a 'representative of the government.'

I was up at five and lost myself in the joys of a Kariba morning. Daylight crept across the lake and my fire was comforting as water boiled for coffee. Waves slapped gently against rocks and a fish eagle shrieked his greeting to the new day. Guinea fowl chuckled nearby and I could hear movement in the village. The Tonga were early risers and I approved.

It was still quite dark when the first canoes knifed across the water and the lady crew called out and waved as they went past. I wished them luck with their fishing and wondered why it was that although Tonga women were generally shy in my presence, their grasp of English was usually so much better than that of their menfolk.

Sidney had promised to take me through a short cut that went directly across the Western end of the Binga Basin and we set off at eight. This time, I walked in a convoy of young men, Sidney in the lead and my pack carried by a hefty youth called Amos.

The going was hard but at eleven, we arrived in Simuzunga where Sunday service was in full swing. Church pews were fashioned from single poles, supported by bricks and the Minister was a young man obviously well fed. Fat Tonga are a rarity and I sourly reflected that he was living well on the generosity of others.

I might have stayed, but the service was in Chitonga, so I wandered down to the shore, where Sidney and the young men of Chavuma were drinking traditional beer and listening to blaring music on a radio. A boy of about twelve demonstrated nifty dance steps in the dust and Sidney introduced me to the chairman, who was called Staff. I presumed that the same story was told to explain my presence, but Staff did not seem enthused to learn that it was his responsibility to take me on to the next village.

"My Treasurer will take you later," He promised, but 'later' in Tonga society could mean minutes or hours. In this case, it was hours and although I had been given a stool to sit on, the sun was hot and I was bored. I tried reading from the Kindle, which attracted the usual admiring crowd, but I was not enjoying myself. I could see the next village on the other side of a wide bay and wondered about walking to it on my own.

When I mentioned the possibility to Sidney, he was shocked.

"I will get this chairman moving," He growled and was as good as his word. Ten minutes later, my pack was on my shoulders and Staff was ready to go. Sidney and his young men crowded around to bid me farewell and I was sorry to leave them. Chavuma had been a lovely camp and I would remember my Bemba friends for a very long time. I had been taught how to say 'good morning' in Chibemba, but when I tried out my 'Amakai kashuken' on Staff, he looked blank, although Sidney and his group howled with laughter.

It was still hot when we set off around the bay, but I was glad to be on the move again, even though I had to carry my own pack.

*　　　*　　　*

The next camp was the end of my role as a government official. We arrived late in the afternoon, to be told that the chairman was away. Staff asked whether I wanted to meet the village secretary instead. I declined that honour and spent the night in a small bay further along the shoreline. I had enjoyed my second relay-baton existence, but it was nice to be alone again.

Staff had not been the greatest of hosts, but the three chairmen before him had been nice fellows and couldn't do enough for me. Whether this was due to my assumed status as a government official or the generosity of their personalities,

I wasn't sure but their assistance had allowed me to make better progress than I would have done otherwise.

My next target was the crocodile farm at Siansowa owned by someone called Jordaan. At various times, I was informed that I was thirty kilometres, nineteen kilometres and forty-three kilometres from the place. Probably the most reliable estimate came when I met a pair of kapenta fishermen, called Foster and Webster – it sounded like a comedy act – who were relaxing after a hard nights work.

"You have forty kilometres to go," Webster informed me knowledgeably. "You should do that in two days."

I laughed. If I made it in four days, I would have done well and a week seemed a better estimate. I sat with the kapenta men for a while and they told me about the state of fishing on the lake.

Limnothrissa Miodan, the Tanzanian sardine was introduced to Lake Kariba in 1967 and proved an instant success. Conditions suited the little fish and their numbers rocketed until licences were issued by the Zimbabwean and Zambian government to harvest them.

Quick fortunes had been made, as kapenta proved a nutritious staple food for the people of both countries. In recent years the position had deteriorated. A system of open licensing had come about in Zambia and the lake was carrying too many fishing rigs, many of which were hardly viable, let alone safe.

"This is what we caught last night," Foster showed me half a tray of fish, some of which were hardly larger than tadpoles. "On a good night, we will get two trays, but there are no big kapenta left."

That evening, I reflected that if the government were to call an annual four month moratorium on kapenta fishing, it would prove more beneficial than closing down the fishing camps for that length of time.

Webster was a giant of man, shaven headed and very black for a Tonga. He was full of enthusiasm and insisted on lifting my pack to see how heavy it was. While putting it down again, one massive hand gripped the end of my fishing rod and the flimsy fibreglass snapped. I hadn't used the rod much, but it was always there as an alternative way of getting food and that accident was a bad blow. The big man seemed mortified, so I let it go with a smile although I was on my way soon afterward.

I just wasn't enjoying company.

I wasn't enjoying much at that stage and my evenings were spent in fretful wondering about the way ahead. My decision to quit was eating into my soul, yet I knew it was the right one. I could reach Siavonga and that would mean I had walked over a thousand miles, but what would I do then? After my experiences along the Kalomo River and in the gorges, I dreaded the same sort of punishment in the Kariba and Mupata gorges, not to mention the wild countryside around Cabora Bassa. It would take an enormous amount out of me and I wasn't sure I had much left to give.

My body was exhausted and seemingly disintegrating with each additional step, while my mind and soul were weary from constant punishment. In my sensible moments, I knew I couldn't continue beyond Siavonga, but then I would worry about coping with failure. I had always succeeded in my little adventures and wasn't sure how my self confidence would react to not achieving my objective.

Besides, I had sponsors and didn't want to let them down. Cowbell had invested a great deal in me and I felt a sense of responsibility toward them as well as my other sponsors, Fluxcon and the Together Agency.

At that stage I had no option but to continue walking and hope that I could come to a firm decision before meeting Andy at Sinazongwe. Once I told him, I would be committed, whichever way it went, but I had about two weeks in which to make a firm decision.

It was in a troubled frame of mind that I wandered into a fishing camp one morning. Meeting up with a boy called

Peter, I asked the way and was directed to a narrow track, heading inland.

"From here it is but a short way before you come back to the lake and find other camps," Peter told me, but he was wrong. The path wound through desolate hills and forest. I walked for hour after hour without seeing a soul or even a footprint in the dust. I might have been alone in the world and the feeling of emptiness was exacerbated by the fact that there was no sound from the surrounding bush. No birds sang and when I stopped on occasion to listen, the deep silence was oppressive.

I walked for seven and a half hours that day and although I put a lot of kilometres behind me, it was a dreadful experience and made even more dents in my waning self-confidence.

The Jordaans, Sinazongwe and Siavonga seemed a long way away and I didn't think I would reach any of them, let alone far off Chinde on the Indian Ocean.

*   *   *

The Sabi Star bloomed alone in bleak countryside. I was feeling very despondent, but the little pink flowers looked so pretty in that desolation that they gave an immediate lift to my spirits.

The going over the previous few days had been hard and I had fallen repeatedly for no apparent reason. One moment I would be walking along, then I would stumble and inevitably fall. My knees were badly grazed and it was upsetting as well as painful, because it seemed obvious that my general condition was deteriorating rapidly.

Each evening, my socks were full of blood from my cracked heels and walking was becoming ever more painful, particularly over rough ground. My teeth were rattling in my mouth, I was subject to vicious headaches and dizzy spells were frequent. I also had a number of painful mouth ulcers. My evenings were spent in anguished consideration of my problems and constant questioning of myself as to whether I should pack up or keep going once I reached any sort of civilisation.

After seeing that gorgeous little plant in such inhospitable surroundings, I told myself that if the Sabi Star could survive, so could I but it only helped for a while. The days were becoming ever hotter as September rolled along and not only did that baking sun bring sweat streaming from my pores, but it seemed to leech all remaining strength from my body.

A stop at a ramshackle store helped a little. The store was run by a man called Dickson and he proudly told me that he had beer for sale. A warm Mosi lager was produced and if ever a beer – even a warm one – saved a life, this was the occasion. I would have liked a few more, but my finances were precarious, so I stuck with the one.

Dickson showed me a path the following morning and although I started off feeling good, the torment soon began again. Repeated questioning of locals as to how far I was from Siansowa and 'Jordaan,' merely brought a plethora of different answers, which added to my frustrations.

With the nights warming up, mosquitoes added their depredations to the misery of my existence. I would lie and listen to their banshee howling outside the net, but if my skin touched the net, it was quickly chewed by the little monsters. When I awoke in the mornings, they would still be buzzing around and that was never a pleasant start to my day.

I had been walking for thirty-five days since leaving Livingstone and was averaging less than five kilometres per day - hardly speedy progress by any standards. I calculated that at that rate, it would take me a couple of years to reach the sea, rather than the ten months I had originally anticipated.

In one village, a young man called Survival gave me breakfast of *nshima* and very tasty meat. At my query, he told me that it was impala and produced the horns to prove it. Survival was employed as the village security chief and as such, was issued with a shotgun. I wondered where on earth he had found the unfortunate impala, but felt it probably wasn't politic to question him too closely.

I later learned that there was a small game farm attached to the crocodile business at Siansowa, so that probably explained a lot.

At Tachitemba, a strapping fellow called Merius showed me around. There were two shops and five churches in the village and I wondered why the churches didn't get together and use one building. Merius shrugged at my question.

"Perhaps they worship different Gods?" Was his answer to the anomaly.

When I asked the inevitable question as to how far I was from 'Jordaans,' he was more forthcoming.

"I work there sometimes," He said. "It will take you an hour and a half to get there."

That should have been excellent news, but an hour and a half to a young fisherman who played lots of football – he had proudly shown me his boots – probably meant a day and a half to a tottering geriatric like me.

Nevertheless, Merius was up early to show me the first road I had seen in weeks. In fact it was the first road I had seen since Livingstone. Surely it meant easier times ahead?

It didn't. Within an hour of setting off, I had not only lost my way twice, but come across tracks in the sand that could only have come from Courteney boots. I couldn't understand where I had gone wrong, particularly as the road was wide and distinct, but unless there was someone similarly shod in the area, I had to have walked in a circle.

By ten in the morning, I was staggering beneath the onslaught of the sun when two cyclists told me that I still had fourteen kilometres to go. It was a bitter blow, but shortly afterwards, a grand little chap called Phineas – also on a bicycle and coming the other way – turned around and walked with me to show me a short cut. He told me that 'Jordaan' was a friend of his and showed me the man's number on his cell phone.

"Do you want to tell him you are coming?" He asked, but I demurred. I didn't think Mr Jordaan would appreciate it.

I had taken short cuts before and ended up doing more mileage than intended, but Phineas was enthusiastic, so I followed the path he indicated. I was moving slowly in the heat and hardly noticed the villages I passed, but late in the morning, I was stopped by a lady – also on a bicycle – called Mavis.

She offered to take my pack on her bike and we walked together, Mavis chatting about her life and her husband, who worked for Jordaan somewhere up country. At one point on the edge of town, children ran screaming into the bush and Mavis smiled at me.

"They think you are a Satanist," She said seriously. "There have been rumours of people taking children for body parts in this area.

'I don't think the rumours were true though."

She was a kind soul was Mavis and as we walked with her pushing the bicycle, I couldn't help reflecting that her assistance had saved me hours of torment. Walking into Siansowa, she showed me the road to take.

With my spirits lifted by the kindness of another Tonga, I walked with a lighter heart. I had no idea what Mr Jordaan would be like, but he was obviously held in high esteem by local people, so I hoped, he would assist one very weary traveller.

CHAPTER NINE

(Bush Club to Sinazongwe)

I had heard of the Kariba Bush Club, but never intended to visit the place. When I staggered into Johan Jordaan's office that morning, he must have been shocked to have a skeletal apparition with a wild expression interrupt his work, but he hid it well. Calling for tea and orange juice, he listened to my stammered story, then called his wife Christine from the adjoining office.

As with everyone else I had met along the way, they wanted to help and when I mentioned that it was time to move on, Christine was horrified.

"You should stay in our Bush Club, tonight," She told me firmly. "You must be very tired and hungry."

I was and went with Chris to the nearby Bush Club, where she handed me over to Denise Mazhandu with instructions that I be looked after.

An hour later, I was showered, my clothing had been taken away to be laundered and I found myself walking on soft green grass with a round bar and a spectacular view. I was due to meet Andy in Sinazongwe six days later, but it was another forty-five kilometres away and if I stayed at Siansowa long, I wouldn't make it. I sent a message through to him and he promised to do the resupply at the Bush Club.

"I can't make it before Wednesday," He warned. "Ask them to charge your food and drink to Cowbell."

What a treat that was. My money stocks were low and I had been wondering how I could afford supper, so this was another Cowbell lifeline. The camp manager, Muftau seemed pleased to put me up.

"We have a fishing tournament this weekend, so I will be busy, but you can stay as long as you want and it will give us a chance to talk. I am dying to hear about your trip."

My room was a rondavel near the kitchen and if the staff became fed up with my constant requests for tea or coffee, they treated me with friendly courtesy and huge smiles. On that first day, I even bought myself a couple of beers in the afternoon and a generously poured whisky and soda in the evening. What the assembled fishermen thought about the skinny geriatric propping up one end of the bar, I wasn't sure, but despite a few curious looks, they were friendly and tried to include me in their conversations.

It was the first of a few magical days and I went to bed that evening with my troubles temporarily forgotten and a feeling of satisfied repletion in my soul.

The main problem still remained however and few of my nights at the Bush Club were truly restful. I would fall asleep, but a few hours later would be awake and wondering. Should I pack up at Siavonga before my system let me down or should I take my life in my hands and push on to the distant ocean. I had to make the decision before Andy arrived, so I spent a lot of time thinking on it.

The fishing tournament was a success and I was touched when competitors came to say good bye and wish me well before they departed. So many people were rooting for me to succeed in my venture and packing up before it was properly completed would surely mean I was letting them down. It all added to my confusion.

The Jordaan's crocodile farm was an impressive enterprise and I spent a morning being shown around the breeding pens by the staff. The pens were set up in the form of shady creeks and the crocodiles seemed supremely content. When I told him about my broken fishing rod and asked whether he had someone able to repair it, Johan took it away and did the job himself. It was typical of the generosity that I received from Zambians from all sectors of society and whenever I use that little rod in the future, it will remind me of a wonderfully relaxing stay at the Kariba Bush Club and some special people.

My only disaster at the Bush Club was the fact that my camera died. There was no reason for this – it just stopped working, but yet again Cowbell came to the rescue. I had asked Andy for an old one, but when he arrived, he had a brand new Samsung for me to use. At that stage, I had been through four pipes and three cameras, so was doing well in the destructive stakes.

Unfortunately, Andy could only stay for a day, but we went fishing in the afternoon and for once I proved the more successful fisherman. I caught two tigerfish and photographs were taken. These were later published in the Lusaka Daily Mail. With two sons and a son in law who are passionate fishermen, I can now boast that I have been featured for my angling prowess on the front page of a national newspaper.

They can't.

Over dinner on Wednesday evening, I told Andy I was going to end the walk at Siavonga and he seemed sanguine about it. So the die was cast and although I was to go through more soul searching over succeeding weeks, I felt better having made the decision.

There was still a long way to go and after an excellent dinner with the Jordaans and their family, I set off again the next morning, my stay at Kariba Bush Club having been extended from an overnight stop to almost a week.

It had been wonderful though and undoubtedly did me good. I had made new friends, relaxed and enjoyed every moment.

I might even have put on a kilogram or two.

*　　　*　　　*

Moving on from the Bush Club, I couldn't help reflecting that the folk there were typical of all those Zambians who had been good to me over the months. From Johan and Chris down to the lowliest members of staff, everyone had been concerned for my welfare. When Andy tried to pay for our accommodation, Muftau told him they were honoured to contribute to my walk. Andy had forgotten to bring me sweeteners, but Denise rummaged in her pantry and came up with enough to last me a few weeks.

For me, it was heart warming and I couldn't help feeling that I was letting them all down by finishing the walk at Siavonga. I should surely keep going until I could keep going no longer.

I hadn't been back 'on the road' for long when my troubles returned in force. With the resupply, my pack was back to its thirty kilogram weight and when I stumbled on loose rocks, the weight drove me earthwards. Another rock broke open the grazes on my right knee and my clean shorts were soon muddy and sticky with blood.

Limping slightly, I called in at a village and was told that I should take a road that would cut off a large headland. A young man called Kembo offered to show me the way and carry my pack, so off we went. Kembo set a brisk pace, but soon began to wilt and after only three kilometres, told me that the pack was too heavy for him.

I took it back and our pace slowed considerably, but I wanted to be back on the lake and Kembo took me down a track until there it was – Lake Kariba, stretched out before me in all its glory.

I set up camp in a copse of tall trees while Kembo wandered off, looking somewhat disconsolate. I think he had been expecting a reward for his porterage, but as I had done more carrying than he had, I was not in the mood for unnecessary largesse.

My camp was comfortable, but no sooner had I spread my things around me than I was approached by Oliver, who announced himself as an important personage in the area and asked whether I would join him for lunch. Leaving everything on the sand, I accompanied him to his huts and on the way, he asked whether I ate *nshima* and whether I enjoyed guinea fowl. I answered yes to both and when we arrived at the village,

Oliver produced a catapult and disappeared, leaving me on an uncomfortable wooden stool.

I heard a truncated squawk and a meaty thump before Oliver reappeared with one of the village guinea birds dangling from one hand – very dead. He handed it to his wife and joined me, intent on learning about the world he would never know.

"We will eat in thirty minutes," He told me and I shuddered inwardly. Guinea fowl needs slow cooking to be tender enough for the strongest of teeth. Thirty minutes was surely being ambitious, even for the Tonga.

In fact it was closer to an hour and that unfortunate guinea bird tasted delicious. It could never be called tender, but it was easy to chew, even with my loose teeth. After lunch I returned to my camp and my next visitor was the headman Robson Machadi.

Robson told me his son had met me months previously near Chitokoloki Mission. I couldn't remember the meeting, but Robson was a nice fellow and we chatted into the dusk. His family had been among those unfortunates, uprooted from their riverside homes with the building of the dam in 1958. He confirmed Sidney's story about Bemba people being brought in to teach the Tonga how to fish and told me many tales about the hardships of the time. He had only been a boy, but his memory was clear and I found his story fascinating. It was dark when we parted and I wished there was time for more talk.

But I was heading for Sinazongwe and was on my way early, turning my face to the East and plodding on. I had another dilemma to sort out in my mind.

I had no idea how large Sinazongwe was, nor how far I still had to walk, but Sandy Dankwerth had offered me the use of her holiday cottage and I wasn't sure whether to take up the offer or not. It would be nice to have a roof over my head, but I didn't feel comfortable accepting such a generous offer from a relative stranger. I had time to make up my mind, but the problem kept spinning around in my tired brain.

Thinking of Sandy brought Karien back to mind. I had phoned her from the Bush Club and she had sent me another cake. What a Lady that girl was and what a delicious cake. I don't know what it was, but it was heavy – which meant I had to eat it quickly – and full of nourishment. She had even sliced it and wrapped each slice individually. Despite the extra weight, I eked that cake out and it was delicious. How I blessed the day, I had been so rudely turned away by the farmer North of Livingstone. If that hadn't happened, I would not have met Karien and would not have been enjoying cake under a tree, in my favourite part of Africa.

With thoughts of Sinazongwe, Livingstone and cake tumbling over each other in my mind, I reckoned I had about six weeks to go before reaching Siavonga and with everyone trying so hard to ease the way for me, was sure I could do it.

*   *   *

Champagne in the bush – who would have thought it?

It was Sunday morning and a few days previously I had left the Kariba Bush Club feeling ready for the way ahead, but that hadn't lasted. A number of heavy falls had dented my confidence and the weight of my newly filled pack was an enormous strain on my muscles.

I only needed to do eight kilometres a day to make Siavonga by the end of October, but at the rate I was moving, it was going to take me considerably longer. The going was becoming ever more mountainous and repeated climbs over rocky ridges were sapping my strength. I wasn't even sure I could reach Sinazongwe.

Emerging on to a wide beach, I found myself surrounded by boats, ranging from fragile canoes to burly kapenta rigs. People called cheerful greetings as I wobbled past and I waved half-heartedly. I could see a wide bay ahead with hilltop buildings visible on the other side.

An aged crone, puffing away on the calabash pipe, called *ncelwa* that is favoured among Tonga women cackled an answer to my question.

"You are in Sinazongwe," She told me, blowing acrid smoke around my shoulders. I had once taken a puff from one of those pipes and it was akin to being kicked by a buffalo so God only knew what they put in them. "But you will have to get a boat across the river before you reach the harbour."

Sitting on the sand, I pondered the situation. I was hesitant about approaching Sandy Dankwerth, but she had given me her phone number, so I sent her a text message, asking whether the offer of her cottage was still available.

My phone rang moments later.

"Where are you? We are in Sinazongwe at the moment and if you are close, will delay breakfast till you arrive."

It was almost unbelievable. They only used the cottage every month or so, yet I had chosen the weekend they were in residence and at a time when I was in desperate straits. Somebody up There was definitely pulling my strings.

I told her that I would get a lift across the river mouth as soon as I could. She promised that I would be met at the harbour and off I went to find transport.

High class transport it was too. Peter had a banana boat with an outboard motor and for five US dollars, he took me across a wide estuary, so that I arrived at Sinazongwe in style. A truck was waiting and Sandy's husband Patrick held out a hand.

"Welcome to Sinazongwe," He said cheerfully. "You look a mess but we will soon clean you up."

It turned out to be Sandy's birthday, so not only did I have an excellent breakfast of scrambled eggs, bacon and mushrooms, but there was Champagne to wash it down with. Her parents had also come down from Choma and the Old Man had been a member of the BSAP, so we enjoyed a session of 'did you know....'

The only name I recognised was that of my old mentor in the Force, Ken MacDonald who turned out to be a relation of Sandy's. He had been a true gentlemen among senior Rhodesian police officers and I found myself stammering when Patrick handed me his telephone.

"Here; speak with Ken. I have just rung him in Bulawayo."

It made me want to cry. From being a solo wanderer in trouble, I was suddenly part of a family and speaking with a man I had always admired. Ken told me he had been reading about my exploits in the Zambezi Traveller and that he was 'very proud of all that I had achieved.'

Tears threatened to overwhelm me and when the call ended, I sat there with a silly grin on my face.

Patrick Dankwerth was an interesting character. He was farming in Choma and was a keen photographer. When I told him about my camera problems, he said it was due to the extreme heat.

"These little digitals can't take high temperatures," He mused. "The bigger cameras are built to cope, but the cheap and cheerful ones die when the temperature becomes too much for them."

That sounded reasonable and I remembered how Lace's camera – a wedding present – had similarly 'died' when we took it to Kariba many years previously.

Patrick also had an interesting theory as to why kapenta stocks were dying away in the lake.

"People say it is because they are being overfished, but I am sure it is due to the lack of nutrients in the water. Kariba has only been here sixty years and the water is still uncontaminated. Now we have a huge fish population feeding on what few nutrients there are so inevitably, sizes drop off."

He pointed out that if the problem was overfishing, there would still be a few larger fish caught in the nets. It was a reasonable theory and as the larger fish fed off the kapenta, I decided that Patrick might be right.

It was a lovely morning, spent in idle discussion about this and that. We had a light lunch and in the afternoon, the family drove home, leaving me to use their cottage for as long as I liked. I told them I would move out the following day and both Sandy and Patrick were horrified.

"You can't do that," Sandy told me. "Patrick has to come this way tomorrow and he can drop in anything you need. Please stay on for a few days. You look all in."

I was, but I had only just been resupplied so didn't need anything. I agreed to stay on for an extra night and when Patrick appeared the following lunchtime, he had come with goodies to make my walk more pleasant.

There was bread, cheese, pork chops, salad, beer and even a small bottle of red wine. Patrick declined my offer to share it with me and was soon on his way. He left me musing again on the kindness and generosity of the Zambians I was meeting.

I had many memorable stops during my walk along the Zambezi, but two nights spent alone in a cottage on the Sinazongwe cliffs will live on in my memory for a very long time.

Once again I had been incredibly lucky.

*　　*　　*

After weeks of roughing it and sleeping in the bush, it seemed that I was going from comfort to more comfort. Sleeping on mattresses – even laid on the floor – was infinitely preferable to sleeping on hard ground and I was enjoying myself.

The Dankwerths had asked me to call in on 'David and Ann,' who were apparently hoping I would. They worked a farm for Zambeef, the Zambian meat company and according to Patrick, lived 'just down the road.'

Probably so when driving, but on foot it was a long road indeed. Despite the rest and the food I had been enjoying, I was soon aching badly and although my decision to quit at Siavonga was giving me sleepless nights, I knew in my heart it was the correct one. I could not go on and my beloved Courteney boots were giving up on me. Despite the repairs done in Livingstone, more stitching was working loose and a small hole had appeared on the top of the right boot. This was bad news, as Siavonga was still a hundred and fifty kays away. I needed those boots to last.

Courteney boots are hand-crafted in Bulawayo and made from buffalo and impala hide, making them incredibly strong and durable. I had worn them for years and when my original pair died while walking around the southern shoreline of Kariba, I contacted the company and asked whether they wanted any advertising.

They didn't, but Gale Rice who owned the firm with her husband John offered me a replacement pair of boots. It was the start of a long-distance friendship, conducted by email and at the beginning of 2012, Gale asked what I wanted for my prize. Gently telling me off for not reading my emails properly, she told me I had been their 'Adventurer of the Year' in 2010 for my Kariba walk and was entitled to a free pair of any footwear I wished.

With the Zambezi Walk in mind, I asked for more boots. They arrived and I spent weeks applying Dubbin and wearing them in. They had done me proud through the flood plains and rocky gorges, but now that I was walking on paths, they were giving up on me. Offering a prayer that they would last for another hundred and fifty kilometres, I plodded on.

I was feeling decidedly anti social and my first impression was that Zambeef must employ a large number of senior staff as I was surrounded by chalets, interlinked by paved paths. Spotting a line of washing outside a larger house, I approached cautiously. I was met by a glamorous lady, who looked as though she should be adorning the cover of a fashion magazine rather than farming in the bush. She stared somewhat askance at my tattered appearance.

That was how I met Ann Mynhardt, who later told me that she had a doubly hyphenated name.

"I am actually Ann-Marie Duncan-Mynhardt," She told me and inevitably I have always thought of her as 'my hyphenated friend.'

"Would you like some tea – or breakfast perhaps?' Was her first question and I probably began salivating as she laughed and ordered breakfast from her maid. I was shown to Chalet 3B, where once again I found myself with a bed to sleep in.

"Please stay a few days," My hyphenated friend asked. "We have a lovely pool on the edge of the lake, which you can use whenever you like."

With daytime temperatures reaching into the mid forties, that was tempting but there was one problem.

"Will anybody be using the pool?" I was becoming paranoid about my skeletal appearance.

In addition to being the farm headquarters, Zamarula was a tourist resort which accounted for the chalets. There were visitors in camp, so although I sat beside the pool and dipped my feet in, I resisted the impulse to plunge into that lovely cool water.

Yet again I had fallen on my feet. Ann-Marie and her husband, David made me welcome and I shared their meals over two glorious days. My clothes were laundered, while Ann-Marie and I enjoyed long conversations.

David was South African and interested in my walk and my motives for making it. I don't think I explained myself adequately, but he seemed to understand and when I left Zamarula two mornings later, I felt a familiar feeling of regret. Would I ever see these lovely people again? Would they remember the skinny apparition who had shared their camp and their lives for two days in 2012?

I didn't know, but much as I would have enjoyed staying longer, it was time to move on. I had thirty one days to cover the last hundred and fifty kilometres. The extra rest did me good, but I knew my target of five kilometres a day could easily become unattainable if things went wrong.

It was a wrench to walk out of Zamarula. Nobody else was up when I left and although walking was easy and I made good progress, it wasn't long before the familiar aches and pains returned to slow me down.

*　　　*　　　*

David hadn't agreed with Patrick Dankwerth's theory as to why kapenta caught in the lake were getting smaller.

"It is because people fish where they like," David was scathing when I put the theory to him. "They don't obey rules and have no idea of conservation. Just as in the rest of Africa, people live for the day and make no provision for the morrow."

He told me of an incident on the farm wherein mosquito nets had been donated by an Aid agency.

"They didn't last long," He smiled ruefully. "They made excellent fishing nets and although they were donated for local children, the men appropriated them and caught thousands of fingerlings. It is a problem and although they will never die out completely, kapenta in the lake are doomed to get ever smaller."

It was a depressing prospect, but I believe David was correct. Lake Kariba provides nourishment for two nations, but that can't last forever and then what?

At Zamarula I switched my phone on and was delighted to see I had messages waiting to be read. Deborah had announced the end of my walk on Facebook and so many folk sent me messages of support and understanding that I became quite emotional. A number of people suggested that in view of my condition I should stop right away, but I didn't want to do that. If I made it to Siavonga, I would get something out of the adventure, so I was determined to reach the place.

The messages lifted my spirits, particularly as many of them were from strangers. In time, I managed to thank some of them, but if you sent me a message and haven't received an acknowledgement, please know I wasn't being rude and was truly appreciative of your kindness.

Walking was becoming more difficult and at times, I was barely hobbling along. My bleeding heels were giving me trouble and while people were feeding me, I had no opportunity to lighten the load in my pack. It was tempting to discard a few packets of food, but misfortune could strike at any moment and I might end up in need of every mouthful.

One hot morning, I was hobbling along a dusty road, when I came across a corpse. It was sprawled in the centre of the road and I could see no signs of life. Approaching cautiously, I nudged it with one foot, but nothing happened. The man appeared to be dead, but as I started taking my pack off, another man pedalled up.

"Don't worry about him," He called cheerfully. "He drank too much beer last night and it has caught up with him."

He must have seen the concern on my face.

"He is not dead, that one. Later he will wake up and curse us all because his head is sore."

Not overly convinced, I walked on without carrying out a detailed check of the body, but I heard no more about it, so presume the cyclist was right.

Although it skirted the lake, the road I was following was very sandy and the surface tugged painfully at my calf muscles. The sand was less in the crown of the road, so I took to toiling up the middle, hoping I would hear the approach of any speeding vehicle before it wiped me out.

There were hills to climb and these caused further stress to my aching body, but the sun was blisteringly hot and there was no shade. Well into the afternoon, I left the road to follow a track through the bush. It brought me out at a fisherman's hut, where I was greeted with amazement. I set up camp a hundred metres away and settled down to read under intense scrutiny from the fisherman's five children.

"They have never been close to a white person before," The fisherman explained. "They think you have come from the sky."

I had a few sweets in my pocket, so handed them out. They were received with childish courtesy, each recipient bending his or her knee in a curtsey and accepting the gift with both hands to show how big it was.

Then they left me alone and I wondered whether I should have stocked up with sweets as I went along. I bought them in village stores and when I was hot and thirsty, sucking on something sweet was a treat.

Suddenly tired and irritable, I told myself that my own need was far greater than the need of any stray children. Besides, the sweets would rot their teeth.

What a grumpy old man I was becoming.

*   *   *

As the distance to Siavonga lessened, the calendar moved into October and the pace of my faltering steps slowed even more.

Not for nothing is October known as 'suicide month' in Central Africa. As rain builds up behind distant horizons, the temperature rises – and rises – and rises. As it rose, so my days grew shorter. I would leave camp at first light, but within minutes my shirt would be sodden and sweat would flow freely down my back, my arms, my legs and my face. Although my shoulders should have been accustomed to pack straps, the sweat caused chafing, which added to my discomfort.

By nine in the morning, the sun was like a furnace overhead and by midday, the arid countryside seemed to creak in the heat. Once I had three hours walking under my belt, I would search for a camp site, preferably close to water and beneath a large, shady tree. That sort of ideal combination was difficult to find however. I seemed to spot the best sites early in the morning and later on, suitable trees were far from water and pools or river banks would have no shade.

If I was still walking at noon, I would be fretful, with sweat pouring down my face and my eyes searching desperately for somewhere to rest. On occasions, I would wriggle beneath a bush and either sleep the afternoon away or read from my Kindle.

That Kindle earned its keep during the listlessly hot days. Some of the stories I had downloaded proved to be badly written and the lay out was often lousy, but being able to read kept me sane. Police procedural stories made me forget about

DAVID LEMON

my discomforts and transport me back to heady days as a British Bobby.

Those long afternoons also gave me time to think – not only about what I was doing or the future, but also about the strange world I was wandering through. This was the twenty-first century, yet in rural Zambia, people lived as they had since time began. As long as their stomachs were full, they were happy. Clothes were a minor detail and entertainment was provided by singing or playing on home-made instruments. Many folk had cell phones, which appeared to be more of a status symbol than anything else. Some were programmed to belt out African music – tunelessly repetitive to Western ears, but loved by the Zambezi River People.

There were no roads in the area and transport was restricted to canoes, the occasional banana boat and scotch carts, drawn by oxen or donkeys. Firewood was collected on wooden sleds, and I looked longingly at these as they crept through the bush. I even considered buying a donkey to carry my pack, but the local animals were poor specimens with ribs showing through scabby skin and I felt that the weight of my pack would prove too much for most of them.

Since leaving the source at Mwinilunga, I had walked among Lunda people, Luwale, the Lozi, the Toka Rea and now I was with the Tonga, but they had all been friendly and eager to help. I had spent time with a number of white Zambians and it seemed sad that few of them shared my regard for their black neighbours. Although they mixed with them daily, there was an air of mistrust among the whites, for which they could hardly be blamed.

For their part, black Zambians seemed to regard it right to purloin anything that was left unattended by their white neighbours. Even Gavin Johnson, a devout Christian and a true friend to the folk among whom he lived, told me that when he moved his camp to Lukulu for the annual fishing expedition, he had to take everything with him or it would not be there on his return.

"On one occasion, we even lost a water tank," He told me sadly and indicated a similar tank, perched on a heavy metal stand eight metres above the ground. To take it down must have necessitated a great deal of work and I could only wonder what the thief or thieves would use it for.

Yet wherever I went, I left my own kit and equipment lying around without worrying about theft. My electronic gear must have been tempting to people with nothing and although my food was hardly appetising, it must provide huge temptation to folk, living on *nshima*.

Nevertheless, I lost nothing in all the months I walked and this was in cruel contrast to the Zambian camp owners and missionaries. Perhaps it was because to the locals, they were merely other Zambians and fair game. On the other hand, villagers did not seem to steal from each other, although I came across one village where a thief was tried, convicted and punished by his peers.

It was all bewildering, but thinking on it seemed to lessen the pain and frustrations of my own problems.

*   *   *

I had a strange introduction to Blue Waters crocodile farm. I had been walking through the morning and faced with closed gates, knocked wearily and waited to be let in. A slot in the gate opened cautiously and I found myself under scrutiny from two strange eyes and a set of teeth that would have been an orthodontist's nightmare. The eyes looked in different directions and the teeth jutted at all angles from a full-lipped mouth.

I didn't have time to consider this odd assortment of facial features however, as the peephole slammed shut after a few seconds. With a sigh, I eased my pack from aching shoulders and wondered what I was getting into.

Minutes passed and nothing happened. I hammered on the gate again and shortly afterward, bolts were drawn back, the structure swung open and I found myself face to face with the eyes and teeth again. They belonged to a young man who obviously thought I looked even weirder than he did, as he backed away from me and stayed at a considerable distance.

Having learned that I wanted to see Mr Mulder, he led me to an office, where a well-dressed, gentleman was working on accounts. He greeted me courteously, provided a chair and chased the weird-looking fellow away with a burst of Chitonga. Learning what I wanted, he picked up a telephone and dialled a number. Gesturing for me to follow, he called the man with the eyes to carry my pack.

Outside another building, we met a petite lady who introduced herself as Peta Mulder and invited me into a spacious office. My bearer – he with the teeth – followed me in and she gestured for us both sit on comfortable lounge chairs. Coca cola was produced and the Toothy One glugged at his with enthusiasm.

"Bill is out with the DC," Peta told me, "but I hope you will stay over for a day or two. I am sure we can fix somewhere for your friend to sleep."

She was referring to the young man with the teeth and eyes.

"He works for you," I said quietly. "I met him at your gate a few minutes ago."

Peta looked bewildered and the toothy one seemed to realise that he had outstayed his welcome. He smiled – I think – at me and left the office. Throughout our brief friendship, he hadn't said a word and I later learned it was his first day on the job. With his talent for meeting up with senior staff, he should go far and I have often wondered what became of him. I didn't even know his name.

Billy Mulder bustled in with his son Kevin and we sat down to lunch in a dining room that lacked nothing in grandeur. In conversation, it turned out that Joe Brooks – the wonderful old fellow I had lunched with in Livingstone – was coming down the following day to collect an albino crocodile and when I mentioned that I had met him, both Mulders were enthusiastic.

"Joe is our oldest friend," Billy told me. "Everything I know about croc farming and the bush was learned from him. You had better stay for the weekend and meet him again."

I didn't need a second invitation and when I was shown to my bedroom, had difficulty not whistling in amazement. It was a suite rather than a bedroom, but I was quite prepared to rough it for a change.

Every bedroom had a television set and on Saturday night, we all sat down to watch the South African rugby side beat Australia. Somehow it seemed incongruous in the middle of the Zambezi Valley. When I retired to bed that first evening, I felt like shaking myself to see whether I was dreaming. Twenty-four hours previously, I had been dirty, hungry and uncomfortable beneath a tree that was home to a million mosquitoes, yet here I was, surrounded by luxury with a kettle as well as a massive television screen. It seemed unreal and I felt I would surely wake up with a bang.

On Saturday morning, Joe Brooks arrived. His wife had died a few years previously, but a lovely lass called Mirrin was keeping him young and I envied them the way they held hands as they wandered around the garden at Blue Waters. For months on end, I had been starved of affection and even at my advanced age, I found myself missing it.

I think that house at Blue Waters was the only double-storied dwelling I encountered throughout my walk and it seemed to contain every electronic gizmo known to Mankind. It was truly incredible, but despite the unashamed luxury, a delightfully homely place to spend a weekend. The gardens were spacious and there was a fountain surrounded by massive chunks of petrified wood that took my breath away. Petrified wood is millions of years old and I've collected a few pieces, but it is an incredibly heavy substance and the labour involved in building that fountain must have been enormous.

Billy showed me the crocodile pens and I met a newly-born donkey that had a good life ahead of it, but one of the best aspects of that weekend was that I was left alone to read from Peta's extensive library of books.

When we spoke about the life she had led, I urged her to write her own story, as it would be a sure-fire best seller, but even though I offered to assist where I could, she was reluctant.

Perhaps I will write it for her one of these days.

*   *   *

Even in Paradise there are bound to be thorn trees and although they lived in what has to be one of the most enchanted spots in Africa, Billy and Peta Mulder had their own problems.

"I worked my socks off for all this," Bill was showing me around the crocodile pens. "We came up the hard way and everything had to be fought for. Now it is all threatened by politicians. They have just brought in a massive hike in the minimum wage, which means we will have to lay people off or go broke. With the current problems in the kapenta industry, we cannot survive."

In addition to his crocodiles, Billy ran twenty-six kapenta boats, but he was feeling the pressure from unlicensed rigs.

"They crowd in wherever they can find a space. They don't care about breeding grounds and fishermen lay their nets in creeks and shallow water. The fish population can't take the hammering and with no fingerlings being allowed to survive, the population in the lake will plummet."

He was right about the netting. Two days previously I had watched nets being laid in a creek not far from Blue Waters. The fishermen had cheerfully told me that they would have a good catch of 'the young ones.' Those same young ones would not get a chance to grow up and become proper fish because there was no escape for anything swimming along that creek.

There was a village beside the croc farm, from which Billy obtained most of his casual labour.

"Every so often I make the villagers spend a day cleaning up," He looked angry as he told me the story. "We join in and collect tons – and I mean tons – of litter that has been thrown away. I have provided every house with a dustbin, but of course they don't use them – at least not for rubbish. It is a never ending battle to keep the area clean."

This was in direct contrast to most of the villages I had passed through, where everything was kept spotlessly clean and tidy. Ann-Marie at Zamarula had made a similar complaint when we were chatting and I wondered whether this unusual apathy toward cleaning stemmed from proximity to places occupied by white people. It seemed possible, although I couldn't figure out where the connection lay.

"This bloody lot," we were in the village and Billy was cross, "were sent five tons of maize by the British government. Do you know what they did? They sent it back because it hadn't been milled. They said they didn't have time to mill it themselves.

'Time – I ask you. Look at them."

Billy's frustration was understandable. Village men sat around in the shade and not one of them was working. A few wandered around with catapults, looking for birds to shoot, but most of them just sat. In this, the place was no different to other villages I had passed through and unless something is done to get the youth working, the future for Zambia looks bleak. An entire generation of work-shy people will be running the country.

I have always tried to deter my British friends from donating money to Africa and my walk down the Zambezi was reinforcing my convictions that little of the cash donated does any good. I know that NGOs and Aid Agencies act with good intentions, but pouring money and food into Africa is not the answer.

*   *   *

The albino crocodile was disappointing for me. Its eyes were blue, but to my inexperienced eye it was just another croc, although Billy pointed out white patches of skin that apparently didn't exist in other crocodiles. Joe Brooks was also enthusiastic and assured me it would take an honoured place in his own croc farm back in Livingstone.

"I will call it Billy Blue," He grinned, but the last time I saw Billy Blue, he was looking thoroughly disgruntled in the back of Joe's pick up. The poor creatures snout was taped, but I could have sworn there was a murderous glint in those blue eyes and didn't envy the unfortunate, whose task it would be to remove the tape.

Kevin Mulder was an experienced, off-road motor cyclist and spent time showing me the easiest way to Siavonga, but with my worries about water, I needed to stay as close to the lake as possible.

"Chipepo will be a problem for you," Kevin mused. "There is a game farm, owned by an Italian and you will need a long inland detour to avoid it. He doesn't like people going through his land. Apart from that, you should be fine, although the journey is much hillier from here on in."

Bad news for me, but Kevin felt that by sticking to the shoreline, I would have just under a hundred kilometres to go, so my daily average could still be under ten kays and I could afford a few more days off. I was enjoying my rest periods with lovely people and despite my anti-social tendencies, everyone really did seem to be nice. I have wandered the length and breadth of Africa, yet the hospitality and kindness I was experiencing was second to none.

Hugging Peta in farewell, I reminded her about the book she ought to be writing. What a life the girl has enjoyed. Refused permission to marry because she was too young – I had experienced the same problem – she had joined Billy in this remote spot and living in a tent at the time, the pair of them built a business. During their years on the lake, they had kept a lion, a pair of tigers, a chimpanzee and a Cape buffalo. How this slip of a girl had coped with all that, I could not imagine, but she needed to get it down on paper. She smiled at my enthusiasm and as I waved the Mulders good bye, I felt that familiar ache in my chest. Would I ever be back? I didn't know, but I still had a long way to walk.

CHAPTER TEN

(Disaster and Disappointment)

The October heat was appalling. Sodden shirts would dry in minutes when hung on a bush, but I had to shake the garments vigorously to get rid of encrusted salt.

I wanted to finish my journey on or about 26th October as that would be six months since the start at Mwinilunga. With less than a hundred kays to go, I could afford to take things easy, but found myself forcing the pace more than was safe in that heat. One morning it caught up with me.

I was walking along a path when I stopped. I don't know why I stopped. There was nothing in my way and the going was easy, but stop I did and when I tried to start off again, I couldn't.

It sounds ridiculous, but I was stuck on that path and couldn't move forward or back. My legs would not obey my brain and I didn't know what to do. It was as though I had become paralysed and fearful frustration welled in my mind. Could something have bitten me and led to some sort of instant paralysis? What was happening to me?

It was a terrifying moment. How long it lasted, I have no idea but it seemed to go on for minutes. Standing helplessly, I winced at the crushing heat from above and tried desperately to move, but without warning, my knees suddenly buckled and I fell forward into the dust. The weight of the pack drove me downward and I spat sand from loose teeth.

Knowing I couldn't continue in that state, I looked around for shade, but there was little to be had and I spent a miserably uncomfortable hour, wondering what to do.

That was the only time I was stuck like that, but whenever my legs felt tired in the days ahead, I would sit down for as long as I could. A doctor could probably have pin-pointed the cause of my temporary paralysis, but the memory haunted me.

Hearing distant singing one morning, I walked toward the sound and found myself in the middle of a Tonga funeral. It seemed a happy occasion and to much clapping from the elderly men present, I did an impromptu dance with some of the ladies. They ululated in glee, *nshima* and *nyama* was produced and the day was given up to partying.

Many of the Tonga built thatched shelters in their fields and I took advantage of these whenever I could. Just having something between me and that awful sun was a relief and I would lie on the ground and read from my Kindle or dream the day away.

At one shelter, I was visited by a teenager on a new bicycle. So new that it still had brown paper wrapped around the struts. His name was Alvin and he proudly announced himself as head coach to the Blue Rivers football team. He was coming to a nearby village to check on his players as the team were playing Nyakasanga the following Sunday.

He was a pleasant young fellow, Alvin but he was horrified when I told him what I was doing.

"You are too old, My Father," He protested. "You will die along the way. If I had a lot of money, I would take you to my home where you could rest your body and eat *nshima* all day. Then I would drive you to wherever you wanted to go. 'You surely cannot walk."

I assured Alvin that although his was a kind offer, I could walk and intended to do so. Even had he enough money to feed me up and drive me to wherever, I would not have accepted the offer – generous though it was.

Poor Alvin; he could not understand why I wanted to walk. At last, he wished me God speed and mounted his bike, shaking his head in sorrow as he peddled away.

I never did learn who won the game between Blue Rivers and Nyakasanga.

Rivers were becoming more frequent as I approached Chipepo and although most of them could be waded across, I needed a canoe on occasion. I was comfortable in a dugout now and enjoyed the feeling of being driven, even if it was in a hollowed-out tree. The boatmen were interested in my travels and nobody asked for payment, although tobacco was gratefully accepted.

I arrived in Chipepo on a Sunday morning. Chipepo Harbour held memories for me and I wanted a boat ride across, rather than trying to walk all the way around. I was again suffering from mouth ulcers and as I hobbled down to the water, I was not a happy man.

Stopping beside a rundown motel, I looked across the water and my heart quailed at the size of the harbour. I had been in the same place many years previously, but that was in time of war and I had not been there legally. We had come in at night from Paradise Island, just off the Zimbabwean shoreline and the plan was to take advantage of a howling gale to set fire to Chipepo itself. We lit a wide grass fire and it burnt for days, but whether it did any damage, I will never know.

Back in the same spot forty years later, it seemed politic not to ask.

There were two boats below the motel and a group of youngsters told me that the boatman had gone into town. They didn't know when he would return, but as it was Sunday, it seemed he could be a while.

"He will be drinking beer with his friends," Opined one young woman and I sighed. It was not turning out to be a good day.

A kapenta rig chugging across the bay gave me an idea. I had passed the gates of a kapenta firm and perhaps they would have a rig going out that evening which could drop me off on the other side of the harbour. My young friends told me that the firm belonged to Mr Crunchie and agreed that he would have rigs going out, so I walked back to see. Passers-by called cheerfully, but I was still feeling down so didn't stop to chat until I saw a man wearing shorts.

In rural Africa, trousers are the norm, but he laughingly assured me that like myself, he preferred having his legs unencumbered, so wore shorts whenever he could. Cheered by this little exchange, I walked into the kapenta company and met the Cronjes, who cheered me up even further.

Pierre and Theresa had started kapenta fishing in Cabora Basa, but decided that Zambia would offer less bureaucratic hassles. They had been proved wrong, but were enjoying their simple life in the bush.

"We are the only white people in Chipepo," Theresa smiled over tea and biscuits. "The locals seem to enjoy having us here, although none of them can pronounce our name."

Remembering the 'Mr Crunchie' comment, I laughed and after having a shower, shave and sandwich lunch, decided that walking down the Zambezi was quite a nice experience after all.

Pierre arranged for me to be taken across the harbour in his own banana boat and it was a lovely evening ride that ended with me being handed over to the headman of another village. The next day I was back on the road.

*   *   *

Heat and mosquitoes were making sleep difficult at night, while one reason for the malaria scourge among African children had become apparent. Whenever I camped near a village, I heard the shrill voices of kids playing well into the night. I was being mercilessly attacked inside my mosquito net, so dread to think how often those little mites in their flimsy clothing were being bitten in the course of an evening.

But I suppose children have to play and there was nothing else for them to do.

At Simililunga school I was made a fuss of by pupils and staff alike. The school was financed by a Canadian organisation and was well equipped, but the plaques announcing donations given by various individuals struck a sour note for some reason. Why on earth would these people want their names so prominently displayed in rural Africa? It made no sense to me.

I spent much of that day in company with teachers, Elemony and Victor and we set the world to rights. Intelligent young men, they questioned me about the writing of George Orwell as well as life in the West. At one stage while we were discussing books, Elemony commented that future generations of Zambian schoolchildren would read about the travels of David Lemon.

I laughed, but it was a satisfying thought and I preened inwardly. Would I really be part of Zambian history long after I was gone? I didn't know but perhaps that was what prompted the Canadian donors to have their names on plaques. Human beings want to be remembered.

From Simililunga I was to take a 'straight road' over steep and rocky ridges to Sinofala, where I could get a lift across the Jongola River, but I lost my way and arrived at the river without ever finding Sinofala.

Fortunately, I stumbled on a camp where two Bemba fishermen named David and Darius were making fish traps out of cane. They had come from Lusaka and did not have a boat of their own, but David went off to borrow one.

Although they were at pains to impress me with the fact that they were Bemba, they paddled the dinghy backwards in the Tonga manner. David apologised that the boat was 'far too small,' but I assured him that I was happy to ride in it. I told them about my 1985 adventure in an identical craft called Hobo and they were full of questions. We parted with God's blessing being called down upon me and once again, I walked on feeling that Zambians were nice people indeed.

But the going was hard and depression was ever more of a problem. I couldn't understand it, because although my journey was nearing its end and I had failed in my major objective, I had covered in excess of a thousand miles and enjoyed fantastic experiences along the way. I thought back repeatedly to the wonderful folk I had met and knew I was privileged to have shared their lives, even fleetingly. I was letting them down and found it difficult to shake off the awfuls. It was an elder called Sylvester who brought me out of it.

Sylvester was even older than me and perhaps due to the empathy of age, I found him easier than most to talk with. We sat on tiny stools across brimming bowls of *nshima* and fried bottlenose, while I tried to convey my feelings of frustration at not being able to achieve my ultimate goal.

Speaking in the usual mixture of languages together with much gesticulation, I struggled to get my point of view across and he frowned as he dipped one hand into the *nshima*. Rolling the stuff into a ball, he dipped it into the fish gravy and transferred the parcel to his mouth. He chewed with his eyes on me.

"But why should you stop?" He asked. "You can go away and rest, then return and do the next bit."

My brain had been so scrambled since my decision to quit that Sylvester's suggestion took me by surprise. Why hadn't I thought of that? I had been absorbed with feelings of failure and the obvious solution had escaped me. I could have hugged that old Tonga for making me see sense.

"Sylvester, you are a genius," I told him fervently and although he probably didn't know what the word meant, the implications must have been clear. His eyes lit up and he smiled before going back to the *nshima* and bottlenose.

It was with a lighter heart and a feeling that all was not yet lost that I continued the following day. Walking the Zambezi in two parts was not according the script, but it would mean that the river hadn't beaten me, even if we ended up with honours even at the end.

Like so many other River Folk, Theresa Cronje had given me a bag of food to take with me and in addition to boiled eggs, sandwiches and bananas, she included a small packet of wine gums, which thrilled me to the marrow. If ever you read this narrative Theresa Dear, those sweets kept me going for a week and I savoured every little taste.

I was also given a brace of cassava roots, dug up and presented by a lady called Gertrude, who lived in a remote spot with her husband Sensa. She approached as night was drawing in and shyly presented me with her gift. I didn't have the heart to tell her that I didn't enjoy cassava, so I accepted with due grace and two days later, gave them to a cyclist I met along the road. That was ungracious of me, but I would not have been able to prepare those roots in any case.

A brief stop at a road workers' camp – they were building a bridge – allowed me to try out a new form of chair. Instead of the normal Tonga stool or plastic chair, I was given a wheelbarrow to sit in and very comfortable it was too.

Spotting blue away to my right, I abandoned the path I was using and cut through bush toward the lake. It was always a special moment when I emerged from vegetation to see that vast expanse of water stretched out before me and even the fact that the shoreline was heavily populated didn't dampen my mood. Wandering along a path that skirted the water, I came across a thatched shelter that offered reasonably cool comfort, should the wind ever blow. Throwing my pack into this, I spoke to a man called Nicholas, who told me my new residence belonged to him, but I was welcome to stay as long as I liked. He even promised to bring me *nshima* and chicken later on.

Buoyed by my new sense of optimism, I set my Kindle to charge, while I explored my surroundings. It was early in the day, but I had already covered more than my intended distance of five kays, so decided that if this place proved comfortable, I might even spend an extra day. There was a store belonging to Nicholas' uncle and plenty of water on hand, as my shelter was only twenty metres from the lake.

An older man called Noel arrived to chat and told me that he came from Siavonga.

"You will reach there in two days," He assured me. "I will show you the best road when you are ready to leave."

Two days at Tonga walking speed probably meant a week for me, but that would still get me to Siavonga before Andy was due. Suddenly my worries changed direction and I fretted about getting there too early. This was becoming ridiculous and I chided myself for a silly old fool.

Thinking about walking, I reflected that throughout my journey, indigenous Africans had marvelled at how well the white man can walk, yet this is hardly the case. Tribesmen and women walked all day and every day while most of my kind only walked when they had to – or perhaps when they lost their mind! In the normal course of life, Noel and others like him would walk hundreds of kilometres more than I ever would, but everyone found this difficult to accept.

Noel wanted a Cowbell cap and I promised him he could have mine if he carried my pack for five kays when I started out again.

The bargain was struck but before the restart, I was to suffer my worst disaster yet.

*   *   *

It had not been a good night. Although my shelter was open, there was no wind and heat built up until sweat poured down my face and body. The mosquito net didn't help, but I could hear the little pests whining happily around my head, so didn't dare come out for air.

Soon after I retired, Nicholas arrived with the promised *nshima* and chicken. I had already eaten, but he had made the effort, so I invited him to eat with me. We were joined by Noel, who was chuckling as he sat down on my pack.

"What is your problem?" I was tired and irritable, but Noel wasn't fazed by my tone.

"Do you remember the senior headman who came this afternoon?"

The man had been one of a fairly inebriated party that included Nicholas, Noel, the store keeping uncle and a couple of others. He had been introduced as 'the Headman of Headmen,' so I presumed he was an important personage, but he was as drunk as his companions. Nevertheless, we enjoyed a chat and he told me that he had been born in 1949, which made him five years younger than me. We both laughed when I teased him for being a mere baby and they left soon afterwards.

"He said he was younger than you," Noel said thoughtfully, "but he must have been lying because he looks much older."

That was the first nice comment I had received about my age since Sesheke and I grinned at Noel. My mood lightened by the compliment, I settled down to sleep with no inkling of the disaster that was about to befall me.

It happened when I was packing my kit as the day was dawning. The shelter was cramped and while I was rolling up my bedding, I stepped back, heard an ominous cracking sound and felt plastic giving under my booted foot.

Instinctively, I leaped forward, only to crack my head on a log beam and as I staggered back again, I stood on my spectacles. Totally beaten, I slumped down on my pack, reluctant to inspect the Kindle that had been charging on the floor. The screen picture was in jagged segments and no amount of fiddling would make the text readable. With a feeling of utter despair, I began unpacking again.

The Kindle had kept me going for over five months. When it was too hot to walk or I was too weary to expend any energy, I could read. Now I had no Kindle and no reading matter, so although I had less than three weeks to go, they were likely to be long weeks indeed. The temperature was rising by the day and without the Kindle, I could look forward to long, sweaty, boring afternoons. In fact, the days were becoming so hot that plastic on the case holding my spare specs had melted, leaving a sticky mass that added to the horrors of my morning.

Noel approached with daylight, but I waved him away. I was not going anywhere. I would take a day off and do my laundry, while sulking over the loss of my most treasured bit of equipment. He seemed to understand my despondency, even if he didn't know what had caused it and promised to return later for another chat.

"Tomorrow we go to Kota Kota," He finished cheerfully, but I didn't care where we went on the morrow.

Moving disconsolately down to the water, I waded out to wash my clothing. Both shirts were caked with salt and I wondered how much damage that loss was doing to my system. Not that I cared at that stage. All I wanted was to finish this terrible walk.

A call from behind me interrupted my gloomy reverie.

"Mr David, Mr David," It was Nicholas carrying a large bowl. "Please use this for washing. We don't want you to be eaten by a crocodile."

Such a fate might have proved welcome relief from my miseries, but I did as I was asked and settled down to face a very long day.

Noel returned during the afternoon and once again, we set the world to rights. He told me about the game reserve at Kota Kota, which was run by an Italian called Masimo and contained up to three hundred elephants.

"They have an eleven-strand fence to keep the animals in," he shook his head in wonderment, "but Masimo hasn't been down in fifteen months and none of the staff have been paid. A few months ago, they rioted and took a lot of equipment as well as a lot of fencing. I don't know what will happen to the elephants now."

It was not a good advertisement for the conservation measures being trumpeted by government officials, but it meant I could go through the game park without having to do another major detour.

As a bleak day drew to its end, I told Nicholas that I did not want an evening meal – his wife had given me lunch – but as night enveloped the village, two ladies appeared with a large, fried fish on a plate and I didn't have the heart to refuse the offering. It was delicious too and my heart went out to these simple folk who shared what little they possessed with a bad-tempered stranger.

At six in the morning or 'zero six' as Zambians told it, Noel arrived to perform his guiding – and I hoped bearing – duties. I presented him with my Cowbell cap and off we went at a pace that I hadn't enjoyed for weeks. In the first hour, we covered what had once been my usual four kilometres, but then Noel began to flag. The weight of the pack was wearing him down and eventually he turned to me with a gesture of helplessness.

"It is too heavy, Mr David," He said simply. "I don't know how you carry this, but I will leave you here. You have only another kilometre before you get to Kota Kota and someone else can carry the luggage from there."

I thanked him for his kindness and we parted with God's blessings again being rained on my head. Hitching the pack into place, I wandered on but the impetus had gone. My steps were leaden and I wanted to rest. It was still early and I needed more kilometres under my belt but when I passed a delightful little village on the edge of a lagoon, I wandered in to find the place empty. Needing solitude to soothe my troubled thoughts, I settled down beneath a large tree.

The view was magnificent, fish eagles called from nearby trees and a hippo gurgled his welcome from the other side of the bay. It ought to have been idyllic, but I was not a happy man.

I was missing my Kindle.

*   *   *

With the loss of the Kindle, a great deal had gone out of my walk. I still started walking at first light, but by eight thirty, the sun would be burning holes in my strength and my pace became more laboured. By mid morning, I would have completed my five kilometre allocation for the day and would find a camp, but that would leave the entire day to get through. Time passed slowly and although I would try to sleep through the worst of the heat, it was never easy. It was too hot for comfort and I knew my remaining strength was ebbing fast.

The countryside was becoming more rugged and that didn't help. After Kota Kota fishing camp I had two massive ridges to cross and although the views were spectacular, I needed frequent stops to rest trembling legs and heaving lungs. I was no longer hungry and had to force myself to eat. Loose teeth made chewing difficult and the effort of preparing my 'health gruel' (all I had to do was mix powder with water) was often too much for me. Whenever I passed a tree offering a modicum of shade, I would throw myself down and rest for as long as I dared.

One evening, I watched two fishermen laying nets and couldn't help admiring their skill in handling their canoes. These men were consummate boatmen, even though they spent much of the time baling water out of their craft. The boats themselves seemed to disappear beneath the waves, but seconds later, they would bob into view once more. Handled with deft flicks of home-made paddles, they could attain surprising speed and despite their clumsy appearance, were highly manoeuvrable under the control of an expert.

On this occasion, I smiled as I listened to their conversation. One of them had moved in close to my camp and waved a greeting. When he rejoined his fellow fishermen, their voices carried across the water.

"There is a *mukuwa* sleeping over there."

"Yes, he must be a tourist."

"Ah but he is very old, so I don't know how far he can go."

That seemed to sum me up and I sourly wondered how much further I could go. The fishermen disappeared into gathering darkness, not realising how much they had added to my depression.

Somehow I seemed to have bypassed the Italian's game farm, but on the way to Kole fishing camp, I was assisted by a little fellow called Isaac, who told me that he was a Lunda from Mwinilunga.

"I came here to buy fish but my money was stolen, so I had to learn about fishing myself to earn more."

On my query as to when this had happened, he informed me that it had been five years previously, so I could only assume he was enjoying the career change.

Carrying my pack, Isaac set a cracking pace through hilly countryside, but much as I would have liked to take things easier, I didn't dare ask him to slow down. I was walking unencumbered, while he was carrying that damned pack – and he was half my size.

When Isaac left me, I walked slowly on to Kole. From there I would need a lift to take me across the Kole River, but in the meantime, I was given an enormous bunch of bananas by a cheerful chap called Phineas Muzuma, which he proudly told me meant 'a sudden thunderstorm.' Phineas had a market garden where he grew bananas, mangoes, paw paws and various vegetables. The plants were fed by a spring and looked extremely healthy.

Phineas told me that he gave most of the fruit and vegetables to local orphans and 'poor people.' Now he was looking for a government grant to expand the business and wondered whether I knew anyone in authority who would approve his claims.

I didn't and delicious though they were, wasn't sure what to do with so many bananas. The village headman, Seward had promised to arrange a boat to take me across the river, but not until the day was cooling down, so perhaps I could eat most of them before departure time. In the meantime, I explored the village, signed the visitors register at Kole school (Headmaster Francis Siadimbe called his pupils together and gave them a little speech) and tried to relax as much as I could. I had the usual retinue of curious children and was greeted cheerfully by people, interested in what I was doing.

I bought biscuits from the local store and listened with half an ear to a programme on local radio station, Kariba FM. Listeners were phoning in to forecast the score in the return football match between Zambia and Uganda, being played the following day.

It seemed that everyone was supremely confident in *Chipolopolo*, as I only heard one person forecast defeat, but I was interested in the radio station and wondered where it operated from. Later on I was to have direct dealings with Kariba FM and a cheerful 'Scottish Tonga' called David Dunne, but that was still some way in the future.

In the meantime, I had a river to cross.

*   *   *

I arrived in Kilelezi Village shortly before sundown and it seemed that every adult male in the place was drunk. Although a few were drinking from bottles, the majority sucked on the little sachets - banned by the Zambian government for the brain damage they caused – known as '*kajilijili.*'

I am not sure what these sachets contained, but from the reports I read, they were pure alcohol, made into a sort of jelly. I had been given the chance to partake at various villages and wherever I went, empty *kajilijili* sachets could be found along the path. In Kilelezi, men were staggering about and I shuddered to imagine the hangovers they would suffer the following day.

Kilelezi was one of the dirtiest villages I had walked through and although I was offered a hut to sleep in, I made camp on the end of a point, where at least I would get fresh air. Perhaps sensing my disapproval, the locals left me alone and I was on my way early in the morning, unsurprisingly not seeing a soul as I wandered between huts.

I was travelling through the Kilelezi District and if ever there was an indicator of how leadership among human beings defines the way they live, this was it. The smaller villages I passed through were scruffy and badly littered, while the people were surly and uncommunicative. There were flies everywhere and these would follow me in a dense cloud when I was close to a settlement. This was such a contrast to the villages I had already passed among that it saddened me.

Following the lake shore, I lost my way continuously and had to backtrack on many occasions. This often resulted in hapless blundering through thick undergrowth where thorns and vegetation ripped at my exposed skin, so that I was leaving a trail of blood. In my already weakened state, this was depressing and from worrying about arriving at Siavonga too early, I suddenly began to wonder whether I would make it by the end of October.

The rains were drawing nearer and dark clouds built up during the day, while spectacular bursts of thunder and lightning illuminated the evenings. It was exciting to watch, but did nothing to cool the air. At four one morning, I was awoken by a heavy shower and had a choice of jumping out of bed and digging my poncho out or lying where I was and ignoring the discomfort. I chose the latter course and although I didn't get too wet, the rain caused a steep rise in humidity and next morning, I felt as though I was walking through an oven. Even before the sun was properly up, I was streaming sweat and cursing myself for a foolhardy idiot.

Later that day, I was given a lift across a tributary in an Indian canoe, piloted by a man called Simon, who insisted that his craft was a 'boat,' rather than a canoe. Feeling irritable after the bad night, I assured him that it was a canoe and nothing grander than that.

"No," Simon was indignant. "Canoes are made from tree trunks. This is a boat."

We left it at that. He was correct of course and I had been a tactless fool for trying to prove different.

In another village, I struggled to make myself understood as nobody appeared to speak English. This was unusual for Zambia as there was normally somebody with at least a smattering of the language, but I was still in Kilelezi District and it was an area that was proving ever more disappointing. On my seventh attempt at finding a path to Siavonga, a venerable old gentleman – he was probably my age but had fewer teeth – told me that 'there is no transport.' I stifled a desire to yell at him that I had my own transport and moved on, hoping that I was going in the right direction.

Although I was trying to stick close to the lake, this led to additional problems in that I had to make long detours to get around inlets and occasionally had my way blocked by tributaries, flowing into the lake. On one occasion, a trader called Godfrey asked me where I was going and when I explained that I was trying to get around a particular stretch of water, he escorted me to a spot where I could get a lift in a dugout. The boatman's name was Boyd and he had a body that most men would die for. Muscles rippled in his arms and torso and if there was an ounce of spare flesh in his frame, I couldn't see it.

Boyd was a cheerful soul and told me he had spent his entire life – he thought he was twenty-seven – in the area of that inlet. I asked him whether he exercised and he laughed.

"Paddling my canoe is all the exercise I get. I have all I want and life is good."

So much for the dieticians, gym fiends and nutritionists. Here was a man living on a basic diet of *nshima* and fish with a minimum of exercise and he possessed the traditional build of a Greek God.

"Take that path and you will arrive at Henga village within one hour," Boyd told me when he dropped me off. I thanked him, but knew that his hour would mean at least a day or more for me. I enjoyed the time I spent with Godfrey and Boyd and after the unhelpfulness I had been experiencing from Kilelezi residents, these two friendly young men helped restore my faith in human nature.

With my pack in place, I put my head down and headed for Henga, but it wasn't long before I was too tired to go on and was forced to find a camp site. I was losing energy at an incredible rate and began to worry that I might not reach Siavonga at all.

The thought of death has never worried me, but I felt it would be a pity if I failed so abjectly after all the pain, weariness and discomfort I had endured along the way.

*　　*　　*

The split in my right boot was widening by the day, but in a perverse way, it made me feel better about my own performance. If the going was bad enough to split tough buffalo hide, it was no wonder it had taken such a toll on my strength.

Stopping for a rest in a small village, I chatted with the elders present and a dapper young man called Martin Bafaana introduced himself as a headman in Henga village. Apparently he was one of several headmen, which seemed odd, but he invited me to stay the night at Henga.

It was probably too early to stop, but when Martin offered to carry my pack, I could not refuse. Leaving the others behind (one wore a Saddam Hussein shirt, but didn't seem to know who Saddam had been) we set off at a brisk pace and it wasn't long before I was thankful that he was the loaded one. The track wound through hilly countryside and the pace my guide set left me gasping for breath.

Henga was a large fishing village with its own school and a couple of stores. Martin had asked me whether I watched hippos – or at least that was what I thought he said. It turned out that he was asking whether I worship, but my vague reply must have satisfied him as we joined a couple of village men, named Alec and Wonder in a deep discussion on religion and the attendance of church on Sundays.

I told them that my religion did not necessitate a church.

"Look at the wonders of the world around you," I enthused with a sweeping gesture toward the lake. "Isn't that cathedral enough for anyone?"

They were not convinced and when the discussion went into the correct day for the Sabbath – two of them were Seventh Day Adventists – I lost patience. I had met many devout and lovely people in the course of my walk, but I had also met some who were intransigent in their views on religion. My suggestion that village churches should club together and use one building was met with horror, but it seemed reasonable to me. Everyone was worshipping the same God – or ought to be.

Once his friends had moved off, Martin and I sat beneath a shady tree and discussed life in general. He did not enjoy being a fisherman, but because he had only reached grade eight and his parents could not afford school fees, he had been forced to drop out and his lack of education hampered him. Nevertheless, he spoke excellent English which he claimed to have 'picked up here and there.'

He had four children of his own and while schooling was free until they reached grade eight, subsequent fees were too much for many and Martin looked doleful when he told me that he was worried sick. His wife Gertrude – a charming lady, who whisked my clothes away to be washed – was heavily pregnant, so that would be more fees to find if the Bafaana brood were to be educated.

It was an intractable problem and applied to so many of the Zambezi River people. My heart went out to them and I wondered whether Aid Agencies and Government Quangos might do better by investing their largesse into the education system rather than handing out unwanted food, clothing and cash that disappeared into the system and made a few people rich. With so many uneducated youngsters being foisted on Zambian society, it can only lead to problems in the future.

During the afternoon, we wandered slowly – it was fiendishly hot – across the village to Henga School, where I was shown around by Howard Kayaya. At the age of thirty-seven, he was only a junior teacher and when I queried this, he told me that his education had been interrupted by a hippo attack, he had been fortunate to survive. Lifting his shirt, he showed me his scars and very impressive they were too.

"But I wanted to learn," He said fervently. "I worked in Lusaka and when I had enough cash, returned to school and to College, even though I was already old and had a wife and two children. Now I am at Henga, but my wife stays in Lusaka."

Henga School had only half its complement of six teachers, even though it was set in a grove of tall, shady trees, the buildings looking out over the lake. I couldn't imagine anyone turning down such a posting, but Howard didn't agree.

"The buildings are broken down, there is no running water or electricity and the weather is very hot. They get transferred here from Lusaka or Kitwe, come down for a pre-transfer visit and refuse the posting. We have asked for repairs to be done to the houses, but nobody bothers – perhaps because we are too far away from the government.

'At the moment," he went on, "we have eighty-four pupils, but at the beginning of this year, there was nobody. There were four of us then and we had to go around the villages, recruiting children to attend school. Their parents are generally uneducated, so they don't see the point of learning."

It seemed very sad, but I fear that Henga is symptomatic of a small cancer that is currently eating away at the heart of Zambian society. All is well at the moment, people have jobs and food, roads are being built to assist communication and the economy is booming. But I wonder whether anyone has considered what might happen when the next generation and the one after it are adults.

For me, it was a frightening prospect for a lovely country, but I enjoyed my stay at Henga village. Martin escorted me on a long walk the following morning and I met the senior headman for the Henga area, whose name was Edward. The young men with him were roaring drunk at eight in the morning and Edward was the first Tonga I had come across, wearing a watch.

A nice watch it was too, but when Martin asked for a canoe to take me across a wide inlet, Edward sharply told us there were none available. My companion started to argue, pointing out that a fish catch was being counted in the village, so boats must have brought it in, but I gestured to him that we should walk on.

So walk we did and when Martin finally left me on a bush path late that morning, my GPS told me that we had covered twelve kilometres.

As I still had ten days to go and less than fifty kays to cover, that really was unnecessary haste, so I set about finding a comfortable camp.

*   *   *

I woke slowly with the feeling that something was wrong.

It was; I had been enjoying an afternoon siesta under a thatched shelter and while I slept, all the women and children of the village had come to see the weird old *mukuwa* who was walking to Siavonga.

I opened my eyes to find them staring at me with rapt attention. It was a curiously embarrassing moment and I hoped I hadn't been snoring. As I rose from my sleeping mat, the crowd – and there were at least twenty of them - moved nervously backwards, but I tried to reassure them with what was probably a pretty strained smile.

My hosts for the day were a middle aged couple called Richard and Tabitha, who with Richard's brother Dennis had hailed me as I wandered by that morning.

All three spoke excellent English and were fascinated by my story. We chatted till noon, then Richard asked whether I would like to accompany them to an *nkololo* ceremony in a neighbouring village. As he explained it, I decided that it was the Tonga version of the Lozi 'coming of age' ceremony, I had watched before Livingstone. It was an excellent opportunity to learn more about it, but my legs were rubbery and I was close to exhaustion, so I pleaded great weariness and retired for an afternoon nap instead.

Richard had told me that I was but a couple of kilometres from the Lufua River. He felt it would be easy for me to take a boat across and then walk on to Nanchowa. He must have seen the doubt on my face.

"It is not far, Mr David," I quite enjoyed this form of address. "Dennis can escort you tomorrow and find you a good boatman."

Dennis was enthusiastic about the idea, but when the new day dawned, he remembered other things he had to do. My escort duties were handed over to Richard's son, Latto – a giant of a man who picked up the pack that had almost broken my back over the months as though it was a lady's handbag.

Off we went on a path heading directly inland and threading its way through rocky hillsides that tugged and tore at my waning strength. Latto tucked the pack over one shoulder and strode ahead without the slightest hint of effort. Unencumbered for once, I struggled to keep within calling distance of his wide back and eventually, we began descending again until we reached the edge of the Lufua – not in itself a mighty river, but one that I could not have crossed or even gone around without a boat.

Negotiations with various fishermen ensued and eventually a diminutive fellow called Douglas offered to take me across the water for ten pin. It seemed exorbitant for such a short crossing, but I had little choice in the matter. I had to cross the river and Douglas knew it.

As I was settling myself into the boat, Richard and Tabitha appeared on the shore. They had decided on the spur of the moment to go to Nanchowa themselves. Squeezing themselves into Douglas' boat, they mocked him for taking advantage of an elderly wanderer. My ability to follow Chitonga was getting better by the day and I smiled inwardly as the little boatman went into a huge sulk.

Across the river, Douglas – obviously peeved at being told off by my friends – offered to show me the way and carry my pack. He only came up to my chest, so it was a generous offer and I decided that I might as well get my ten pin worth.

Forty minutes later, we were sitting on rocks beside the water, waiting for another boat. This didn't make sense and I asked whether it was possible to reach Nanchowa on foot.

"Ah, but it is a long way," Richard told me. "For you perhaps, it is not so far."

Taking that as a challenge, I hefted my pack on to my shoulders, but Douglas jumped to his feet.

"I will show you, Mr David. Let me carry the luggage."

So off we went again, the little man leading with my 'luggage' across his shoulders and me strolling behind with nothing but a walking pole. Passing a group of huts, a burly young man called to my guide, asking about the *mukuwa*. Making his way over to us, he grinned at me.

"Good morning," He said. "My name is David."

How could I resist the obvious riposte?

"Good morning," I said. "My name is David."

Roaring with laughter, he shook my hand and he was still chuckling as we resumed our journey.

Perhaps ashamed of his pecuniary greed, Douglas began to ask questions and when I told him I had been on the road for nearly six months, he looked stunned.

"Walking for half a year – you must be a strong man indeed."

Thinking to myself that 'half a year' sounded much more impressive than six months, I allowed that I was and after we had walked four kays, Douglas had finally had enough. For me, it had been an easy morning and somewhat reluctantly I took my pack back from the little fellow. He had more than earned his ten thousand kwacha and as he walked away, his shoulders were up and there was a jauntiness to his step that had not been there before. I didn't doubt that he would have many tales to tell by the fire that evening.

It seemed that I was still a few kays from Nanchowa, but I had done more than my allotted five kilometres and Siavonga was less than twenty kays away, so I had all the time in the world. I made a basic camp under a tree and settled down to endure the afternoon heat. I had little to do but think, although a number of folk came to see who I was. Few of them spoke English, so it was a question of smiling and shrugging at each other, although they all said 'bye bye' when they left.

That evening, a fisherman named Eric brought me a fresh bream for my supper and in front of an audience of hopefully impressed youngsters, I roasted it over my fire. The operation left my hands and face in a sticky mess, but the fish tasted excellent.

Another somewhat lugubrious fellow named Contract offered to 'escort' me the following day and told me he was going home to write in his diary that he had met David Lemon, the Zambian explorer.

It was all very flattering and despite the heat and boredom of the day, it had been a pleasant one. A number of folk had offered to arrange a lift to Siavonga for me and I had been given the choice of boats, motor cycles and trucks for the purpose, but I was close now and still anxious about arriving too early, so I smilingly told them I would walk on.

I went to sleep that night, feeling better than I had for a long time though the following day began badly. Contract – he told me he was named after a doctor – arrived to escort me to Nanchowa, but when we arrived at the place, there was nothing to it. I had been expecting a business centre with shops, but all I saw was a few tattered huts and a wide, dusty road.

'Where is the lake?' I asked. Contract pointed back the way we had come.

"You must take the road to Siavonga," He told me. By road, Siavonga was less than fifteen kilometres away, but I would be moving ever further from water, so for me it was impractical. My escort could not understand this.

"Your destination is that way," He was a stubborn soul was Contract. "There will be plenty of transport."

Eventually he seemed to accept that I didn't want transport and we parted on less than amicable terms. There was a river to my right, so I left the road and made for the water. A cheerful lady told me that if I took a canoe across the river, I would find the road to Munyama, so that was what I intended to do.

It wasn't to be easy however. I managed to get a lift across the river and set off east, but on arriving at a village store, I popped in to ask the way. The proprietor was enormously fat and when I asked him about the road to Munyama, he shook his head.

"Wrong way," He muttered. "Come with me."

That was all he said apart from the occasional grunt over the next hour and a half. Shuffling ahead of me with his shirt flapping wildly, he set a cracking pace and despite his bulk, I had difficulty keeping up with him.

I had been going in the wrong direction so it was as well I had asked, but as the heat built up, I could feel my strength ebbing away again. Sweat poured down my body while my lungs heaved with the effort of getting enough oxygen to keep me moving. The fact that we were walking straight toward a high ridge of rock and scrub made my overtaxed brain quail at the thought of more punishment, but that ridge turned out to be the first of four – each one higher and rougher than the one preceding it.

My guide picked his way unerringly between the rocks and I stumbled in his wake, wondering whether I would survive. Somehow I managed to keep moving and suddenly, my overweight companion stopped and turned to me. He had escorted me well over four kays and saved me from going completely wrong, but my only thought at that moment was relief to see that he was sweating even more than I was. Mind you, he had more to sweat off.

"Road to Munyama," He pointed to a barely discernible track through rocky forest. "Perhaps four kilometres."

With that, he turned and disappeared into the trees. I mumbled a weary thank you, but he ignored it and walked off, presumably heading back to his unattended store. I never even learned his name, but he had been an enormous help in spite of the pace he set.

The sun was high in the sky when I resumed walking and there was no shade anywhere. I plodded along, taking occasional sips from my dwindling water supply and wondering how far I was from the lake. I needed water badly.

It must have been close to midday and I was barely shuffling along, body and brain leeched of purpose when at last I arrived at a village. A man called Patson brought me water and wondered whether I wanted to eat.

I didn't; I was far too hot and sweaty to even think of food, but Patson misunderstood my refusal.

"Ah, you will probably be fed by Mr Danie," He said with a smile. "*Mzungu* food will taste better for you than *nshima*."

To be honest, I wasn't too interested in any food, but wondered what white folk would be living in Munyama.

"They are missionaries," Patson was a mine of information. "They are at home too because I saw Mr Danie earlier in the day. Do you want me to take you to him?"

All I really wanted was to get out of that fiendish sun, but I had met some fine missionaries over the months, so followed Patson along another road that inevitably went uphill.

Dan and Adrie Van Aswegen met me at their front gate and I was hurried into the shade of an awning where I was plied with orange juice and lemon cream biscuits. Best of all, I was able to remove my boots and let my swollen feet ease back into their normal shape. It had been a particularly gruelling morning and Dan pointed out the main reason for that.

Wandering into the homestead, he came out with a look of bemusement on his face.

"Do you realise that the temperature inside is forty five degrees?" He demanded. "You must have been walking in fifty degrees or more, because there are no trees along that road."

I was too weary to work out the conversion from Celsius to Fahrenheit, but I knew that was pretty hot. No wonder I had been sweating.

Mind you, from Patson's manner of speech, it seemed that I was back to being a *mzungu* rather than a *mukuwa* and that was a relief.

*   *   *

When I arrived at the gate of the Van Aswegan's place, I was in a mess. Both knees were badly grazed and my arms and legs seemed to be one large bruise. There was no particular pain apart from the usual overtaxed muscles, but I probably looked pretty unsightly.

However, with a shower and lunch behind me and a stretcher bed laid out in a barn-like classroom, I felt content. I was almost there and my 'half a year' adventure was about to end. For once, I had no worries as to how I would cope with a return to civilisation and this was probably because I had been in so many wonderful spots along the way. I had lived in unashamed luxury at Blue Waters and the Moir residence and spent time in comfortable homesteads and lodges, as well as an assortment of mud huts and basic shelters. There had been few days when I didn't meet with people, so my usual fear of how to make conversation and be pleasant when back in society wasn't there to trouble me.

That evening, we had a wonderful supper of oxtail and rice with gem squash and I felt even better. If there is a better combination of foods in the world, I don't know it and even though I struggled with a second helping, it was just too delicious not to take full advantage. Patson had been right. I enjoyed *nshima*, but this *mzungu* food tasted better to me.

Dan and Adrie were an interesting couple. Both South Africans, he had held down an excellent job in a platinum mine.

"I had a company car and a big house." He told me with a smile.

She had also been in a responsible post and they had thrown it all up to start new lives as missionaries in Zambia.

"I was never a practical man," Dan admitted. "When we arrived here, I had no choice but to do everything myself, even building this house."

'This house' was a basic construction, but it was comfortable and like Gordon Hanna in far off Chitokoloke, the Van Aswegans were freelance missionaries who prayed for everything they needed – and got it.

"We had a boat here when we came, but no engine," Adrie told me. "We prayed hard that something would come up and were having dinner with some people, when they asked whether we needed an engine. Dan told them that we were desperate for one, so they went off and bought it for us. Our two trucks came the same way."

As with Gordon, they seemed content with their pioneer life and despite my reservations about organised religion, I couldn't help admiring what they had achieved. They told me that I was only a few bays away from Siavonga now, so when they invited me to stay on a while, I was only too happy to take another day of rest.

"There is a fellow countryman of yours just down the way," Dan said after supper. "Do you know Glen Tatham?"

I knew of him. Glen had been Head Warden in the Zimbabwe Parks Department and I wondered what he was doing in rural Zambia.

"He runs a camp for Ian McFaddean," It was Adrie again. "Ian lives overseas, but he has this lovely little camp and is talking about setting up a game reserve."

"Ian who?"

A memory was stirring in my brain. In the late eighties, I had been running a charter boat called Queen Two on Lake Kariba. I took tourists on day trips to Sampakaruma Island and for eighteen months, I probably had the best job in the world. One Saturday, I had a young English couple come along and they were the only passengers, but I took them out and we had a lovely day. They were back on Sunday and again it was just them, but we enjoyed another excellent day on the island.

It was the start of a friendship that lasted until we lost touch when I left Zimbabwe. His name was Ian McFaddean and she was Helen Harwood. I vaguely remembered a Zambian connection, so this had to be the same bloke. I wondered if he had married Helen and determined to get hold of him at the first opportunity.

Thus it was that when I arrived in Lotri Bay a couple of days later, one of the first things I did was question Glen Tatham on the subject of Ian McFaddean. He gave me Ian's cell phone number and told me that he was often at the camp with his wife, Helen.

What a coincidence that was and when I finally sent a text through to Ian, he replied straight away, remembering the trips on Queenie and wondering what I was doing with myself. Our long lost friendship was back on the road.

One sad story related by the Van Aswegens concerned the previous occupant of their camp, Jenny Goodfellow. She and her husband Leo had done a huge amount for the local area. They had built roads and set up clinics and schools, till Leo was killed in a home-made microlight. Jenny had also lost a son, killed by a cricket ball in Zimbabwe and the double tragedy had understandably affected her mind.

"She had all the records of Operation Noah as carried out on the Zambian side," Dan told me sadly. "There were photographs, letters – just about everything that could be of interest, but a few weeks ago, she burned the lot in her boiler. Why, we will never know, but some weird idea made her do it."

What a tragedy that was and how many wonderful stories of those exciting days were thereby lost forever. As far as I knew, the only surviving member of those animal rescue teams was Joe McGregor Brookes and he had only played a peripheral part in proceedings. Others, such as Rupert Fothergill, Frank Junor, Mike Van Rooyen, Tommy Orford, Tinky Haslam – all of whom I had known and admired – had gone on to that great game reserve in the sky and I mourned the loss of those papers almost as much as I had mourned the loss of fine men.

But it was done and there was no going back. Nor was there any going back for me and after another lovely day with Dan and Adrie, I moved on to Lotri Bay with a sense of huge excitement in my soul.

Less than twenty kilometres to go and over a week to do them in. What a lovely prospect that was.

CHAPTER ELEVEN

(The End of the Line)

Glen Tatham was a curious anomaly. An abrasive fellow, he wore a large wooden cross around his neck, almost as a badge, proclaiming himself a good man. Of all the missionaries I had met over the months, he was the most flamboyant, but underneath the image was a man with genuine belief in what he was doing.

A fluent Shona speaker, Glen was another freelance missionary, following the doctrines of no particular church. He told me of his plans to develop a mobile mission station in Zimbabwe that with the overwhelming need for God's comfort in that country could prove a boon in the future.

The camp was idyllic. Whitewashed chalets nestled under mahogany trees and birds set up a constant chatter. Sitting in the shade, I listened entranced to some of Glen's stories about life in the Zimbabwe department of National Parks and Wild Life Management. He had met with the Great and the Good – and the not so good – and it was probably the fact that he was a very knowledgeable white man that had enabled him to survive for so long in a hostile government department.

But that was in the past and Glen's concerns lay with his fellow men rather than the wild animals that were decreasing daily across the great lake behind us.

A local woman had been bitten by a crocodile and when he told me that he was going in to Siavonga to see her, I asked if I could accompany him. It was a fifteen minute boat ride and I enjoyed walking around the little town. There was telephone reception there, so I took the opportunity to tell Andy where

I was. He replied saying that he would not be down until the following Friday, but that Karen (I hoped he had the name correct this time) at Eagles Rest would put me up until he arrived.

I rang friends in Kariba and thereby started a flood of calls and text messages. It seemed that everyone was worried about my health and I was repeatedly told to stay where I was and either a boat or vehicle would be sent to take me to Siavonga at the earliest opportunity. Smiling to myself, I didn't tell anyone I was actually in Siavonga. I wanted more time in Lotri Bay.

In the local hospital, we found the lass who had been mauled by the croc and she was in a pitiful state. There were no fans operating in the hospital, although I could see where they had been ripped from the ceilings. The temperature must have been in the high forties and patients lay listlessly on their beds, unattended and dripping sweat. I couldn't help feeling that they would be better off in their villages.

Glen sat and prayed aloud with the woman, while I tried to find a vaguely cool spot, eventually opting for the shade of a tree outside. How those patients must have been suffering, I could only imagine. There had been another crocodile victim in the male ward and he had been attacked at Nanchowa of difficult memory. His injuries were more severe than the woman's and he was in a semi-comatose state, muttering in his sleep and turning his head restlessly from side to side. Glen prayed over him as well and was then called by an Aids sufferer in the ward, who also wanted someone to intercede on his behalf with the *Nkosi Pezulu*.

I have no idea what the mortality rate is in Siavonga Hospital, but it was surely one of the most primitive such establishments I have ever been in. The place had little in the way of drugs to alleviate the plight of patients and Glen paid twenty-three thousand kwacha to one of the nursing staff so that they could buy some hydrogen peroxide to use as antiseptic.

"They can get four litres for that," He told me grimly. "It has to come from Lusaka, but they have promised me it will be here tomorrow."

I left that horrible hospital, thanking God I could do so, but the marauding crocodile still had to be dealt with. This necessitated a taxi ride to see the local representative of ZAWA, the Zambian wild life people. He was a pleasant fellow called Pearson. Although Glenn suggested the croc be captured alive so that it could be shown around the schools as a warning, Pearson felt that shooting it was a better option.

When asked whether he had weapons, he produced an AK 47, but Glenn shook his head.

"You can't kill the brute with that," He said firmly. "Crocodiles are too heavily armoured. Don't you have a proper rifle?"

Pearson produced a gleaming Brno .375 but forlornly admitted that he had only two bullets for the weapon.

"Never mind, bring it with you and I will find more ammunition," Glenn told him impatiently and they made a date for the following Tuesday. I wondered how wild life in Zambia could be properly managed when a government official was sent to a remote place like Siavonga with two bullets to keep him going.

Shopping was carried out while my phone continued to bleep its messages and it was only when we were back on the boat that I read any of them. Only one was important.

'Hello, this is Karen from Eagle's Rest,' It read. 'We are coming out to Lotri Bay tomorrow and will pick you up.'

I wondered what to do. If I was brought in over the last few kilometres, it would not really be cheating and in truth I had had more than enough of walking, but if I accepted her offer, it meant that my Zambezi Cowbell Trek was over.

Fortunately perhaps, the phone signal had disappeared and I couldn't reply to Karen.

I often wonder what I would have said.

*   *   *

I didn't know quite how I felt when I awoke that Sunday morning. I hadn't had a chance to reply to the mysterious Karen, so whether they – whoever 'they' might have been – would pick me up as promised, I wasn't sure.

The one thing I did know was that I didn't want to walk any more. I didn't want to feel the weight of that pack tugging on my shoulders or face the blistering heat of midday when there wasn't any shade in sight. I didn't want to boil water on a small fire or lie on hard ground, frightened to turn over in case my 'bed bruises' protested. I didn't want to fight with thorns or mosquitoes. I didn't want to watch for puff adders on bush tracks.

Nor did I want to tell my story or try to explain my motives again. Suddenly, I had just had enough. If Karen didn't come for me, I would hitch a lift to Siavonga when Glen collected Pearson.

In short, I was at the end of my tether and not prepared to go any further.

Glenn and I spent a quiet morning, chatting over innumerable cups of tea. We discussed the future of wild life in Zambia and his doubts on the matter reflected mine. Rural Zambians would need a change of cultural mindset for people to live in harmony with animals. How could a farmer like Malindi cope with his crops being ravaged by wandering elephants? When lions were brought in, what would happen when livestock was taken? Zambians had lived in harmony with wild life many decades previously, but the world had changed and from being merely a source of food and warmth, wild animals had assumed the status of dangerous nuisances.

A change of attitude, particularly among the rural poor would have to be brought about and that could only come through extensive education. Schemes like the Zimbabwean Operation Campfire in which professional hunters were encouraged to bring clients into particular areas, provided local people took a percentage of profits might work. My companion was doubtful.

"Campfire worked well for a time," He mused. "But it needs extensive government backing and sponsorship or it will fizzle out, just as it has in Zim."

Inevitably perhaps, we also discussed God and religion. He seemed to agree with my somewhat cynical attitude toward the plethora of religions that abounded in Zambia and when I told him of missionaries I'd met who were able to send their children to private schools on the donations of a flock amounting to less than twenty, he nodded fiercely.

"Too many people make money out of God's work," His tone was heated. "But there are others who live on the bones of their bums and give their all to the community they serve. The Lord looks after them and in return, they look after the people."

I had to agree and the morning passed pleasantly, although my eyes kept wandering to a gap in the hills through which any approaching vessel would appear.

It was early afternoon when a houseboat pulled majestically through the gap and I studied it through Glen's binoculars. The name on the bow was Bateleur and I smiled at the thought that ending my walk in a vessel so named would be wholly appropriate. The bateleur eagle is a fiercely competitive bird, his aggressive nature belied by his clownish colouring. I had long admired the species and seen quite a few in the course of my walk down the river.

The houseboat moored on the other side of the bay and a tender was soon streaking across the water. Two young men alighted from the craft and advanced across the grass. I stood up at their approach and the taller of the two stuck out his hand in greeting.

"Hi, I'm Peter," He said cheerfully. "You must be David Lemon and we have come to take you in."

I felt an overwhelming urge to weep, but held it in and started hefting my pack on to my shoulders.

"Let me take that," Peter urged and my long walk was over. No more carrying that awfully heavy 'luggage' for me.

On the Bateleur, I met Steve and Carol Thompson who own Eagle's Rest, as well as their daughter Karen, who was married to Peter and ran the resort. Also present was an old friend, Liz Lywood, who had last seen me when I was a strapping fellow with weight on my bones. I fear my emaciated appearance shocked her somewhat, as she quietly asked whether I was feeling alright.

I assured her I was fine and with a final wave to Glen Tatham, we pulled out of Lotri Bay. I allowed taut muscles to relax and settled down to enjoy a leisurely ride to Siavonga. Lunch was served and although I could do little justice to the delicious food on offer, I enjoyed answering the few – and very polite – questions from my companions. Eventually, I moved up to the driving console to join Steve Thompson.

"Heavy weather ahead," He indicated a bank of black cloud stretching across the near horizon.

That suited me. I love storms on Lake Kariba, particularly when I am safely ensconced on a craft like Bateleur. I have seen so many of them in various boats and although I have been scared on occasions, they never fail to thrill.

This one was a big job. As we passed Siavonga Town, the evening became very dark.

"Nearly there," Steve told me and guided the houseboat into a deep bay. As the bow grounded beside a small jetty, the heavens opened. Lightning flashed across the sky and thunder set up an ear-splitting din.

"Welcome to Eagle's Rest," Steve commented wryly. "This is the first storm of the season, so quite a greeting for you. Anyway, let's go ashore and get you comfortable."

Walking through drenching rain, I looked up at the sky and decided that the storm was a message from above, but whether it was congratulation from the *Nkosi Pezulu* on my achievement or a snide comment on my inability to complete what I had set out to do, I wasn't sure.

Feeling confused and relieved at the same time, I put my pack down in the beachfront chalet that had been allocated to me. There was no electricity in camp due to the storm, but I didn't care. There were plenty of candles and I had done without electricity for months. I was protected from the weather by solid walls and didn't have to worry about walking anywhere the following day. I could eat, sleep and do exactly what I liked. I could even stay in bed the entire day if I felt like it.

My Zambezi Cowbell Trek was well and truly at an end.

Reflections

As with Zambians everywhere, the people of Siavonga were wonderful to me over the week I was there. Steve and Carol Thompson entertained me in their lovely home, while Karen and Peter kept a careful eye on me, ensuring that I had everything I needed and was eating well. David Dunne, the *Mzungu* Tonga of the Kariba FM radio station interviewed me one evening and we ended up in fits of laughter when the station telephone batteries died in the middle of a phone in. It could only happen in Africa.

Mind you, David also introduced me as a seventy-six year old and when I remonstrated with him, I could see in his eyes that he had taken me for being much older than I am. He stumbled through an apology, but I didn't mind. I had mirrors in my lakeside chalet, so knew how I looked.

I felt somewhat flat at having finished part one of my walk, but at the same time, I was glad it was done. My chalet at Eagle's Rest looked out over the lake and the wonderful hills of Matusadona, so I spent hours enjoying the view while I thought about the walk and what I had achieved.

Although still vaguely ashamed at stopping when I did, I knew I could not have carried on and I had done far more than any sane person in their late sixties would dream of. The track manager on my GPS informed me that I had covered eighteen hundred and thirty nine kilometres and that I had roughly twelve hundred to go. I knew there was a lot of difficult terrain ahead of me, but with rest and a bit of strength back in my body, I felt I could do it.

I had been walking – with a few breaks here and there – for a hundred and eighty four days, so I had averaged just over nine kilometres a day, which surely wasn't bad for a geriatric. Although there had been bad moments in Luena Plain and the gorges, together with bouts of depression in the latter stages, in general I had had a wonderful time.

One of the aims of the trip had been to raise awareness for elephants, but in truth, I hadn't seen too many, although there was a lot of sign around in some places. I had met a number of people who cared though and that was heartening. With folk like Chief Inyambo Yeta, Gerald Chibanda and the dedicated staff at Lilayi Elephant Orphanage doing their best, the future of Zambian wild life is in capable hands.

I had met some incredibly fine people too. I had mixed with cabinet ministers, senior government officials, lordly chiefs, missionaries, drug smugglers, villagers and bandits but everyone had been kind and anxious to assist where they could. I had spent happy hours in remote villages, luxury homes and safari camps or tourist resorts. Without exception Zambians had taken me into their homes and treated me right royally.

I had eaten everything from tender fillet steak to boiled monkey, roast rat and fried flying ants – helped down with handfuls of *nshima*. I had enjoyed them all, but the food had not been sufficient to balance the hammering I was giving my body and the loss of weight had contributed more than anything else to my decision to stop when I did.

Sitting on my veranda with modern amenities to hand, I remembered the frustrations of building a fire with wet wood and the smoky taste of my bush tea. How I would miss that, even though it was grand to merely switch a kettle on.

I remembered the long dusty paths, forcing my way through bush so thick that I was forced to crawl and other times when the effort of ploughing through thick sand tore at my calf muscles and left me gasping for breath. I remembered the horrific effort required to get across the rocks in the gorges, the lapping of water around my thighs on the flood plains and the cruel ripping of my skin by *wag n bietjie* thorns. That had all been traumatic, but now that I was away from rough countryside, the painful memories were already beginning to blur.

I couldn't help smiling when I thought of spectacular sunsets, magnificent panoramas and crystal daybreaks along the way, as well as the bands of shy children who watched my every movement with wide eyes and little hands stuffed into their mouths – presumably to prevent them laughing. I remembered the dignity of village elders – some of them younger than myself – who quizzed me on my movements and motives. I had been treated with huge respect wherever I went and even the grilling I received by Chief Inyambo Yeta's Court of Ndunas had been done tactfully and with great dignity.

Wherever I had been in Zambia, people wanted to chat and many asked to have their photographs taken with me. It was all very flattering and I had enjoyed a brief taste of what celebrity life must be like. Newspaper reporters like Clever Mutinta and Gethsemane Mwizabe had penned glowing accounts of my fortitude and fortunes, while to my great delight, Monica Mwenda and Alpha Ngoma of the Inter Air office in Ndola offered me a free flight to Johannesburg – business class too - which was a real treat.

All in all, I had memories enough to last me into my dotage and even though my heart was heavy when I looked out over the lake on my last morning in Siavonga, I consoled myself with the thought that I would be back, not only to walk the remaining twelve hundred kilometres of the Mighty Zambezi, but also to mix once again with simple rural folk, each of them battling to make a living from the harsh Zambezi Valley.

Be they black, white or in between, Zambians had done me proud and I knew that I was privileged to have wandered among them.

The End

Glossary

BSAP : British South Africa Police.

Banana Boat : Canoe like vessel, made of wood or fibreglass and usually propelled by paddles.

Barbel : African catfish from the genus *barbus*.

Bobbo : Commonly used abbreviation for baboon.

Bream : Indigenous fish of the *tilapia* family.

Chilapalapa : *Lingua franca* of Southern Africa. Also known as *fanagalo*.

Chipolopolo : Word meaning 'bullet,' applied to the Zambian national football team.

Chitenge : Wrap around garment worn by both genders. Known as a kikoi in East Africa.

Crooks' Corner : A wedge of land close to the Limpopo River, which became a refuge for criminals and ne'er do wells in the late nineteenth century.

Dagga : Commonly used name for cannabis or marijuana.

Inamorata : Lover or swain.

Kays : Slang word for kilometres.

Kajilijili : Sachets of pure alcohol, banned by the Zambian government, but much enjoyed by rural drinkers. Said to cause brain damage.

Kapenta : *Limnothrissa Miodan* – Tanzanian sardine, introduced to Lake Kariba in 1967.

Kwacha	:	Monetary unit of Zambia.
Leatherman	:	An American made multi tool, built around a pair of pliers.
Litunga	:	King of the Lozi People, appointed by the Chiefs.
Manyatta	:	East African dwelling used by the Masai tribe. Invariably windowless and terribly claustrophobic.
Mealies	:	Maize or corn on the cob. From the Afrikaanz word *mielie*.
Mealie meal	:	Maize porridge.
Miombo	:	*Brachystegia* woodland - tropical and subtropical grasslands, savannas, and shrublands
Mombies	:	Cattle.
Mopane	:	*Colophospermum mopane* – a tree that grows in hot, dry, low-lying areas and only in Africa.
Msasa	:	*Brachystegia spiciformis* - a medium-sized African tree with compound leaves and racemes of small fragrant green flowers.
Muti	:	Medicine.
Mzungu	:	White Person in many African languages.
Mukuwa	:	White person in the Lozi language.
Mvuu	:	Hippopotamus
Ncelwa	:	Calabash water pipe, smoked by Tonga women.
Nduna	:	A Chief among many southern African tribes.
Nkosi Pezulu	:	Literally, 'Lord Above' – a slang name for God.
Nshima	:	A stodgy maize porridge that is the staple diet of rural Africa. Known as 'ugali' in East Africa, 'sadza' in Zimbabwe and 'pap' in South Africa.

Nyama	:	Meat.
Paw paw	:	Papaya.
Rondavel	:	A small round building, usually used as a bedroom.
Tigerfish	:	*Hydrocynus vittatus* – freshwater fish, armed with formidable teeth and famous among anglers for its fighting qualities.
Wag n'bietjie	:	Afrikaanz name for *Acacia Caffra* - literally, 'wait a bit' – a cruelly hooked thorn on a small, creeper-like bush.
Wazungu	:	Plural of Mzungu – white people.